Tickers:
And P

By Kimberley W. Eley

To Lisa —
Always follow your
passion!

i

Eley, Kimberley W.
    Tickers: What Makes People...Tick! And Pursue a Career They Love!

Copyright © 2016 by KWE Publishing LLC

ISBN 978-0-9974025-0-6 (paperback) – ISBN 978-0-9974025-1-3 (ebook)

Kimberley W. Eley
www.kwepub.com
804-536-1972

Cover design by Michael Glass

Dedication

To my mother, Shirley Wells, who taught me to draw outside of the lines. Every beat of my heart is because of you.

Acknowledgements

Thank you so much to Erin Nunnally and Randy Shavis, who edited "Tickers" and kept me from getting my degrees revoked. You guys are so wonderful! Thank you to very talented Mickey Glass who created the amazing cover and designed the logo for KWE Publishing. Thank you to my Aunt Peggy and Uncle Russell who cheered me on! To my darling Ruth, who always fills my life with joy, and to Russ, Jen and Jake too! Thank you to my wonderful sister-in-law, Vicki, for all your love. Thank you Anne Baird, my soul sister, who encouraged me to interview Mr. Bradshaw, and has been so supportive – you rock! Thank you Sandi Wiggins who helped me bounce ideas around and kept me inspired! Thank you Tracy Long, my dear sweetheart friend, for letting me pour my heart out to you that day, and for introducing me to Danielle! Thank you Kay Long for just being your wonderful self! Thank you, Will Marshall, for inviting us to see the cat circus! Thank you Mike Lawrence and Robert Bryant for taking a chance on a crazy kid from Texas all those years ago. And thank you Kevin Wells! You helped me become the manager I wanted to be. Thank you, Markia, our "black daughter," for being such a wonderful, inspiring young woman. Thank you Donna Highfill and to the members of the River City Express Network for encouraging me. Thank you to all of the Tickers who agreed to interview with me! Your stories inspired me more than you will know. Thank you to all the amazing friends in my life – love you all!! To the late Scott Short, my "brother from another mother." Being your friend was one of my greatest pleasures and biggest honors. To the late Mike Nunnally, my brother-in-law, who loved reading and enjoyed books so much.

And most of all, to my two favorite men:

Thank you Dad who told me I was his author, his buddy and his DD – darling daughter! I wear all these titles with pride – love you so much!

And most of all, thank you so much Jerry, my best friend and the love of my life. Thank you for reading the book and giving me your honest feedback! Thanks for believing in me and making me take breaks from the book with some forced television watching. Love you to the moon and back!

Table of Contents

"Make sure your life is a rare entertainment!
It doesn't take anything drastic.
You needn't be gorgeous or wealthy or smart,
just very enthusiastic!"
~Bette Midler

"Follow your passion. It will lead you to your purpose." ~Oprah Winfrey

Introduction

My career awakened when my butt fell asleep. Sitting on hard cubicle desks, shifting from foot to foot, my coworkers and I waited. All of us had just been called unexpectedly into a central conference room. With just over 40 employees, and a decades-long history of working together, you could say we were a family. Looking out for that "family" was Mike, our Senior VP. Mike was part father-figure to our "family", part jokester, and all heart. Mike had suffered a major break to his leg from a recent race which required surgery, a huge cast, and crutches. No one expected him back in the office so soon, so we were all anxious when we saw Mike arrive that day.

Many women claim to have a "work husband" in their office. My work husband was my actual husband, Jerry. I scooted over on the cubicle desk to allow him to sit next to me. Both of us had returned to the office that day from a vacation together. I eyed Jerry to say, "What's up?" He shrugged.

Crutching into the room, Mike arrived flanked by Kevin and Robert, our other managers, grim expressions on their faces. Sighs and mumbling that had broken out immediately stilled.

Mike broke the news to us. Layoffs. We just couldn't believe it. As defense contractors, we knew our contracts were finite. And we had suffered through furloughs and sequestration along with our Department of Defense employees the previous year. But this was June, not September, the end of our fiscal year, so the timing was wrong. And unlike those furloughs that affected us before, the United States Congress did not cause what had happened this time. This time, there was a budgeting issue, a major miscommunication. Mistakes happen, but this one was going to cost the jobs of our coworkers, our family. Mike told us to go back to our desks. "We'll call you if you are being impacted." We were one freaked out group of people walking back to our offices. Everyone dreaded having their phone ring. The collective tension was really intense.

Jerry and I actually met at work years earlier before we became husband and wife. As a married couple working in the same office, we had enjoyed some nice perks. We went to lunch together, talked during the day, and collaborated on some projects together. My predictions that working so closely together would result in bickering or other issues were thankfully wrong. Without a blow to the ego, Jerry even dealt well with my tasking him to work on projects. But being married coworkers on this day meant we could both be laid off right after returning from our vacation.

We were fortunate. Neither Jerry nor I received a phone call stating we were laid off that day. Fifteen of our office friends weren't so lucky. They were laid off and given two weeks' notice. The rest of our team would be impacted too, although not as severely. The remaining employees had to take three weeks of unpaid leave. The result of taking this time without pay meant that we prevented some other of our office friends from losing their jobs; however, some employees had little to no leave time left due to the prior furloughs and shutdown. In fact, Jerry and I had just burned most of our leave balance going on vacation. Learning that the leave time we took for vacation would not count towards our three weeks of unpaid time caused us great concern. This worry was minor, however, compared to our friends who were losing their jobs.

Saying goodbye to three loyal members of my team was an especially hard blow to me. As a project manager, I had become close to my team, and really was impressed with how well they had worked together and how much we had achieved. At a farewell luncheon, I thanked them for all of their work. With only one member of my team left employed, my team – and much of my project - was decimated. After the goodbyes, I started to think about what this change meant. Why is this happening, I thought.

Being human means suffering. That's a given, and a fact I knew very well before the layoffs. Four years earlier, I lost my mother. She had beaten breast cancer into remission and for three years, she seemed healthy. When the cancer came back in stage 4, and she died a month later, I learned that life can be unexpected. As much as I wanted to stamp my feet and scream, 'Life is not fair!' I realized I had to let go. If you focus on the fact that nothing is fair in life, you are preventing yourself from moving on. And change is inevitable.

Before that day in the conference room, work-wise I thought I was Kim Eley, Documentation and Training Manager at ManTech, seventeen-year employee. I loved my job. I loved my managers and coworkers. But career-wise, we had just endured a seismic shift. And I felt like I was standing on the San Andreas fault. After I said goodbye to most of my team, and other coworkers, I knew my career and my company would never be the same.

For the first time since I graduated from college, I really started thinking about who I am and where I want to be. When I was an undergrad, I didn't know myself that well. I had general ideas about what I liked or disliked, but I had no idea how to channel these ideas into a career path. I am a middle-aged woman now. This was more serious, and the stakes were higher. I had a husband, a house, and people who count on me!

What really matters to me, I asked, at this stage in my life? I couldn't shake this thought. How do I even start to think about this? Moving out of my sadness from losing my friends, I experienced stirrings I hadn't felt, and suddenly my formerly great job seemed two sizes too small. Wheels turning, I started thinking about people I have met that inspired me. And many of those people have chosen a career path that reflects their passion.

Through my own career path and personal travels, I have been fortunate to meet some incredible people. Some of the people I have met stood out because they truly love their jobs. I thought about how these people who deeply loved what they did impacted the world around them with their enthusiasm. They had gifts they were offering to the world, and their spirits made deep impressions.

With my world now in flux, my mind traveled to these astonishing people. What did they have, what did they know, to get to where they are today? I've always heard the expression to "follow your dreams" but how did I apply this "pie in the sky" concept to my day-to-day life? How did these amazing people start their journey? What could I learn from them? I thought about the presenter I met at a conference who dazzled the room and captivated everyone's attention…the woman with the spy-like name I met at her mysterious and curious mansion…the man who started a cleaning empire and dedicated a museum to all things clean…a couple whose passion for spreading a craft beer gospel lead to the creation of an amazing beer restaurant…and who knows whom else I would meet along the way?

Wow, I thought. I wish someone would write a book about them! And figure out how they got to where they are! How awesome would that be? For the first time since the layoffs, I got excited. I started thinking about how cool it would be to meet these people and find out what made them tick. Then something clicked. Oh….wow….maybe I should write that book! Flying in the face of my distress over the layoffs, I began a year and a half of spelunking into myself, and listening to my own beating heart, and figuring out what makes me tick…what makes people…and figuring out if I have what it takes…

Part 1 What does it mean to tick?

Having an educational background, a lively curiosity, and a love of words, I began my new career path – writing this book and exploring my own passion - by researching the expression, "What makes you tick?" When we say, 'do what makes you tick,' what do we mean? I started my journey where many modern searches start... I Googled it!

My first search produced a horrifying series of tick pictures…um, gross! After I recovered, I made my search more specific: "What does 'what makes you tick' mean?" This definition from a contributor named Rybar from Yahoo resonated with me: "It means, what motivates you... what causes you to go about life and do what you do... sometimes a job makes someone tick, sometimes money, sometimes love. The things that make you tick are the things that keep you going in life." [i]

That was a satisfying answer. What makes each person tick may vary and represents an individual state of being. What makes <u>me</u> tick might drive another person crazy or make them miserable. Also, the things that could make a person tick are endless. It could be a career, or another person whom you love, or the dollar amount in your savings, or something else altogether. The common denominator is that the thing that makes you tick makes you want to live. Or more specifically, what makes you tick is what makes you <u>feel</u> alive.

I continued thinking. If someone is in sync with what makes them tick, that would make that person a "Ticker", wouldn't it? Turning once more to Google, I typed in the word "Ticker." Hits on stock tickers and ticker symbols appeared. Nope, not it. Clicking "next", I searched additional hits. The Urban Dictionary's first definition for ticker is "a hardcore drug that is anally absorbed." Eew! Not where I was going with this quest! Second definition: the "affectionate nickname for the city of Penticton, British Columbia, Canada." Charming but again, not where I was going. I read the third definition: "A person's heart." **Ah-ha…**

I began processing the definitions. A Ticker, meaning a person who knows what makes them tick, is similar to a countdown ticker on a clock. The clock represents the person's life, or rather, represents a measure of all the moments that make up a person's life. A countdown measures out the seconds, minutes, hours and days to any date. Related to my quest, I asked: When does your life start? **When you become a "Ticker".**

More than defining a person as a countdown ticker, however, I kept gravitating to the definition of the ticker as a person's heart. Everyone's emotional heart yearns to do what makes them tick. When a person is a Ticker, could it mean that they have tapped into their emotional heart's desire? If Tickers were devoting most or all of their time towards their passion, they would be following their emotional heart. I looked further. Healthy physical hearts beat in a specific rhythm; their rhythmic contractions move the blood throughout the body. This rhythm could be described as a "tick"…and probably is where the term "ticker" came from in the first place. For these people, the Tickers, it would be as though every beat of their heart aligns with their passion. In other words, their emotional hearts have synched with their physical hearts. Their time can be measured by the number of beats of their hearts spent doing what they love.

Part 2 What makes someone a Ticker?

So now that I had a definition of a Ticker as someone who follows what makes them tick, I needed to figure out what makes someone a Ticker. I thought the most obvious answer initially was that a Ticker must have passion as they have become in touch with their emotional heart. Continuing my efforts to define the Tickers, I searched the word "passion" on the Internet. The first definition in the Merriam-Webster dictionary for passion is:

"a strong feeling of enthusiasm or excitement for something or about doing something."

So…passion is a feeling, and feelings are connected with emotion. That makes sense. When you are bored or unexcited about what you are doing, you want to stop. I mean, there are always things we have to do in life that aren't exciting…paying taxes, dealing with bureaucracy, etc. We usually don't have a choice with those things. But what if your job bores you to tears? Or if the way you make your living makes you feel uncomfortable or even forces you to do things you don't like to do? And you're stuck like this all the time, for hours at a time? That will inspire negative emotions. That's not the kind of job that will make you feel passionate or excited, unless you count that it makes you passionate about running away or quitting!

According to a 2013 Forbes magazine article, 70% of employees are not "engaged" at work. More than half, 52%, say they are not enthusiastic or committed and are essentially sleepwalking through their day. Another 18% are truly unhappy, or "actively disengaged". According to the same survey, only 30% of American workers really love their jobs. [ii] That's a great deal of unhappiness happening in the work world every day!

So then I thought about the people I know who are passionate about what they do. These are people who have followed their desire, and made a career out of that craving. I realized that I had more questions about them than answers. I wanted to know: Did these Tickers choose their path, or did it choose them? How did they move past the "idea" phase to the "action" phase of following their passion? Are they any different than anyone else, including me? Maybe if I could find out how the Tickers found their path, I could use that information to find my own new road.

When I compared the people whom I consider to be Tickers, I realized they all have in common the ability to awaken an interest in other people. Obviously they had made a big impression on <u>me</u> because I kept thinking about them! But what I didn't know is, how do the Tickers get other people excited about their passion? I had witnessed others who have made a connection with someone who doesn't share their passion. Yet their excitement and enthusiasm about their passion makes others respond. But how?

Many of us have also met people who are really excited or passionate about something, and they managed to turn everyone off from their favorite subject! I recall being cornered by some passionate people at a few parties where I just wanted to ask the person chewing my ear off to STOP! "Um, no, I don't want to see your lint collection, thanks." These people were not Tickers...just annoying! So what makes the difference?

So many of us have dreams but we don't pursue them. Maybe we think our dreams can't come true – we've "drunk the Kool Aid," and think that other people's dreams are special but not our own. It is one thing to acknowledge that you have identified your dreams. But what do you do about them? Do you really look at your dreams and help them out, instead of drowning them in the bathtub? The Tickers have dared to pursue their dreams. What makes Tickers so special?

So I got to thinking about entrepreneurs and innovators. If Tickers are exploring doing things in different ways, doesn't that bring innovation to others? Wouldn't an individual following his or her passion lead them to take a different or new approach? Wouldn't taking this new approach lead them to create something brand new? And wouldn't taking this new approach, and creating something brand new, become an innovation?

And then my mind expanded...How would this innovation improve the world? Would it make the world better for others? Is there evidence that this new way of viewing the world that the Tickers have can influence other people to view their world differently?

Focusing on the idea of viewing the world differently made me think: If a particular thing is new or a new way of looking at things, by definition it is different than the old way of looking at things. We have to look at whether the old way is accepted because it has become the norm or if it actually has value. If the old way is accepted just because it is the norm, it might be that it had value but it doesn't anymore.

If the old way actually has value, however, then we have to look at whether the new way has value too. And what if the value, too, is showing others the ability to look at the world in a fresh new way? Isn't that valuable in and of itself?

And which is more important, the Ticker, or the thing that makes the Ticker tick? Are they one and the same? Is it just that the person "ticks" so that anything they put their mind to will become energized simply by the fact that they pay attention to it? Or is it their single-minded devotion to their passion that makes them "tick"? How do Tickers identify what they want?

I want to find out what the catalyst is, the 'kick in the pants' that will make someone want to pursue what makes them tick. But I had had it with books and articles that only encouraged you to pursue your dreams without the reality of how to get there. I wanted to know the good, the bad and the ugly. What did the Tickers know that I should know…that all of us should know? As a person devoted to process improvement, I wanted to know what stumbling blocks the Tickers had that I could avoid.

With my own experiences in mind, and the relayed experiences of the Tickers, I was ready to document a journal of what makes up a successful, creative person's path. My head full of questions, I was ready to begin my journey.

Part 3 Wouldn't you like to be a Ticker, too?

When I decided to write about Tickers, I also decided at the same time to examine my own life and career choices. Prior to the layoffs I had convinced myself I was happy in my career with ManTech. But was I? I had been at the same job for seventeen years. During the time I was there, I had worked in a number of different positions which made my work interesting and challenging – for a while. But as I examined the previous few years, I realized that my work had become stagnant. I was not learning anything new. I also realized that I had worked to the top of the food chain at my employer, and unless someone quit or something else drastic happened, I was not going to be promoted anymore. As a "Type A" person, this realization bummed me out.

As I started making my list of people to contact about Tickers, I also dusted off my résumé and started looking for a new job for myself. I made a list of the things that are important to me. I knew I wanted to write about the Tickers, so that too was part of my new path.

Throughout my life, I have been told that I have a talent for writing. As an English major who loves words, linguistics and rhetoric, I found it was easy for me to write papers for school and for work. What was hard for me was writing stories. I know now I was trying to force it – I was not writing about things I truly loved. When I started thinking about Tickers, however, I got very excited about the project. I was really enjoying the planning, including writing the questions to ask. Then I really enjoyed scheduling the interviews and meeting with the Tickers in this book. I felt such a rush of excitement whenever someone agreed to talk with me and when I started looking at the websites for my interviewees and preparing my questions.

The part that had made writing Tickers just the coolest, most fun and interesting project I've worked on is because I am part of the experience! I too am a Ticker. At the same time that I was tracking down people to interview, I was exploring my own passion: to find out what makes people tick and writing about it. I can say that writing Tickers has been my Ticker coming out party!

So I kindly invite you to join my journey of a year and a half. Along the way, I will explain what happened in my life as I introduce you to the most passionate, interesting people I have ever met. Let's go!

Story 1: Bill Smith, CMMI Instructor: Why can't I have fun at work?

Flying monkeys with shiny black capes whizzed past my head as the booming chords of "Back in Black" shook the seats. A tall, striking bald man strode past wearing a KISS T-shirt and a blazer, flashing a dazzling smile. Immediately the participants became engaged with the music, almost dancing in their chairs, turning their heads, and anticipating what was to come.

Why aren't more presentations like this? Why isn't work like this?

It was back in November 2009. I had just been on vacation in Rio De Janiero, picking sand out of my bathing suit and drinking out of a coconut. Two days later, I shivered as I tromped through the snow into the Hyatt Regency Tech Center in Denver for a work trip. I thought I left fun behind on the plane in South America. I had no idea I was about to be entertained by one of the delightful people I have ever encountered.

Two years earlier, I came into work and learned that I had been "volunteered" to lead our quality management system effort. Our newly won contract required our software development team to have a quality management system established. We could choose either International Standards Organization (ISO) 9001 or Capability Maturity Model Indicator (CMMI) development compliance. We had just won the contract to support a major legacy system, and with the exception of a couple of people, no one knew much about it. And now we were required to ensure we had a quality management system? Yikes! So, lucky me, I was "shanghaied" into leading the project.

To "smarten up," I signed Kevin (my boss), Mike (Kevin's boss) and myself up for a conference held by the National Defense Industrial Association on CMMI. It seemed like a good idea when I registered a few months prior, but on this day, to say I was not looking forward to the conference was an understatement. I was jet-lagged and dehydrated. I anticipated being treated to "Death by PowerPoint" on an endless loop for four days.

In reviewing the conference agenda's list of presentations, I opted to go to see "9299 – Creatively Applying CMMI®-SVC in a Very Small Consulting Firm". It was the last presentation of the day during the 4:15 to 5 PM time slot. Kevin, Mike and I had split up to attend different presentations at the conference so we could compare notes. Besides feeling like I was still on Brazil time, I was exhausted from the boring presentations I had already attended, looking for the right conference room (and the nearest coffee station), and making small talk with people I didn't know. I was hungry and cranky, already Googling the location to the sushi restaurant in downtown Denver where we would eat dinner. One more presentation, I said to myself. Should I just sneak off and go to my room before dinner?

And that's when Bill Smith entered the room and rocked my world.

As a young person going into the work force, I aimed for a white collar job after graduating from college. The advice I was always given was, "Act like a professional." I think what people meant by "act professional" included dressing well for an interview, speaking in a way that you will be taken seriously, and standing out from your competition by being (or appearing to be) the smartest person in the room. Or as George Thoroughgood sings, "Get a haircut and get a real job." Besides being well-dressed, the 'smartest person in the room' is supposed to be serious. Once the person has a job, they are encouraged to remain serious, keeping their emotions in check.

But life is so very short! Why do we feel we have to live it on someone else's terms? Are we afraid of authority…afraid of the naysayers to the point where we let the naysayers run our lives? But if we resent what they say, why are we listening? Why pay attention to them at all? Who made the rules anyway?

The emphasis on this "serious" work environment stems from the Protestant work ethic. Turns out the rules were made many years ago by a fellow whom most office workers wouldn't realize they were following...Martin Luther!

All I remember about Martin Luther from high school was that he was the dude who nailed his thesis to a door. (I tend to zone when it comes to religious history.) But when I started researching the American work culture, I realized that almost every place where I have ever worked had a touch of ML lurking around. I went to my trusty source of information, Google, and did a search on Puritan work ethics.

According to Wikipedia, "It is argued that Protestants, beginning with Martin Luther, had reconceptualized worldly work as a duty which benefits both the individual and society as a whole. Thus, the Catholic idea of good works was transformed into an obligation to consistently work diligently as a sign of grace. Whereas Catholicism teaches that good works are required of Catholics as a necessary manifestation of the faith they received, and that faith apart from works is dead (James 2:14-26) and barren, the Calvinist theologians taught that only those who were predestined (cf. the Calvinist concept of double predestination) to be saved would be saved."[iii]

Basically, the Calvinists thought you had no choice about whether you were good or not…you were pre-programmed before you arrived here on Earth. "Since it was impossible to know who was predestined, the notion developed that it might be possible to discern that a person was elect (predestined) by observing their way of life. Hard work and frugality, as well as social success and wealth, were thought to be two important consequences of being one of the elect; Protestants were thus attracted to these qualities and supposed to strive for reaching them."

So according to the Calvinists, the way a person lives their life is supposed to demonstrate that they are in fact one of the chosen people…that by appearing to be successful, they are favored by God.

According to Samuel Gregg on *Mercatornet,* "These forms of Protestantism ingrained the belief among their adherents that they should avoid superficial hobbies, games, and entertainment. Instead, Christians should commit themselves totally to whatever calling to which God had summoned them. These forms of Protestantism, especially their central doctrine of predestination, helped to foster the type of focused minds and disciplined work habits that are essential for market economies."[iv]

The effect of this is obvious in typical white collar offices in America as this work ethic seems to linger. Anything seen as frivolous in nature is perceived as unprofessional. Anything unprofessional is seen as taking time and energy away from the pursuit of business and therefore is nonproductive. It is interesting to me that this Calvinist theory of good v. bad would still exist in workplaces today. Many human resources departments would likely bristle at the idea since most strive to be tolerant of all workers' religious freedoms. This notion seems to fly in the face of the American dream where we tell children if you work hard, you too can achieve whatever you want. However, having a serious workplace seems to be ingrained in many people's minds as the correct way to be "professional."

There are of course notable exceptions to the rule. The Google corporate office famously has a casual work atmosphere with tons of awesome perks. When I watched the movie, "The Internship" (which was set at the Google work campus), I kept thinking, "Why don't we have nap pods? For God's sake, we need nap pods at our office!" I really admire the people who have opened their minds and made their offices a more creative and open space for ideas. However, these are the exception, not the norm.

This attitude towards being professional (aka seriously boring) can sadly carry over to all aspects of the office. Unfortunately, this includes office training. Training classes, both online and in person, are usually a dull affair. Having been "treated" to numerous online training presentations, I can attest to this. Many presentations of the facts are presented in bullets, and narrated in a matter-of-fact manner. The presentation is given in a way that is fact-laden, with an emphasis on the information.

But this is not how people learn.

People retain facts when they are linked with emotion. Many people relate to stories because they experience the emotions which are presented in the story. In stories, there is a problem which must be addressed. There is a crisis where something can be lost. And then there is a conclusion where the story wraps up. In stark contrast with the monotonous recitation of facts that is performed in most training classes, the telling of a story is an exciting buildup where the listener wants to find out how the tale ends.

Why do we continue to cling to a dull approach if it is not effective? I think it is because people are insecure about looking unprofessional. We want to be taken seriously. We don't want to be laughed at or made to feel foolish. We have been told we should be the smartest person in the room, and anything that might make us look otherwise should be avoided.

While there are fewer practicing Protestants in America, and many American offices include people of many faiths (or atheists, or worshippers of the Flying Spaghetti Monster, etc.), many offices cling to this approach like a life raft. How much are we losing by holding this outdated approach in a death grip? How many employees are bored to tears during meetings? How many students sit in classrooms to learn business practices and end up spaced out and miserable? How much information can be retained if students are tuning out?

Enter Bill Smith. He started as a CMMI trainer for a corporation. Then he discovered his own style, branched out on his own, and became a successful CMMI Entertainer, CMMI Institute-Certified CMMI Instructor and the President and CEO of Leading Edge Process Consultants LLC. And he is a purveyor of flying monkeys, devoted rock fan and self-proclaimed geek. And his students love him. One quote on LinkedIn states, *"Bill has...a lot of enthusiasm...a pleasure to work with...great learning experience."*

As the owner of Leading Edge Process Consultants, Bill describes himself as the CIO, CFO, and Chief Marketing Officer. Until recently, his license plate was "CMMI ROCKS!" But honestly, everything about Bill rocks. He is charming and unexpected. His face lights up one minute into an amazing smile, and then he starts into serious discussion, and then launches unexpectedly into a song.

In 2014, Bill was one of the first people who came to mind when I started writing Tickers. I just had to pick Bill's brain about his presentation since it knocked my metaphorical socks off. Bill and I stayed in touch after the conference in Denver, so I gave him a call and asked about whether I might interview him. When I told him how amazed I was in that conference room in Denver back in 2009, he said, "Oh my God! Really? I think I just peed myself a little!"

There is a talk Bill gave called "How to Deliver a Presentation that Rocks!" A few years ago, the CMMI Institute asked him to give a presentation to a mass audience at one of their workshops. Thankfully this presentation is online, and it allowed me to have a peek at how he crafts his presentation magic. Bill gave the presentation on presentations to about 200 professionals.

"It was a little bit intimidating at first, but fun," Bill said. "It was something that I had to put a little bit of time into preparing because I realized if I am going to be talking about delivering a presentation that rocks, and the presentation doesn't rock, then I am disproving what it is that I am talking about because I am not rocking as I am talking," he said, energetically. "But it was a blast, and I had fun with it. I think I even jumped off the stage at the end and I didn't break or strain anything! I knew that I had the audience when the new CEO of the CMMI Institute was sitting in the front row and he was actually watching and looking. A lot of times people in that position would be fiddling with their power tools but he was actually getting into it."

One of the methods Bill has used to make himself stand out and to market his energizing personality is social media. Bill has a presence on Twitter, Facebook and YouTube. He uploaded a video on YouTube called "CMMI Rocks! You Know You're At CMMI Maturity Level 1 When…"[v] Maturity Level 1 is when a company has not adopted any quality management standards, so they are essentially in chaos. The video includes Bill speaking to the camera. First, he is surrounded by album covers from the Beatles, Van Halen, Jimi Hendrix and The Doors…not your usual CEO surroundings. He describes a Maturity Level 1 company as having management that creates the major source of risk of a company, then holds up a picture of the Three Stooges implying that they are managing the company which is in trouble. He goes on to say maturity level one managers get their training from Darth Vader, maturity level one companies get their modeling not from CMMI but from Tyra Banks and Heidi Klum, and lip syncs lines from Star Wars and song lyrics from Lady Gaga. These pop culture references are presented humorously to capture the audience's attention. And they work!

Bill's techniques in class include the use of flying monkeys, using CMMI as a means to choose heavy metal and pop songs for his jukebox, and implementing CMMI services for the upcoming zombie apocalypse. The flying monkeys, stuffed animals which can be flung sling-shot style across a room, are also a clever marketing device, as their capes display Bill's company's name, Leading Edge Consultants. Social media also helps display Bill's humor and advertise his company.

"I started using social media a lot in 2008 and 2009 when I was first becoming recognized in doing this stuff because no one knew me." Bill left his previous company, Systems and Software Consortium, and had signed a non-compete with them, so he was starting his business with no ready clientele. He had to get "famous" in a hurry, and social media helped him do that. He has attracted a couple of thousand Twitter followers. "I don't even know who these people are. And frankly I was into [Twitter] for a couple of years, but I really don't Tweet that much anymore. And part of it is because I kind of did succeed in getting a name for myself, and frankly right now I am coasting a little bit. Maybe I shouldn't say this, because I love where I am right now in my business, and I am just kind of coasting and enjoying the ride. I'm not really trying to grow it at this point." Bill said he did not intentionally ratchet down his social media presence, but he slowed mainly because he has "real actual work to do." He found doing work interfered with time to blog, for example. He said that now that he is getting a ton of business without social media and that he is not really worried about it.

Bill graduated from Carnegie Mellon University with Bachelors in Applied Math (Operations Research track) – according to him, stated tongue-in-cheek: "Arguably when their admissions standards were a bit easier." He also received an MS from University of Pittsburgh (Information Science track).

After talking back and forth, I coordinated to meet Bill on a summer day in 2014 in his apartment complex in Reston, Virginia. We got cups of coffee from the nearby Keurig and sat by a gas fireplace (which countered the overabundance of air conditioning in the room), a comfortable place for our chat. Bill was relaxed and entertaining...thankfully we were in a separate area because Bill made me laugh really loudly.

***

K: What is the story of your life as you were growing up? Who was Bill Smith as a kid?

B: If I had to give a headline to it, it would be 'Small-Town Nerd Makes Good' or something like that. I am from a very small town in Pennsylvania, New Castle. It is a Rust Belt town nowadays, and even when I was growing up, there were elements of a Rust Belt town. It was a booming place to be, I'm sure, when my parents were working there in the '60's, '70's and the '80's, but it was a place...where I needed to get out of there. I went to school in Pittsburgh. I found out when I was in high school, I was a complete nerd, a complete geek.

And <u>now</u> I find that nerds and geeks are embraced by the world. At least maybe by the people I hang out with. Back then, I was not cool at all. I am at least a little bit cool now because I am geeky and nerdy. So I would say that would be my story in one headline, at least so far. Hopefully I have many years left in which I can fail. And I will fail many more times because you have to fail sometimes in order to succeed.

I was the guy with the real huge thick glasses; I was the guy with the overbite, with the large front teeth. I was the guy with acne, and I was the guy who didn't get a date because I figured, 'Why try?' At that point of time, books were much, much more appealing than girls. I knew if I wanted a book, I could get that book. But if I wanted a girl…um, never mind!

I graduated first in my class in high school. It was a small class…there were only the three of us. But still…[Laughs] No, actually there were about 120 or so of us. I was the stereotypical, prototypical nerd, until I graduated and I started my undergrad at Carnegie Mellon, and then I realized, 'Whoa, now I'm just like everyone else!' And all of a sudden I went from this über excellent student to like, 'Whoa, now I'm an average student! And wait a second, are you kidding me, I just took chemistry, and I got a C?' I didn't even know C was a valid grade!

I instantly became more worldly because I was very sheltered in New Castle. I was an only child. In my first week at Carnegie Mellon, I was getting breakfast and grabbed a doughnut for breakfast from one of the cafeterias. I sat down there with my doughnut, my orange juice, and probably my fruit, and I'm biting into the doughnut and thinking, 'Dammit, this is the worst doughnut I ever ate! Oh my God, how college sucks!' And then someone sitting next to me said, 'That's called a bagel.' And I said, 'Oh!' They explained it to me because I had never had a bagel before. Now I don't really consider a bagel to be a food from another culture, or associated with anything other than America. I don't really know for sure. I'm not a bagel expert!

New Castle is about 60 miles outside of Pittsburgh. Growing up, Bill loved going to Pittsburgh for baseball games, loved going to the zoo and the museums. There wasn't a lot of culture in New Castle, and Pittsburgh was the closest big town.

When I was growing up in the '70's, the Pittsburgh sports teams were totally rocking. The Pirates in baseball were winning world championships, the Steelers were winning four [championships] back then, so it was an awesome sports place to be.

Bill developed a love of sports, especially football. He discussed the Terrible Towel.

It came about in the early '70's. Myron Cope, a sportscaster, came up with the concept. I think I remember the original broadcast…it was in the early days of the Steelers winning the playoffs. I hate to admit this, but my first thought was, 'How bogus is this? Really, we need a gimmick like a towel? What?' I thought it was going to be a one game kind of thing. I mean, if you were to ask me if this kind of thing would catch on, I would have said, 'What? Are you kidding me? A terrible towel? I'm not even sure I like the name of it!' But the rest is history. I am guessing I own about 10 or 12 Terrible Towels right now.

Since playing rock is a big feature before and after Bill's presentations, I wanted to ask him about his love of music.

Rock music is a big part of your presentations in your classes and at conferences. When did rock music become part of your life?

B: Pop music became part of my life in the early to mid '70's. I was totally into popular music. I would listen to Casey Kasem's top 40 every weekend, his countdowns. I would write down the songs and chart them myself. 'This song is number 2 this week, and it was number 4 last week.' Sometimes Casey would say that, but if he wouldn't say that, he didn't have to, because I would know!

At the time, I was listening to middle of the road, perhaps you would say the softer side of music. Elton John was a big hero back then. I was listening to Fleetwood Mac, Billy Joel. I appreciate all those artists and their music, but what I kind of wish I was listening to back then was the Who, and Led Zepplin, and Van Halen, and AC/DC, and the Rolling Stones. Those are the groups from that era that I love and totally embrace now. I probably went through a rebirth in the year 2000 or so where for some reason, I started getting into hard rock. Maybe some of it might have been because I started doing more working out and exercising, some weight lifting. I mean, come on, you're going to lift more weights if you are listening to Led Zeppelin than if you're listening to the Eagles!

My musical taste diversified a little bit also within the past 10 or 15 years. I didn't like soul, Marvin Gaye, Jackson 5 or Stevie Wonder. Now I love all that stuff! Now my philosophy of music is there is no such thing as bad music. There is only music that you play at an inappropriate time. If you're holding a happy hour for some friends, Motown might be just what the doctor ordered. But on the other hand, if I am running or lifting weights, maybe Motown, or maybe something else would be better. If I am ever sitting around depressed, which thankfully doesn't happen a whole lot, maybe I would gravitate towards, I don't know, country? 'My wife left me and my mom died, and my dog got run over by a train.'

[Laughs] Your presentations have elements of humor. Where do you get your sense of humor? Do you always remember gravitating towards funny things?

B: You know, I struggle with that a little bit. I think probably I used a sense of humor when growing up. I think I used it as a little bit of a defense mechanism, or a little bit of…I struggled…I'm fine with the way I look now. I'm not Brad Pitt and I know that. I'm more like George Clooney, and don't you dare laugh! [Laughs]

When I was growing up, I had self-image problems, especially with the way that I looked. And I guess I used a sense of humor as a way to help get friends and to get dates or impress people. People generally like other people who have a sense of humor. I've always been relatively witty when it comes to words and word play, and I've always enjoyed puns.

Now for me [my sense of humor] is pretty spontaneous. It's nothing that I actually have to try for. I'm not a joke person. I don't really tell jokes. I find humor in life. I think life got better for me when I started finding humor in life. I can find humor in the most ridiculous things in life. Even in bad things that I might be going through in life. There is humor in just about every situation to be found. Now, that doesn't mean you always need to share it!

I can share the humor I see in my life, and generally that is perceived by people as good. It's called self-deprecating humor, and it is kind of making fun of yourself. People kind of like it when other people make fun of themselves. People don't like other people who are arrogant or are braggarts. Actually, that's how I get through some of the stories that I tell in my classes. The problem with presentations or delivering in front of a live audience is if you make it too much about yourself, it is unappealing. People start thinking, 'Oh listen to this guy. All he can do is talk about himself! How egotistical can he be?' But, if you start interjecting humor into it, even if it is about yourself, people kind of like that. That's one of the ways that you can tell a 'me' story. I tell a lot of 'me' stories, about me, from when I was developing software or managing projects, etc. I tell a lot of these stories in my classes, but the way that I can get away with that is because I kind of make them funny. There's something funny in just about any story that I can think of, especially if we consider things like project management.

In my online research, I found that you have an educational background in Math (Operations Research) and Information Science. How did you feel about math as a kid? Did you love it or hate it, or was it just there?

B: This will sound weird…even though my undergraduate degree was in math, I wasn't passionately drawn to math. In fact, I still kind of really don't like math. It is sort of OK. When it comes to higher math, like calculus, trig or above, I really don't have a fascination with it, which sounds weird for a math major. I think I was drawn to it because I was good at it. Just because I don't love it doesn't mean I wasn't good at it.

Interesting…so you can be good at things you don't love. So being good at something doesn't mean it makes you tick!

When I went to college, I didn't have a clue what I wanted to major in. So something like applied math seemed like a default thing to get into. If I wanted to move into some kind of engineering or computers or whatever, that would be a decent foundation. So that's how I got into math.

Nowadays, and in fact over the past couple of decades of my career, I realized I use the liberal arts part of my education so much more than the math part of my education. I can't remember the last time I used higher level math. Duh, I use algebra all the time, right? We all do, I guess. I had a class at Carnegie Mellon called 'Aesthetics.' I had another class called 'Theories of Painting'. These were classes that my engineering friends laughed at! They just could not believe it. But you know what? Nowadays, what do I do? I design PowerPoint presentations, web sites, and that sort of stuff. For several years, I did user interface design, and I was programming for other people, and guess what? That aesthetics class came in much more handy than any of my math classes!

Did you think at the time that these liberal arts classes would be helpful?

B: No, I had no clue. I was drawn to it because I thought it was cool. I loved the 'Aesthetics' class, and I loved the 'Theories of Painting' class in ways I never, ever loved my math classes. Did you get 'ever'? You can write down several 'evers'! I don't want come across as a math hater, because math is very necessary and very fundamental, but there is just so much more.

Carnegie Mellon is where CMMI was developed when Watts Humphrey joined the Software Engineering Institute in 1986. You were at Carnegie Mellon between 1979 and 1983. You have included quotes from Watts Humphrey in some of your presentations. Did you meet Watts Humphrey at Carnegie Mellon as an alumnus (since you were in grad school when he started working at CM)? Were you familiar with CMMI while you were an undergrad? If so, were you interested in it?

Bill said he never met Watts Humphrey as an undergrad, and actually SEI came into existence later after he graduated. Bill did meet Watts Humphrey a couple of times at conferences.

B: I can't really claim I had a conversation at all [with Watts]. It was probably me and a group of people thinking, 'Oh my God! That's Watts Humphrey right there! He is an über rock star in my world, and here I am standing six feet away from him, and this is kind of unbelievable!'

I forget exactly what he was talking about at the time, but I think he was probably talking about something like his basement. At least when I heard him, he wasn't really talking about intellectual theories of software development. He was just talking about regular life. From what I know about Watts, he really applied a lot of these theories of his to his regular life which is kind of cool. I do a little bit of that from time to time, just a smidgen of that. There's a little bit of CMMI in my life.

In reviewing your info online, there is an emphasis on things that rock ("CMMI Rocks!" "How to Deliver a Presentation that Rocks!") What does it mean to you if something rocks?

B: It stimulates your senses in an utterly fantastic way, and maybe even an unexpected way. Maybe not unexpected, because if you go to a rock concert, I guess you expect to be rocked? But short of a rock concert, in everyday life, you just don't expect to be rocked. Right? It's just not something that you expect necessarily in the business world! I have seen some presentations that rocked, and I have been to some classes that rocked…although, as I say, sadly, not a whole lot!

Part of the reason is because for something to actually rock in the business world, there needs to be a fair amount of emotion in it. When you start applying emotion to things, you are almost immediately taking some risk. You start being emotional about something because it's kind of like, 'Whoa! How is this going to end up? I'm being exuberant about this, passionate, emotional. How are people going to receive this?' Because it is out of the ordinary.

You might say something that could offend people. You might say something that could rub people the wrong way. But I also think if you start becoming too careful about things, then you are just going to become generic and vanilla. Honestly, in a lot of my professional world, generic and vanilla is what is wanted. A lot of the government contracts I have worked on in the past – that's what's called for, that's what's needed. 'Give us a system that's generic and vanilla! Don't make it rock!'

Sometimes to make something literally rock, you need to put some more time into it! And some more thought into it, perhaps. There may not be the possibility of doing it…in my presentation "How to Create a Presentation that Rocks!" I know sometimes after I give that presentation, some people will come up to me and say, 'Bill, I understand what you were saying. The problem is that I just don't have the time to do that.' And I realize that! I tell them that I realize that they don't have the time to create a presentation that rocks. And it is not the end of the world!

Not all presentations need to rock. I wish that everyone would, OK? But it is like anything. Whether we are talking about presentations or talking about cars, maybe we don't have the time, the money, the infrastructure, or the right designers who have the right passion to make this car totally rock. So we end up with 'insert name of car here'! I don't want to name a car because I don't want to offend car owners of a specific vehicle! But instead of a Lamborghini, you end up with…something else. For something to rock, there needs to be a fair amount of emotion put into it, passion, and probably a dose of…thinking!

You have 28 years of software and systems engineering experience. Who were some of your heroes and mentors at work?

B: There were a couple of mentors of mine back when I worked for the Systems and Software Consortium, formerly known as the Software Productivity Consortium. My first manager there was a guy by the name of Joe Seppy. Joe's school of management, I absolutely loved. Generally, the Consortium only hired very experienced people. His school of management was, 'OK, I'm hiring the right people for these engagements. They're very experienced. They know what to do. I just need to facilitate their jobs. I just need to make their jobs easier. I don't need to actually manage them. They can manage themselves! I just need to make sure that they have the right tools to do their jobs, and if they have any problems, I can handle that.'

And Joe was consummate at that. He was consummate at honestly, staying out of my way, out of everyone else's way. But yet, if I needed advice, he would give me awesome advice because the guy was just a font of wisdom! And he was just a really nice guy overall. We could talk about rock music! We loved that! We had some disagreements over some of the bands.

He sometimes would have us come up with a first draft of our own performance reviews. I remember coming up with a draft of my review: coming up with a list of my accomplishments, things I needed to work on, what I think I did well, what I think I did 'not so kinda well'. I remember giving it to him, and he called me into his office after he read it. He said, 'Bill, this would be a wonderful review if only it were true.' And I said to him, 'What do you mean?' And he said, 'You are way too hard on yourself.' And he looked at all the critiques that I had, and he ended up removing all, if not most, of the critiques. And you know what? At that point in time, I decided he's the boss and I'm not going to argue with him! Right? Those kinds of behaviors were where I really grew to like him and respect him.

A lot of the studies say, if you are looking for major dissatisfactions in your job, a lot of them come from your manager. On the other hand, if you get along with that guy or that gal, you may be happy, even if you aren't necessarily making a ton of money. That might be a more important differentiator than the amount of money you are making.

The other mentor that I would mention was a guy named Sean Cassell at the Consortium. He was another one of the people who gave me confidence there, that I could do things that I didn't necessarily know how to do. I remember he came into my office once. He asked me what I knew about configuration management. And I ended up talking about configuration management for a while. And he said, 'Good. I would like you to teach a course on configuration management.' And I'm like, 'What?' And actually at that point in time I hadn't taught any courses previously with them, and I had only taught one course previously in my life! This was a two-day configuration management course! And I said, 'Sean? Really?' And he said, 'Don't freak! We'll give you some time to prepare. Just let us know how much time you need. We'll make sure that it's budgeted.' And I'm like, 'Sean, it's not necessarily about the preparation. I don't know how to teach!' And he said, 'Listen, I know you. In just talking with you, I know you will be fine. Just don't obsess over it; you'll be fine!' So of course, I did obsess over it!

But the first time I taught our configuration management course, I remember looking over at the student feedback afterwards. I remember this one guy saying something like, 'Wow! This guy totally blew me away! He totally blew away the preconceived notions I had about configuration management so now I understand it totally!' When I started reading comments like that, I started thinking, 'Well, you know what? At least I'm going to believe the students! At least as long as they keep tossing me good comments, I'm going to believe them!'

That's great! How did you use this while teaching? For example, in your presentation on Storytelling, you explain how stories engage emotions to make facts more memorable. Where did you learn about storytelling? You gave yourself the title of "Head Storyteller". Have you always been a storyteller? Who taught you, or who was your inspiration, for telling stories?

B: I need to give someone credit. I pulled a lot of that information from an author of a book called 'Presentation Secrets'. [Presentation Secrets by Alexei Kapterev] He also created a presentation going around the Internet several years ago called 'Death by PowerPoint'[vi]. My presentations take a lot of principles from his book which I happen to agree with. I read his book and agreed with his book. Now, had I been telling stories in my classes prior to reading his book? Of course I had.

How did I learn to tell stories? Probably by telling them wrong for a while! This one class, CMMI for Development…I don't know the exact number, but I have taught it approximately 100 times. I stopped keeping track at 90 something. A lot of the stories I have told over and over and over and over again. I'm quite certain that the first time I told them they were probably a little bit on the lame side. OK? But like anything else, if you keep doing it over and over again, you either get better, or if you're not getting better, you're getting fired! Or you lose business. So I got better at story telling because there was no alternative.

I got better at live presentations in general when my attitude became a little more carefree about talking in front of an audience. And I think for years, I probably suffered from the paradigm a lot of people have, and that is when you get up in front of an audience, you'd better know your stuff, and you'd better be the expert.

What I found out is that's not what people want to hear. That's not what people need. People don't need an expert talking to them. I mean, certainly you kind of need to know your stuff. You need to be familiar with the material. Being an expert helps.

The problem with most experts in their fields is when they try to give a presentation, they are utterly boring. And yes! You know this! Why are they utterly boring? It could be that their focus is wrong. They are trying to impress people, or they are showing slides of bullet points. Facts don't resonate. People don't want to see facts. People don't want to see bullet points read to them because they are not going to remember them, and it is quickly turn into 'blah blah blah blah blah', it's not going to register, they're going to start checking their phones, or whatever. We have a lot of competition nowadays.

The secret then, for giving an effective presentation, would be…and this I think aligns perfectly with the topic of this book…have passion! Be passionate about whatever it is that you are talking about. Show some emotion!

People love passion. Even if the passionate person is saying some silly things or maybe making some mistakes along the way, and I am certainly not a perfect speaker! I sometimes stumble over my words, and immediately I make a joke of it because that's what you have to do. Or if I find that maybe I misspoke in a presentation or in class I can correct myself a little bit later on. And that's OK!

I never try to be perfect in a presentation because it's never, ever going to happen. It's never a goal of mine when making a presentation because I never want to set myself up for failure. Because guess what? I'm never going to deliver a perfect presentation. You aren't either. Maybe people have come close. Maybe people like Steve Jobs have come close. Steve Jobs had passion. He was passionate about what he was talking about. And that can go a long way. You're engaging people's emotions and they want to listen to you.

The first time I was called upon by my previous employer to teach Intro to CMMI, they said, 'We would like you to go down and listen to one of our instructors teach this 3-day course. Just listen to her for a couple of hours, and that will give you an idea about how to teach this course.' I came back up after listening to her, and I told my manager, 'Joe, I can't do that!' Because I listened to that instructor, and my jaw dropped as she was training because she was so smart. Honestly she was smarter than me, she probably still is smarter than me, and I'll probably never be that smart. Don't get me wrong, I'm not stupid. In fact, I think I'm above average in intelligence, but not as smart as her. I was intimidated. And what Joe said to me was, 'Bill, what you need to realize is that I'm not asking you to teach the class like her. I'm asking you to teach the class yourself. Teach the class like you would teach it.'

And I don't know that I necessarily heard those words at first because I thought he was joking, but over the years, that has so resonated with me. Honestly that's how I can make money teaching this class is because I differentiate myself from a lot of people that teach the class and that's because I do keep them engaged with stories, I do keep them engaged with passion. I do keep them engaged by not speaking in a monotone. I keep them engaged by not showing them a slide full of bullet points. Instead, there's a picture and then maybe a couple of words. Joe was right!

In terms of engaging an audience, it starts with being authentic. It starts with being genuine. You need to be genuine, you need to be authentic, and you need to not bamboozle your audience. Say things that they understand. Don't use big words! A lot of people when they give presentations immediately start talking in some other kind of language. There's their normal English that they use standing around at the water cooler, and somehow when they're giving a presentation, all of a sudden every word is four or more syllables. That's not how normal people talk! That's why people don't connect a lot of times in presentations. They start talking like they came from a different planet. 'What are you talking about? Dude, use normal words!'

How did you make the leap from teaching for Systems and Software Consortium to creating Leading Edge, your own company?

B: It was so, so easy! It was incredible! It was something called 'process of elimination'.

Here's what happened. I found in the year 2006 I was a reasonably high-income wage earner, and so was my wife, and we were both spending a lot of hours at work and traveling on the road. I was a consultant, and she was an executive. And guess what? Oh by the way, we were kind of raising a kid as well. I started thinking about it in the year 2004 when both my parents died in the same year. That started me reassessing life just a little bit, and priorities. And is my priority all about just working as hard as you can? Is it really all about amassing money? Is it really all about professional development and career? And I started questioning, and started thinking, 'Well, wait a minute? What about other stuff?'

So, I talked to Kathy, my wife at the time, about it, and I had an idea. I would try to drop down to part-time at my job at the Consortium, make less money, but a lot of the house projects, etc., I would do during the week. The groceries, the bill-paying, the laundry, all the stuff, and just bring sanity to our life. I think we lacked a basic measure of sanity there for a little while. She said fine. I talked to my management at the Consortium; after a while, they said fine. In 2006, I put in 1,000 hours at the Consortium. I had this perfect work-life balance! Everything was getting done at home that needed to be done, I was still working enough that I was professionally engaged – I did not want to change that. It was literally awesome.

Then 2007 came. The Consortium started using me less and less. It wasn't because of customer feedback. My customers still loved me. My students still loved me. It was because there may have been some financial difficulties. And the Consortium started to become more focused on making sure that all their other full-time employees were fully billable, as much as possible, as opposed to placating me. I wasn't called a part-time employee; I was called an 'unbenefited employee.' Because of the nature of my work, some weeks I might work 40 hours, and some weeks I might work 0 hours. So that year, they started using me less and less. Towards the end of the year, I realized [I had worked] less than 300 hours. And that's no way to live your life! Then I just didn't feel balanced in terms of the whole work-life thing. So I talked to my managers and tried to figure out if we could do something different. They assured me that in the next year they would try.

But as my good friend Yoda would say, 'Do. Or do not. There is no try.' So that's what I'm thinking. I didn't say these words, but I was thinking, 'You're going to try?' 'Try' wasn't good enough! I had to worry about making actual cash money; I had to worry about my actual career and it not going down the tubes. So I looked at my alternatives. One was just to trust that they would try harder and I would have enough work the next year. ANK! Sorry, no! The other one was to try to get back to a full-time job, either with them or with someone else. Sorry, no! I had tasted work-life balance, and I loved it!

Another alternative was to try to get another part-time job or an 'unbenefited employee' job with another organization, and I thought, 'That's not going to happen.' Or at least it's not going to be able to retain the same level of income. The only reason why the Consortium was able to do that for me was because they knew me, I had worked with them for six years, and they knew what kind of employee I was. Presumably they thought I was a decent one and they let me do that. So, I had an idea, and that idea was, by process of elimination, 'Wait a second! The stuff they've been having me do over the past year or two, is pretty much just me doing training engagements and then coming back. I think I could probably do that on my own!' And I started thinking through that, I started doing a little bit of market research, I started doing a little bit of [CMMI] modeling, and I thought, you know what? I think I could probably do that on my own and probably kinda fail, and still make more money than I did in the past year working for them! So I did that!

So I found out that in 2008, my first full year of business, I was wrong. I couldn't make as much money as I was working with them. I made $11,000. I could have made more money flipping burgers at McDonald's! I don't want to slam McDonald's employees, I'm sure it's a fine place to work…NOT!

What did happen was the next year, 2009, I ended up making more money that year than I ever did previously in my life. So it was that one year of not making a whole lot of money…that year was dedicated to figuring out how to make money. Because with my sort of unique business model, of renting training space and trying to fill that training space, and my income being directly related to how many people am I convincing to take my classes, it's a pretty unique business model in the industry. In fact, even though the name of my company is Leading Edge Process Consultants, since 2008 I can only think of one very brief, one-week engagement where I was paid an hourly rate. Other than that, since 2008, I've made all of my money without billing anyone an hourly rate for anything. And most of that has been from people signing up for my courses online.

I have a part two to my answer. I'm going to answer a different question now – well it is actually a segue. I never wanted to be an independent business owner. Never, ever did I have that as a goal! I never dreamt of that; it was not a lifelong ambition. If you would have asked me just a couple of months before I did it, would I do any good at it, I would have said, 'No! Are you kidding me? How would I figure out how to do that? I don't know how to get business! I don't have a marketing background! I'm not a salesman! I'm not a marketer! I would have no clue!' I didn't want to do it at all until I had no choice.

It was the whole process of elimination thing where I actually felt like I was boxed into a corner and I had no choice. But in the intervening years, now I have found that I love it so much, that I am only exaggerating a little when I say this, I would almost rather be poor but still have my own business than make a good income and work for someone else because I love it that much! That's probably not literally true – I don't want to be poor, there are very few people who have that ambition of being poor. But what I am saying, quite confidently, that I just can't imagine working for another person right now.

Even if I drift into what I might call 'semi-retirement', I'm quite sure it's going to be me launching another business and me doing something else, and me having my own venture. And you know what? Maybe I will not make a whole lot of money on it, but at that point, it may not even be that important.

I've probably become unmanageable! So really, over the past 6 and a half years of doing this on my own, I've become utterly unmanageable. Maybe unemployable? I can't think of why someone should hire me! If I were interviewing for a job, why would you hire me? Because I'm going to want to do things my own way! And you know, I'm not sure that translates into the best employee.

How important is energy to your approach to life? Energy could be synonymous with passion. How do you tap into that?

B: I don't know how I do it! Oh my God, finally you have asked me a question where I have no answer! [Laughs]

We can get kind of metaphysical and even kind of spiritual here. I consider myself maybe not to be the most devoutly religious person in the world, but I do consider myself to be spiritual. And I know some people are going to ask what the difference is there, and I don't even want to get into it. Whether you call it God, or whether you call it love, or whether you call it energy, or whether you don't have a name for it, I do believe that we don't have all the answers. I do believe that there's much more to life than face value, than what we can observe. To me, that's almost kind of self-evident. I tap into…I don't have a name for it.

Love/passion/energy/spirituality/God…all of these things vaguely mean something similar. I just feel like when we're here on Earth in this existence, we need to make the most out of every moment. You know what? I'm guessing that whether you're an Atheist, or whether you're a devout member of some religion – insert whatever, a name of a religion - or anything in between, I think it still kind of applies. Why not make the most of every single moment that you're here? Because if you don't know what happens to you after you die, then of course you need to make the most of every moment that you're here.

And if you do think you know what happens to you after you die, you still realize how precious life is at least in terms of getting to that other place you would like to get to. I believe in making the most of every moment. Part of that probably goes back to…if I had to pick a seminal moment when maybe my personality started changing, maybe in a different way, it would be with both of my parents passing away in 2004. And as an only child, who suddenly had his parents taken away from him, and having no siblings, I really grappled with, 'How is this possibly good? How can I possibly walk away with something good about this?' And what I realized was, I saw my parents suffer. I suffered as well, not nearly as much as them, obviously. I went through a whole lot of emotional stuff back then and I remember walking away from that whole experience thinking, 'OK, geez, I just lost both of my parents. Almost regardless of what happens to me now, it is going to be easy compared to going through that.' And I found that I no longer had fear.

I found that I lost fear of doing things. I found that I lost any potential fear I would have of a client. I would argue that you could put in front of me any client that you want to and I will not fear that person even a little bit. I don't fear anyone. And look at me. I'm not a weightlifter; I don't believe I have a strong, abrasive personality. Maybe I wouldn't correspond with someone you think would have no fear, but…I started riding roller coasters more! I began to not have any fear at all of new situations because again, in the back of my mind, I was probably thinking, 'Geez, I lived through some stuff there, and that was pretty difficult stuff. So other stuff, difficult client? Bring it!'

And since then, I have dealt with some difficult clients. I remember shortly after that experience, I was in a room with two vice presidents in a client organization. I remember them saying, 'Wait a second, we're the client. And you are telling us right now if we ask you to do this that you're not going to do this?' And I remember saying, 'Yeah! That's exactly what I'm saying! There's no way that's happening!' And having no fear about that, of getting fired, or my company not getting used because you know what? I was right, my client was wrong, because guess what? A lot of times, your clients are wrong. I'm all about the truth and honesty. 'You know what, difficult client? Bring it!' Experiences like that, not only client experiences, but experiences with other parts of my life, led me to have little to no fear about getting into new circumstances or situations.

In one of your blog posts online, you discuss commitment and its importance. You discuss that other trainers will cancel classes at the last minute, but you refuse to do that. What does commitment mean to you? Why is it important?

B: It's interesting that you bring up that exact example. As I am sitting here right now, we are only a couple of hours away from a deadline I have for people to sign up for classes I am having next week. One is Intro to CMMI for Development. I have 21 people who are enrolled in that. It's going to be awesome! I'm going to make a nice chunk of change off of that, and it will be fine.

On Friday, I am teaching the Services Supplement for CMMI class and when I checked this morning, I had three people enrolled in that. And in fact, I got an email from someone who wanted to cancel. So it might go down to two people enrolled in that Services Supplement CMMI class. So, one might be tempted to cancel the class. Because guess what? I'm not going to make money! Even if three or four more people sign up for the class, I'm not going to make money. It's not going to be worth my time to teach that class.

If I strictly look at that class in a vacuum as an income-producing event, it will not be worth my time. However, I don't do that class in a vacuum! I view that class as, 'Wait a second! I put that on my calendar, I said it's going to happen, it's going to happen.' Some people's schedules depend on that. Some people might be having an appraisal that depends on them getting through this class. Some people may have made non-refundable travel engagements that depend on them getting through this class. And guess what? I would like to think I have a good reputation in the industry, and I would like to keep it! Word gets around about who are the good instructors and who are the not-so-good instructors, who are the companies that keep their promises, and who are the companies who don't keep their promises. So even though I say it may not be worth my money in the short term to have that class, guess what? In the long term, it's worth my money!

If anything, it might be enhancing my reputation a little bit. These people are going to get something out of the class; they're going to be benefitting from it. When I talk about losing money from the class, it's not going to be a fortune. And I will have made enough money the previous three days that I'm fine with it.

But what I'll do is I will revisit my schedule for next year, and I may decide not to teach that class publicly next year. That's the way I think these things should be handled. If you don't get enough people in your class, don't cancel the class on the people who are depending on it! Instead, revisit your marketing! And maybe there weren't enough people in the class because the marketing failed. Maybe there's just not enough marketing demand right now. Maybe it was the same day someone else was teaching the same class. I don't know. But I have to look at all of these things. I need to get to the root cause as to why I don't have that many people in my class.

When I'm talking about keeping your commitments, I guess that would be an example of it. If you say that you are going to do something for someone, DO IT! Even if it becomes difficult, and not so expedient, and not what you imagined. And sometimes in life you just have to grow a pair. [Laughs]

How different is it working for yourself versus working for someone else? Did you immediately take to it like a duck to water? Or were you like, 'What do I do?'

B: It was fascinating at first. Given my somewhat unique business model, it was like a puzzle to figure out. The thing that made it fascinating was that it was a puzzle, but as I was figuring out the puzzle, this was like real-life money that I'm investing in figuring out the puzzle. Different marketing approaches, different ads on Google, trying different things with my web site.

Very quickly, the fascinating puzzle did give way to a somewhat depressing puzzle. I found that I would try something and it wouldn't work. I would try something else, and it wouldn't work. There were times that first year when honestly I would just go up to bed at 7 o'clock at night because things just weren't working out, and I would get under the covers and I just wouldn't want to deal with anyone. By the same token, at the same time, things would happen. Like while I was sleeping, or in the middle of the night, I would have a thought, at like 2 in the morning, and I would go downstairs and tinker with my website.

Eventually, this puzzle which became a depressing puzzle, I started figuring it out. When I started figuring it out, it became much less depressing and much more fascinating. I began to focus not so much on the failures, but on what I was doing right. And if I found I was doing something right, keep doing those right things! If I failed at something, just don't do that again! I don't have an MBA, I don't have a business degree, I don't have a marketing certificate, so I had to figure out the whole marketing thing on my own. And basically I was able to do that.

Actually, even though there were down times, even the down times were much, much better than working for someone else. Because of the fact that I can be a bit of a control freak, and because of the fact that I owned the problem, and I owned the business, I got incredible satisfaction.

Don't get me wrong...I loved my employers in the past, I loved my clients in the past, but there was much more satisfaction now that I was dealing with my real live money and figuring out how to invest in the company in the best ways. It very quickly got to the point where it was so much better than working for someone else that I can't imagine working for someone else. On a scale of 'How much does it rock?', I would say working for someone else – 4 – working for myself – 10 – on the Work Rock-O-Meter!

What makes somebody tick? If someone knows what makes them tick, then they have found their passion. How did this figure into what makes you tick?

B: I haven't always ticked! The person that you're interviewing now, if you had interviewed me 10 – 12 years ago, it would have been sad and pathetic, and maybe melancholy. I was a different person then, and I hadn't figured out what made me tick. Here's the thing about what makes me tick: We could say that I'm passionate about what I teach. We could say that I'm passionate about CMMI. We can say that, and maybe that's why you're talking to me, and that's fantastic. The problem is, that I'm not sure that that's the whole story. I'm not going to say it's not true. It certainly is true.

But it is only part of the story, because I would not be shocked if four years from now I'm doing something completely different. Don't get me wrong; I love what I'm doing now. I would not be shocked if I am doing something four years from now that has nothing to do with this, and, I know right now, sitting here, that I'm going to be passionate about it. I don't think the passion comes from the CMMI. It doesn't come from there. Don't get me wrong – I love the CMMI, I think it rocks; it's a great framework when you use it the right way. But that's not where the passion is coming from.

I think the passion comes from this thing that I tried to describe earlier, this thing like love, or if you're religious, God, or some amorphous energy, or whatever it is; I don't know where I am kind of tapping into this. I really feel like, and this is going to sound weird too, like there is this reservoir of stuff within me that I'm constantly tapping into.

Whether that is spirit, passion, energy, love, God, whatever, I feel like I'm constantly tapping into that, and I also feel like, OK, I can tap out of that for a while if I want to. Because frankly it is tough to be like that constantly. I can guarantee you that sometime next week when I have dinner and I am up in my apartment by myself, I'm not going to claim that I will be passionate about having dinner by myself. Not going to happen.

So I'm not passionate 24 x 7. If people can be that, that's awesome. That's who my new role model is going to be! If you interview them for this book, I want to meet them! And I would have one question: 'What kind of drugs are those, and where can I get them?' Because if someone is like that all the time, oh my God! I have this kind of energy generally when I am around other people. And I would say, almost irrespective of circumstances, it has to be moderated by social protocols. OK? There would be times where it would be weird for me to be having a conversation and for me to be as animated as I am right now in this conversation.

People do simultaneously energize me and also sap the energy out of me. I am getting stoked by this conversation; I love it! I think it's great. I'm going to have another conversation actually, a business meeting with someone, in a half hour, and then I am going to dinner with some people. I'm probably going to retain pretty much a similar level of energy throughout all of that. And then at 10 o'clock at night tonight, I'm going to crash! If you're calling me or texting me at that time, it's not you! I'm sorry! I just don't want to talk right now!

I mentioned a couple of reservoirs or names for where this passion, where the other stuff comes from. There are other places where it comes from as well maybe that I didn't mention. Namely coffee and Diet Coke! I find that the coffee and Diet Coke help a whole lot! And frankly, in the evening, occasionally, in moderation, wine!

Sometimes passion is stupid. Like I was so passionate about…my son, Connor, said two weeks ago, 'You're the only person I know who doesn't have a case for their smart phone!' And I said, 'Connor, if the folks at Apple meant for this phone to have a case on it, they would have built something with a case! I think it looks perfect!' But then, you drop it in a parking garage! [Holds up his iPhone with a huge crack in the glass.] And so I was passionate! I loved the design of the iPhone! It's like, 'Whoa, this is so cool! I can't make it better by putting a case on it!' I guess I could have made it better.

How do you connect with your inner passion? Are they inseparable, your passion for what you do versus your passion for life in general?

B: They're inseparable. I'm sorry, that's a pretty boring answer. You gave me the answer! Oh my goodness, yeah! You gave me either choice A or choice B! You should know, you should become a better interviewer than that! You gave me two choices so I took one of the choices! Don't do that! You've been awesome up until now! [Laughs]

[Laughs]

Were you always certain of your path?

B: No! I don't even know my path now! No, there is no path. Seriously, there is no path. There is no goal. This is kind of like a new concept for me or something I am just realizing right now, because of recent circumstances, my mindset nowadays is just to enjoy the journey.
It's not, 'Where do I want to be at a certain age? Or, where do I want to be when I die? And how do I get there?' What is the path to getting there? Increasingly, to me that is not as interesting to me as the journey. Don't get me wrong – I am goal oriented. I have lots of little goals here and there. But more and more and more, I'm enjoying the journey, and realizing that for some aspects of life, there doesn't need to be a goal. Just enjoy the here and the now.

I guess that's another thing in regards to passion and energy, is just being in the moment. And not living in the future. I have found recently as I have started to get social more and more, due to some circumstances in my personal life, one of the things I find – and sometimes it can be when you're in a group, and sometimes when you are one-on-one –

there are certain personality types where it seems like, even though you might be talking with them, they might be looking down at their phone.

As if like, 'What? Something on the phone might be more important than what you're saying right now?' Or this is even worse, or maybe this is just a clue to me that I just don't get that I'm getting like freaking boring, they're looking around like, 'Who can I talk to next? How can I get out of this situation?' I would like to think, or I know this is the case, when I'm in a social thingy, I'm engaged and in the moment and connecting with that person. And I'm not thinking in terms of, 'OK, yeah, but what's going on in my business right now? Oh my goodness - let me check my phone. What if someone else is trying to get a hold of me and is trying to reach me?'
Chances are, there are very few things more important as that person in front of me at that point in time. If my son is running cross-country, and he falls and breaks his arm, that's kind of more important, and I need to get out at that moment. Short of things like that, live in the moment! Embrace the moment! Embrace the now! So many people just don't do that.

I actually got a question from a guy who is going to be in my CMMI class next week. He knows about my policy that you really need to attend all class hours. He has a client meeting one afternoon next week. And he wanted to dial into the client meeting and simultaneously attend my class while he was sitting there. I said it in more polite terms than I'm going to say here, I said a variation of, 'That's not going to happen!! Make up your mind. What's more important to you?'

Because guess what? If you're dialing into a client meeting from my class, one of two things is going to suffer. One would be your participation in that client meeting. And if it is such an unimportant meeting that you believe you could actually attend class and get stuff out of the class, then don't dial into it! Explain to your customer why that meeting is unimportant. I don't know how you're going to do that because that's your problem, not mine! And guess what? You're not going to be absorbing the stuff from my class!

So I said no, I'm sorry, that's not going to happen. I gave him a couple of other alternatives, but none of the alternatives involved him trying to multi-process or multi-task. In the real world, people aren't effective at multi-tasking. It just doesn't work.

Do you have a similar policy with cell phones or other devices?

B: I do. I have a kinder, gentler policy with cell phones. I do tell people, 'No cell phones during class, no laptops during class, save your message-checking until breaks.' Now when I say 'kinder, gentler', I realize that a lot of people may need to stay connected in some way, shape or form with other people on their project or headquarters. And if they need to glance at their cell phone occasionally, or need to talk a call for a couple of minutes, and extricate themselves from the classroom, I have no problem with that. I mean, come on! I live in the real world. I really have no problem with that.

Another thing is, to some extent, if someone is looking down at their cell phone a whole lot and it's not because there is something urgent going on, that's a clue to me that I'm boring. That's a clue to me that maybe I need to revisit the way I am approaching whatever it is that I am doing at that point in time.

Bill's answer made me think about how he reacts to students and their reactions.

So are you able to make mental notes as you are teaching a class, like, 'Wow, this is so not working,' or is it more the feedback that you get from the students? How do you learn that?

B: When I'm teaching a public class, it always is working. It never gets to the point where something I am doing in class is not working. And I know that might sound weird, or like a touch of arrogance. But the thing is, with public classes, because of the law of averages, one public class is generally the same as another public class. Because I have taught this class so many times, it's going to go down pretty much the same way as the last public class that I taught. You're going to have a couple of smart guys over in the corner, you're going to have a couple of people who know practically nothing, you might have one person who might be borderline disruptive. All public classes are going to be the same! Never will there be a point of time in a public class when I think, 'Whoa! I'm not connecting.' [This is the Intro to CMMI class that Bill has done over 100 times.] If I don't know how to connect by now, I should have stopped doing this years ago!

It's a different ball game for a private class. Not all private classes are created the same. Not all private class audiences are like every other private class audiences. There you no longer have the law of large numbers working for you. As you can imagine, if I teach a class at Lockheed Martin [a large defense company], that's going to be very, very different from a class at a small, 20-person organization that no one has ever heard of. Just like any class at any big defense contract is going to have a different dynamic than a class at a commercial company. In those kinds of classes, I do have to be more careful about coming up with unique examples for that audience. Again, in my public classes, I don't have to come up with unique examples. My examples are going to work for most, if not all, of the people in that class.

How do I know when something is not working? When people start returning a little bit late for breaks, or when people are excessively checking their messages. Or when I say something, and there are confused looks on people's faces. Usually the main problem that

I have in a private class that I don't have in a public class is people are usually a little bit more secretive and less prone to give examples of what's going on in their workplace because they tend to be intimidated by other people sitting in that classroom. It might include their manager, or someone else from their project. They don't want to air their dirty laundry by giving an example of something.

Private classes are a little bit more challenging to teach in terms of trying to get people engaged. Because sometimes, every once in a blue moon, almost no matter what I did, people just sat there like bumps on a log. I'm going to file that under, 'If you teach a class 100 times, one time that's going to happen no matter how good you think you are, or how engaging you might try to be, that's the one time (and literally one time) it happened in history.' I got pretty good feedback for the class, but geez! I wish I could have gotten them to participate just a little bit more.

Have there been times in your career when you had to do something, and it genuinely made you afraid? I know you said now you have gone past the point of fear.

B: Oh yes! Many times! Many, many, many times! I was afraid to give accurate estimates on projects! We've all done this, right? At least in the software development world! I remember being afraid to give my manager, because I felt in my heart that, 'Geez, this is going to take a whole lot more time to do than he wants to hear', so I would give them an inaccurate estimate! I'm only saying that now, even though it might make me sound like a bad person or a bad engineer, but I only say that now because the statute of limitations on that has probably passed! So I don't think they can get me for that!

But yes, I used to be fearful of that. But certainly now I would not be fearful of that at this point and time. I remember, going back to graduate school, in one of my first jobs as an intern in 1984, there was a manager that I was doing work for, and he was kind of mean. I didn't know how to deal with him. And I was just afraid. What did I know? I was still in school, even though it was graduate school. I just dealt with him by just doing whatever he told me to do, regardless of whether I thought it was stupid, or maybe unethical, or maybe the wrong thing to do. But, come on, I was young back then, and, I hope once people get a whole lot of experience behind them, at least some of that fear goes away.

It's easy for me to say because I'm Mr. 'I-Have-My-Own-Business' sitting here, so I really do live in fear of nothing right now. And even in my business now, I don't fear things. There are things that if they happen, I know how to respond. There have been a couple of times in my history where I have had some new, competitive threats. This new competitor or person has the potential to impact my income negatively. 'What am I going to do about that?' So far, knock on wood, I have been able to almost immediately respond because I am a small company.

One advantage of being a small company is like, 'OK, let's figure out a response,' and then boom! Within 6 weeks or whatever, boom! There's the response, and boom! When I look at the response, and what was happening, or what could have been happening, it looks like the threat was significantly warded off.

I always know that there are threats out there and that I can't anticipate what the threats might be, but at least I've addressed enough of them to have enough confidence in myself that I don't live in fear. In fact, and this might be a weird thing to say, if there was some threat that I couldn't fend off so easily, I might think, 'Whoa! This is an interesting problem!' And it might take me longer, it might take me 6 months or more, to fend off that problem, but I know I could eventually. Or maybe I need a new line of business! It might take a year, but I know that I'll do it! But I just don't know how! Luckily enough, I've been doing this stuff long enough to have some cash reserve that I could withstand that kind of stuff. I'm not living paycheck to paycheck. (I don't get paychecks so that's probably not the right phrase!)

Do you have a motto or words that you live by?

B: Not really. Not like one unifying motto that describes everything in one succinct sentence with a period behind it.

Some mottos have changed. I was in a fraternity at Carnegie Mellon, and our motto back then in Phi Kappa Theta fraternity was 'Give, expecting nothing thereof.' Beautiful, isn't it? Doesn't that sound great? Now, back then, I thought the motto was 'Drink beer, chase girls.' I didn't know the real motto so I'm not sure I behaved that way!

But when I think of it now, it took a long time for that motto to resonate with me, and I think there's an element of that with me nowadays. Which is basically, give of yourself without obsessing too much with what you might get back. Whether we're talking about a relationship, or we're talking about work, whether we're talking about something going on, or whatever it is, if you obsess too much about scorekeeping, that's not the right mental attitude.

I have no expectation that people will behave the same way that I do. That's something that took me a little bit of time. Usually I treat people in a certain way, and I have passion and energy and so forth. For a little while, I was a little bit disappointed when I realized not everyone is like that. But then I realized, 'Well, duh, Bill, you're expecting everyone to be like you and act like you.' And guess what? The way that I act is not the best way to act. It might be one of the best ways for me to act, and that's fine.

I finally have gotten over expecting other people to be like me or having my value system. Or to have my sense of what's ethical and what's not. Or to have my sense of what should happen in a business relationship or in a personal relationship. I have no expectations. I would encourage my customers to keep their expectations low so I can exceed them. 'Give expecting nothing thereof' resonates within me, but it doesn't really describe me. I wouldn't describe myself as a giver because that's really just one part.

Is there anything in hindsight that you would change about where you are now? Meaning, how you got to your professional life. Is there anything that makes you go, 'Aw man! If I had only done this?'

B: No, because otherwise I wouldn't be here.

'Regrets, I've had a few; [Stands up and breaks into song:] But then again, too few to mention/I did what I had to do/And saw it through without exemption/I've lived a life that's full/I've traveled each and ev'ry highway;/But more, much more than this,/I did it my way./ Yes, there were times/I'm sure you knew/When I bit off more than I could chew/Don't know the words/Anymore/Soon they'll be walking/Through the door…' [vii]

I kept looking around as Bill stood up and sang! Was someone going to walk in and hear us? What would they think? I couldn't stop laughing!

OK, I'm sorry! So does that answer the question? Pretty much whatever Sinatra said.

What advice would you give to other people who want to follow their passion? If someone was there on the precipice, and they were trying to figure out if they should take a leap, to try something new, what would you tell them?

B: Other than grow a pair? [Laughs] Here's something that I actually didn't mention which is relevant. When I followed my passion and took that leap with my own business, I had a safety net. The safety net was that I was part of a family where there were two wage earners. In fact, that allowed me to follow my passion. Because if it weren't for that safety net, if I was on my own, I probably wouldn't have followed my passion. At least not initially.

I remember that I was offered a consulting gig very early on. Well, consulting wasn't really what I was passionate about. I was more passionate about the training. I was offered a consulting contract but I rejected it. The reason I rejected the consulting contract was that I said, 'No, no, no, I want to focus on training, training, training. I want to focus on developing my business model because I think in the long term this is the best thing for me to do strategically for my company. Getting involved in some consulting effort, that's not the best thing for me strategically. How am I going to learn from that?'

Sure, I would make money from that. I would not have followed my passion if it weren't for the fact that I actually had a safety net. So maybe these aren't the most inspiring words that I am giving you right now, but kind of make sure that it's practical, that you have a safety net or a plan. Just because I have said all these words, words, words about me following my passion, it doesn't mean that I did it blindly. I've always had a plan.

I've always had a plan for everything that I've done. Even major changes in my personal life, I've had a plan. I've had plans for following my passion. I'm not saying that everyone is like that, or that everyone needs to be like that. The problem is you probably get people who try to follow their passion without a plan. They figure, 'You know what? I'm going to open up a bar! I'm going to open up a restaurant! I'm going to open a vineyard! I'm going to open up a bed and breakfast!'

But you know what? That could be a passion that's cool, but again, if you don't think it through, you're going to be toast. And you're not going to be able to follow your passion. Passion is not separate from the analytical you. Passion is not separate from the planning you. It is not separate from the 'think it through.' Just because you're passionate doesn't mean you suddenly stop thinking!

I'm ending on a little bit of a cautionary note. But because I don't just want to end on a cautionary note, I would say that once you have thought it through, and once you do have that plan in place, and if you are really, truly passionate about yourself or what it is that you like to do, kind of trust in yourself. The 3 key words are 'Don't give up!'

Don't give up, even when things are hard. I'm not claiming to be the most resilient person in the world, but it would have been very, very easy for me to give up. At least for one of my passions, being a small business owner, it would have been extremely easy for me to give up. But I didn't, and I figured it out, and that's the only reason why we're having this conversation!

***

When I replayed my conversation with Bill while transcribing the interview for this book, I laughed just as hard as I did during the interview.

The more I thought about it, the more I realized that Tickers have either looked into finding something that excites them, or they have happened into something and recognized that it excites them. I wanted to know what happened that made them choose their current path.

Bill Smith said that CMMI is not necessarily where he gets his passion, and in fact, he could see himself taking his passion to another subject. So is it that the Ticker is like a musical instrument, and the "tick" is just one song? Just because someone picks a profession does not mean that subject is the only thing that person is good at.

When I followed up with Bill, he said, "I'm doing GREAT --- and thank you for asking! New house, new (and improved) girlfriend... but otherwise the same old/new me." So glad....Bill is fantastic and I wouldn't change a thing!

Story 2: James and Aimee Hartle – Craft Beer Bar Owners: All You Touch and All You See...

I have always hated the question, "What are you going to do with the rest of your life?" GAHHH!! It is loaded with pressure. As a kid, I wanted to be a veterinarian because I thought it meant I could play with dogs and cats for the rest of my life. When I realized the truth, that it meant sometimes cutting animals open, I didn't just say no, but hell no. Not for me.

And after that initial occupational desire, I could never quite put into words what I wanted to be. It got to be a minor concern that grew larger and larger every year. I looked sideways at kids who proudly announced, "I'm going to be a doctor!" or whatever profession. How the hell did they know? I felt like an aimless loser in comparison.

Along the way I was figuring out what I liked and what I didn't like. I like writing! I don't like math! I like nice people! I don't like mean girls! I like chess! I don't like dodgeball! But how to turn these things into a career? It was beyond my imagination. I hadn't lived long enough to know and commit to what I was going to do from age seven until I took my last breath. TOO MUCH PRESSURE!

I really like Pink Floyd's music. However, their lyrics, "All you touch and all you see/Is all your life will ever be" completely freaked me out when I heard them. Part of it has to be the implication of mortality (ohmigod! I'm gonna die one day! WHAT?) But part of what bummed me out is that it implied that living with blinders on meant you would miss a large part of the whole wide world, and that you would only get to experience a tiny strip of it. What if, in the course of your life, you were only doled out one of the crappy parts and you didn't even know it? Unbeknownst to you, there could be some other delicious, wonderful, amazing strip of life out there but your piece was not carved from that part? So all you touch and all you see is limited, and, oh, guess what, sucks to be you! It haunted me.

I thought about those lyrics obsessively for a while. It accompanied my thoughts whenever someone asked, "So, what do you want to be?" I stumbled, "Um, I'm not sure". But all I touch and all I see is all my life will ever be...so the pressure was on. I wanted to dedicate my life to touch and see some more stuff so I know what I really like and don't like!

It's like trying all the eggs. In the movie, "The Runaway Bride," Julia Roberts' character keeps getting engaged to be married and then running away from her intended on her wedding day. There's a scene in the movie where Richard Gere's character yells at her and says, "You are so lost that you don't even know what kind of eggs you like." Later, she is trying to figure out the root of her issue. In the scene, she is surrounded by plates of eggs: scrambled, over easy, fried, etc. And she tries a bite of them all. She wanted to know herself, what she liked. Until she knew herself, even something as simple as how she liked her eggs, she could not commit to a marriage.

And in my life, I had to try out more stuff, to touch and see more, until I knew what I liked and what I didn't.

At twenty-seven, I had completed my undergrad in English and had completed my masters' degree in Writing and Rhetoric. I had two degrees. Yet I still froze when asked what I wanted to do with the rest of my life. It tortured me.

Well-meaning family and friends offered suggestions. "Become a teacher!" I love and respect teachers. I proudly come from a line of teachers. My mom was a home economics teacher in high school, and my Aunt Peggy was a kindergarten teacher. But I didn't really want to be a teacher.

Others said, "Become a writer!" That seemed like a logical choice given my educational degrees. I love to help people by editing their papers. While I have always loved to write, whenever I tried to write stories, I just didn't feel compelled to say anything. Writing was a logical choice but not my emotional choice.

I took a big leap in 1995. I knew that I like to learn. No, more than that, I love to learn. I feel alive when I am in an interesting class, learning more, and making thought connections. While many of my friends looked at me as though I had lost my mind, I would talk about how much I loved being in the classroom.

Still, I did not know what I wanted to be, but I had at least nailed down something I loved to do. My new path took me to Fort Worth, Texas, to Texas Christian University. I enrolled in a doctoral program. But bigger than that, I moved halfway across the country from Virginia to live by myself. All I touched and all I saw was now going to include the Lone Star state, the state where I was born but had left as a baby. No one knew me there.

I compared everything I knew from Richmond, Virginia to everything in Texas. It was familiar and yet odd, like I had 'Quantum Leaped' into someone else's body. No one knew me; they did not know what an unpopular chick I had been in high school. They thought my accent was as funny as I found theirs to be. My world was expanding. My mind was expanding. I had some lean times and dated the wrong person. It was the hardest two years of my life but without my two years in Texas, I would not be who I am today.

I am hardly the first person to explore new paths. Many of us are on the path of life but haven't arrived at what we will ultimately be. Maybe the question is not, "What do you want to be" but "What are you becoming?"

***

In 1997, I moved back to Virginia from Texas and started doing IT support. It was during this time that I got to know James Hartle because we both worked at the same company. James was always quiet but when you spoke with him, he had a great sense of humor. He was smart and the customers really liked him.

James went to Colonial Heights High School, then VCU between 1990 and 1994. He worked for ManTech, Primedia and General Dynamics doing IT desktop support. James has not always done IT desktop support since he graduated. He worked in retail for a while, and then got into music.

When James got married, he and his wife, Aimee, moved to Atlanta. For a few years, I lost track of him, but then I caught up using that great social media stalking program, Facebook. James and Aimee were posting pictures from craft beer festivals which caught my eye because I am a huge craft beer fan. James and Aimee had a blog called Spreading the Craft Beer Gospel between 2010 and 2012 which I followed. When James moved back to Virginia, I began chatting with him about craft beers.

I was really excited when James said he and Aimee planned to open a craft beer bar. Through conversations with James, and following their progress on Facebook, I eagerly awaited their opening of their place, The Bucket Trade.

***

The Bucket Trade just feels warm and welcoming when you walk through their doors. Part of this feeling comes from the fact that the space is small. The walls are painted a warm golden yellow. Then there is the friendly vibe in the air. The people who come to the Bucket Trade make it their one-stop for craft beer and growler fills. They are craft beer people, people who generally have a more open-minded approach than many towards taste and style. This approach usually isn't just restricted to their choice in beverage.

Just like their bar, James and Aimee are also warm and welcoming. James is laid-back, quiet but attentive and has a quick wit. He may share a new word of the day with you, or show you a new beer that has arrived that they've been dying to try, or just shoot the breeze with the regulars. Aimee is bright and exuberant, has a wicked sense of humor and a lovely laugh. She and James are just plain fun.

At the Bucket Trade, located in Chester, Virginia, James and Aimee have 16 taps which feature both international and national rotating taps by style. They also have the best Virginia beers and hard cider, on draft by the pint and available to take home in to-go bottles called growlers, and a multitude of bottles and cans to go. Customers can drool over the many awesome beers and quiz James and Aimee on their contents. On a balmy night, customers can enjoy the back patio. The scenery consists of the back of a strip mall, but the fire pit burns brightly and you can hear laughing and talking along with the gentle clinking of glasses.

What does that name Bucket Trade mean? Before Prohibition, and before bottles and cans became widespread, if you wanted beer outside of a bar it was put into a bucket. The buckets of beer were then taken by "bucket boys" who usually carried several on a pole. This process was called the "bucket trade." The growler, the large bottle into which draft beer can be poured and stored, was created from the bucket trade tradition.

At the time we spoke, the Bucket Trade had been open for almost a year. I have to admit being a little jealous that James has quit his job and was devoted full-time to the bar. But I wondered - was it everything he thought it would be? Were he and Aimee still excited about craft beer since it was now also their occupation?

I wasn't sure what made James take the leap from IT or how he and Aimee got into craft beers or how they got the Bucket Trade off the ground. What did it take? And could I follow a dream, too, once I identified what it was? Since James and Aimee are friends of mine, I asked James and Aimee if I could interview them for my book. They invited me to attend a restaurant soft opening with them for a place called Betty on Davis in Richmond. Over craft beers (of course!) and appetizers, we started talking.

***

K: James, according to LinkedIn, you have worked for ManTech, Primedia and General Dynamics doing IT desktop support. So it looks like you have always worked doing IT support since college?

J: I have a very firm plan, which is that I will never work at anything more than 10 years, and then I move on to the next thing. First it was the food industry, like Olive Garden.

Then it was music retail, like Digits. That was right out of college. When Digits went out of business, I worked at Plan 9 [a popular record store in Richmond, Virginia]. Then I got into IT because my girlfriend's mother at the time was the CIO [Chief Information Officer] at DeCA [Defense Commissary Agency]. She said, 'You seem to have an aptitude for IT. Why don't you do that?' I overstayed IT – I was there for about 12 years.

In my research online, I read that Aimee, you went to the Medical College of Georgia. I know that you currently work at a hospital…have you always worked at hospitals since graduating from college?

A: I've done it all. So I graduated out in California, and I was working at a computer company. My brother worked there, and basically everyone in my family worked there because he was awesome, so we all kind of started off with him. I said, 'I'm a sister of Gerald,' and they said, 'You're hired!'

I used to dance with the ballet out in California. I just did different auditions all over the place. I wanted to travel, but I didn't have the money, so I used ballet as a way to travel. As soon as I graduated in California, I got a scholarship to dance in Yuma Valley Theater for six months. It sucked! It's Yuma, Arizona! Enough said! [Laughs]

So while I was with Yuma, we went to a dance competition, back in California, which I thought, 'How funny'. There were scouts all over, and I got a scholarship for the Richmond Ballet School. So I went for their summer program on the Fulbright scholarship thinking, 'I'll do it, it'll be great to see Richmond, and then I'll come back home.' I had a chance to dance in Sacramento but I chose Richmond because it was across the country and I figured I would travel and see the East Coast.

While I was there [in Richmond] in the summer program, they offered me to stay as a 'trainee', like an internship almost, except you have to pay. But because I told them [I needed money] they found me a scholarship, which paid for a portion of it. But after two years, they hadn't hired me.

James and I met during that time. I got auditions all over. I made a tape and sent it to every ballet company in the frickin' country, and I got an offer at the Atlanta Festival Ballet. That was an actual position, so I was paid to be there! Yeah! Eight thousand dollars a year, what up? [Laughs]

J: It would barely pay for the gas to get there!

A: But Georgia has this amazing thing where you can go to college for free! It's called the Hope Scholarship. You have to live in Georgia for at least a year as a resident. You just have to pay for the first 30 credits, which is nothing, and then you are eligible for the Hope Scholarship! You don't even have to try! As long as you get a C average, you're in! It's like you just show up and you get free school.

I went to community college for two years, and then I went to the nursing program at the Medical College of Georgia for the last two years. During that time, while I was dancing and making terrible pay, I worked at Einstein Bagels, managed that; I actually worked at Bed, Bath and Beyond for a little bit, and Bath and Body Works; I probably did every stupid job you can think of!

Then I got a job working for an accounting firm for builders. Basically it was just a [jobs] program; I just entered in numbers and paid their bills, and paid the subcontractors. They kind of screwed around a lot...

Aimee ended up quitting and having margaritas with a fellow co-worker who quit too.

A: But apparently I made an impression on one of the builders that I did accounts for because he found out I was looking for a job. And I think it was because I caught a mistake on his paperwork and everyone else was ignoring it and I fixed it. This guy was amazing. He was a British guy. I worked in his basement and basically I was his 'basement bitch'! [Laughs]

He was awesome and he was funny as shit. It was awesome! He paid me really well. We would argue sometimes but otherwise he was a great boss. I would have stayed with him forever.
And then the economy went down. And it was right at the same time I finished my first year at the community college, and I started the nursing program, and you can't have a full-time job. So it was perfect timing because he could pay me enough. So I went from ballet, to construction, to nursing! I was a nurse for three years when I said, 'This sucks!'

James and Aimee ended up moving all over Georgia and sometimes James was in one town while Aimee was in another. They Skyped a lot.

A: Once I started the nursing program, that was when we really started getting into the beer. That's when we started doing beer fests pretty much every weekend. Some of my teachers were like, 'We're a little worried that you're at beer fests every single weekend! What are you going to do when you become a nurse?' And I said, 'Then I'm going to go to more [beer festivals]!'

James and Aimee have been married since 2006. They met in Richmond when they both lived in the Fan area across the hall from each other.

Did you both like beer before you met? One of your blog posts mentions James drinking beer at the Commercial Taphouse in 1994.

J: So way back when, the whole beer thing started for me at the 7-11 on Rives Road. I was working at 7-11 off from Crater Road in Petersburg. At that time, I strictly drank Budweiser because of the cost. One night, the manager said we had a lot of 'one-off' beers from where people took beers from different packs and left ones out. He asked me to throw out the beers. So, of course, I saved them. My friends and I pulled up with two trucks and filled up the coolers.

That summer, James found that beer came in an array of styles and tastes. So this was a turning point for James. A new world of beer had opened up! But he didn't immediately follow his passion...it was a slow progression.

Doing a search online shows that you had the blog called Spreading the Craft Beer Gospel between 2010-2012. Is that correct? The blog included information about events (Raleigh Beer Fest, Myrtle Beach Beer Fest), and included menus too. You reviewed stores (Sam's Quik Stop) and restaurants (Commercial Taphouse and Grill, Legend Brewing). Also it had info on specific breweries. The blog is well-written and interesting!

J: Well, thank you!

James started the blog to provide reviews of macro beers and craft beers.

Did you review beers before writing the blog? How do you track which beers you like and which you don't?

James and Aimee started to notice first which types of beers they liked and writing about them. From there, they tracked which breweries had the types of beers they liked. They mentioned on their website that they don't use "geek speak."

I read on your website about "geek speak." What is "geek speak"?

J: 'Geek speak' is the very pretentious language people sometimes use to review beers. It's similar to when people use fancy language to describe wines and their flavors. We prefer not to use 'Geek speak'. Just explain why you like a beer...or why you don't like it. Is it bitter? Does it taste sweet?'

Can you provide an example? What is the different between a male and female view of beer? [Laughs] What beers do you prefer, Aimee, versus which beers James prefers?

J: I got Aimee into drinking beers when we lived together.

A: He would fill the fridge full of beer, and only kept food in the freezer!

Aimee would try some and after a while she too was "converted".

On the blog, many of the beers received 3.5 out of 5 stars or 4 out of 5 stars. Have you ever rated a beer as 4.5 or 5 out of 5 stars?

James said Duvel is a 5-star beer. He explained that it is light enough to drink in the summer, but has enough spice to drink in the winter.

You also included tasting tips on the blog. How did you guys become so knowledgeable about beer?

J: Practice. The more festivals we attended, the better we got at identifying beers and their characteristics. We began volunteering at beer festivals and we got to know the vendors, and helped with pouring beer and serving people. It enabled us to go to the festivals for free!

A: We became Beer Connoisseur Magazine Sales Reps. We would set up booths at the beer festivals and sign up people for the magazine. We were like, 'Hey, come over here!' We were able to use their connections to set up an interview with Simon Thorpe, CEO of Brewery Ommegang [a notable craft brewery in Cooperstown, NY], and his selection as a member of Knighthood of the Brewers' Mash.

In your first blog post, you state "We'll take a macro beer (Budweiser, Miller, Coors, etc.), a middle of the road beer (Yuengling, Sam Adams, etc.) and a craft brew (Stone, New Belgium, etc.) and do a his and hers taste comparison." Your format started that way, but then gave way to reviews of craft beer "mini-reviews". Why did you change the format?

J: There just aren't as many macro beers to compare to craft beers. After a while, we started just reviewing craft beers.

While reading a review of the Beer Growler from Athens GA, I was struck by the line: "Last night, we had the pleasure of visiting a Georgia first...The Beer Growler-

-a shop that actually sells and refills growlers!" Was that a novelty in 2010? Have you found that more and more places offer growlers? Did that place, The Beer Growler (and/or others like it) inspire you to create the Bucket Trade?

J: Yes, the Beer Growler was the first place to get around the GA law that you had to have closed containers of beer by putting Saran Wrap over the stopper. When we wanted to open our own place, we wanted to have growlers.

A: When James said something about only selling bottles, I was like, 'Unnnh! NO!' I knew I wanted to have a place where people would get growlers filled.

Did you guys know all along you wanted to open a place of your own? If not, when did you decide?

J: We just sort of started talking about it.

A: I became a nurse but I hated it! I gave it a chance for a while but 6 months in, I knew it was not my calling.

James and Aimee started talking about having a place and then they started getting more serious about it.

A: If I hadn't hated nursing, I would probably still be there. There would not be a Bucket Trade.

How long did it take from idea to opening to open the Bucket Trade?

J: After we started talking about it, we just kept talking more and more until we were talking about how to make it happen.

What kinds of challenges did you face in creating the Bucket Trade?

J: It took a lot of work to fix up the space we rented for the Bucket Trade. For a while, I was considering just having a bottle shop.

A: But that just made me depressed. I wanted to have growlers!

I know you have a presence on Facebook, and a website. Your web site uses Trinkin to show what's on your taps currently. Do you use other social media? How has social media helped your business?

James and Aimee have a blog, twitter account, and Facebook presence. They use Trinkin to show which beers are on tap (https://trinkin.com/?city=1). James and Aimee said social media is a mixed blessing. They said they can get a lot of exposure and can publicize events. They can even make the pics look good like there were more people than there actually were.

J: I really liked Trinkin but Aimee was resistant.

A: I just really didn't see the point. At first I was like, 'Save the money!' But we started using it, and it has been really helpful. People can do searches for particular beers through Trinkin.

J: People have sought out the Bucket Trade based on the beers listed on Trinkin. It has been great because people have come out of their way to go to Chester just for the beers we have.

A: I'm glad now we have used it!

As far as other social media is concerned, there are positives and negatives. The positives include publicizing special events like Metal Night or Game of Thrones Night.

A: Social media can make an event look like it was huge and make customers feel like, 'Damn! I missed that event and it looks like it was a lot of fun!' We had a party for one of our employees, Anthony. It was Anthony's Yacht Rock Birthday over Labor Day weekend. Unfortunately, since it was a holiday weekend, the turnout wasn't great. But when people saw the pictures and saw how much fun we had, they all said, 'Sorry we missed it! We'll be there next time!'

Social media also has its downside. People can say whatever they want and they can be somewhat anonymous. It's hard to counter when people say negative things.

How did you select the location in Chester?

J: Richmond [Virginia] has such a big presence now in craft beer. Look at An [Bui] at Mekong. He started off craft beer in Richmond when there wasn't anyone doing that, and now he's been Best Beer Bar in the South for three years in a row. There are people in Chester and the Tri-Cities who wanted craft beer and now they have a place to get it. We get a lot of executives and military people from the region.

What kinds of challenges do you face on a daily basis with the Bucket Trade? Distributors, customers, lease holder, etc.?

James and Aimee are out to "spread the craft beer gospel," but some potential converts are stubborn.

J: We get a lot of people who come in and think they are beer experts. Then they aren't open-minded about trying new beers. They will come in and say, 'I want an ale.' And we're like, 'There are literally hundreds of ales. Can you be a little more specific?' And they get defensive.
They will have an idea about what a stout or some other beer is like, and they won't try other types. Or we will have someone who had a specific beer in a specific little town in Germany, and we're like, 'I'm sure that's a great beer, but we don't have that. Would you like to try this?'

James and Aimee also carry macro brews like Miller Lite and Budweiser for people who prefer to stick with the big name beers.

J: I don't want to alienate anyone. I will let people know we carry those beers, but I will also say, 'Well, if you like this beer, would you like to try this one?' And I will offer them a beer which is a similar style or taste.

James and Aimee agree they just want people to say why they like or do not like a beer.

A: Don't worry about being right or wrong. If you like a beer, tell me why you like that beer. Is it sweet? Once you can say that, then we are getting somewhere.

J: Just say what you like.

They love when they can "convert" someone to try a beer and they really like it. The distributors are a challenge, too. Started originally from the days of Prohibition to ensure equal opportunities for breweries, the distributors' intentions were good. But things have changed, and sometimes distributors cause obstacles.

J: Since you have to go through the distributors to get your beer, you can't go straight to a brewery and say, 'I want this beer.' You have to go through the distributor. And that means sometimes they will tell you, 'Well, you can have this beer if you take some of this beer too.' So you're limited with what you can get. It can be frustrating. Because distributors have this power, if you rub them the wrong way, it can be hard to get the beer you want.

A: You have to order seasonal beers ahead of time. We had to take a chance when we were ordering the pumpkin beers for the fall. We ordered them back in July. I've got 20 f'ing kegs of beer in my basement!

J: We are hoping we ordered the right quantity and styles but who knows until the fall? We'll see.

Aimee, is it challenging being in the craft beer industry since it is a male-dominated field?

A: Oh yeah, there aren't many women involved in the craft beer scene. It's almost all guys.

Do you see a lot of sexism?

A: Yes! All the time. Men will come in the bar and say, 'I want to see the owner.' I'm like, 'OK, here I am!' Sometimes I will be talking about craft beer and explaining a type of beer and I can tell they aren't listening to me.

You both work at the Bucket Trade. What percentage of time do you spend, James, and what percentage of time do you spend, Aimee?

J: At first, we were both working full-time jobs and working part-time at the Bucket Trade. Then I quit to work at the BT full-time.

A: I worked at both the hospital and BT until a few months ago when I quit my job at the hospital to work at the BT full-time.

Mekong [An Bui's bar], also located in the area, has been voted "Overall #1 Great America Beer Bar". What have you learned from An and his path? Do you consider him a competitor or a mentor?

J: Oh An is great, he is totally not competition. He is really inspiring! He and his family came here from Vietnam with nothing and have created this amazing bar. An has been so helpful with providing advice to us.

After dinner at Betty on Davis, James, Aimee and I went to Mekong and An's new bar, "The ANswer Brewpub" the night An received the Best Beer Bar in America vote the 3rd year in a row. He had all craft beers for $1 and the place was packed!

J: It's not a surprise that they are packed here tonight. But they are like this every time we come here. [An] does amazing business.

What annoys you about this business?

J: I hate when people ask, 'How are you guys doing?' They say it like they are concerned. Do they want us to say, 'We're doing terrible!' And then they will feel bad. But it has been a year, and we're still here! That's how we're doing!"

After years of researching and now providing craft beer, how do you connect with your inner passion? Are you still excited about craft beer?

J: There is always something new to try. I still get excited to try something new.

James opened and shared a bottle of Stone Russian Imperial Stout.

J: This is one of the beers that started us on craft beer.

***

I had such a great time talking with James and Aimee that I hardly cared that my digital recorder ran out of memory part of the way through our interview. I took great notes and filled in the parts I missed.

So I learned that James and Aimee still love craft beer, even after quitting their "real" jobs and opening The Bucket Trade. And it is still a lot of hard work. They only have one day off a week. They are constantly communicating with the vendors and distributors; coordinating field trips for their VIP group, the Bucket Heads; and ordering food, beer and supplies. And their work isn't always a party. They have to contend with people who argue about beer even though James and Aimee clearly know their stuff. But even after all the work they put into their place, you can still tell they are passionate about beer and love converting craft beer novices into craft beer appreciators. As far as I can tell, looking at James and Aimee, the saying is true: "If you love what you do, you will never work a day in your life" …with the caveat that you will still have to do some work, but it will be work you enjoy.

After I interviewed the Hartles in 2014, they opened another location of the Bucket Trade in Petersburg, Virginia. Unlike their location in Chester, the Bucket Trade in Petersburg does not serve food or beverages to enjoy on the premises but instead is a retail location for buying craft beers and wines. They have an outstanding selection. They also have been active in regional festivals as the Bucket Trade is one of the sponsors for the Grapes and Hops Festival in Petersburg. And in 2016, they announced they would consolidate the Chester and Petersburg locations into one larger, even more awesome, location!

James had said he changes professions every decade or so. Will he and Aimee ever change jobs? My guts say this job is different. Unlike food service (for someone else) or working in IT, James and Aimee are living their vision. And if for some reason they do change paths, I am sure it will be for something that they have learned, touched, tasted or seen along the way.

Story 3: Don Aslett – Owner of The Museum of Clean: Thinking Differently

One night in June 2014, while driving through Idaho on a cross-country vacation, I got sleepy driving through a town called Pocatello. My first thought was, "Pocatello? That's a funny name!" Jerry and I had been driving past windmill farms and not much else for a while. We consulted Trip Advisor and looked for the top-rated hotel in Pocatello. I love to drive but my butt was falling asleep and my eyelids were drooping. When we drove up to the Hampton Inn, all the rooms were taken due to a big wrestling event at Idaho State University. Tired and cranky, we were bummed until they recommended that we stay at the new Holiday Inn Express right around the corner.

Commanding the counter at the Holiday Inn Express in Pocatello was a petite young woman. I wondered when I saw her if she was old enough to work there. She warmly greeted us and to our relief, we reserved their last room. When she saw me eyeing the flyers on the counter, she asked, "Are you here to see the Museum of Clean?" Um, no…but now we wanted to know more. What the heck is a Museum of Clean?

The young lady explained how she and her brother went to the museum and how much they enjoyed it. She said the owner was very passionate about cleaning and he gave them a personal tour. She said there was a lot to see, and recommended we take a look.

The next day, refreshed and now curious, Jerry and I decided to check out the Museum of Clean for about an hour before we left Pocatello to head for Oregon. Bemused, we were not sure what we would see in a Museum of Clean. Would it look like a grocery store cleaning product aisle? Were we going to have to sweep something? Let's be honest: many of us think cleaning sucks. Sure, we may like the end result of having everything look shiny and new. But the actual work of cleaning is often considered a chore, a pain, something to avoid or pay someone else to do.

When we arrived, the building was much larger than I was expected. We were greeted enthusiastically by Larry, an older gentleman who proceeded to give us a brief overview of the museum. Then he handed us over to a gentleman he introduced as his brother.

Don Aslett, Larry's brother and the owner and founder of the Museum of Clean, is a dynamo of a man. He immediately greeted us and shook our hands. And he started talking about his museum. For three entertaining hours, he walked and talked with us, encouraging us to try out the interactive exhibits, and even talking Jerry into wearing a

Viking hat made of cleaning supplies! While I was pleasantly surprised at how fun and entertaining a museum dedicated to cleaning could be, I was even more blown away by how amusing and compelling Don Aslett is.

***

Don Aslett was raised on a farm in south central Idaho. When he started attending Idaho State College (which is now Idaho State University), he and his friends started a housecleaning business. They named the business Varsity Contractors.

Don, who briefly served in the Army, and then served a Mormon mission in Hawaii, returned to Idaho and financed himself through school with his cleaning business. After graduating from college, he taught and coached at public schools before devoting himself to business full-time.

Don grew his company to reach all 50 states and even to parts of Canada. He is also a prolific author who has written over forty books on cleaning. His books include the colorfully titled, "Is there Life after Housework?" and "Clutter's Last Stand." These books also address business success, time management and being a good employee. In 1993, Don was named the Idaho Business Leader of the Year.

Don's popularity led to television and radio engagements. He was interviewed by Oprah Winfrey. He has also been featured on the Discovery Channel. Products from the Don Aslett Home line are sold on QVC. He was once featured in "People Magazine." Don is also frequently asked to speak. He is hands-on with his business and with his museum. [viii]

The Museum of Clean is one of Don's favorite projects. It took six years to build at a cost of six million dollars. The exhibits in the museum include a 1902 horse-drawn vacuum cleaner, a vast collection of antique vacuum cleaners, a 1600-year-old bronze toothpick, and an antique Amish foot bath.

Don's museum items started with an old pump vacuum he purchased for $250 and his collection grew from there.[ix]

***

Jerry and I shocked ourselves by leaving the Museum of Clean three hours after we arrived. What put us late on our path was the oh-so-worth-it experience of meeting and getting a personal tour from Don Aslett.

When I decided to write "Tickers", I thought about Don. Months after our visit, I started sending a barrage of mail items including a slew of cleaning-related cards. I mailed a package of peanuts to Don with the note, "I'm Nuts About You!" After receiving the peanuts, Don called and spoke with me. When I asked, he graciously agreed to allow me to interview him.

What touched me so much about Don is his passion for everything. As an author himself, he really went out of his way to offer me advice as a novice author during our interview. Don is so dynamic that you hardly have a chance to ask questions! You just settle in and enjoy a great story.

***

K: Thanks for talking with me today! I appreciate you talking with me about my book.

D: You're writing a book; you know what it is like. It takes a lot of time. If you pick the right subject and somebody wants it, they still sell. People come after it. But the market is so flooded. If you are a Sarah Palin or an O'Reilly or somebody, you have built-in sales.

I know a guy who wrote a book on flagging. You know those cars that flag behind other cars. What a stupid book, but the guy sold 20,000 of them. And at $15-20 a book, he made $400k. It's a book you would think would only sell one or two. So he found a niche market and he capitalized on it. He wrote a book that sold so many.

We lack people who have passion and succeed at what they do. Everybody wants to work for everyone else, and everyone wants to be entitled. It's a whole different world out there. I'm very frustrated...you know, for an entrepreneur like me, I have made my own money, I have done my own thing, and I pioneered all of my own stuff, and now I am at an age where my company has switched to a corporation. You know, at one time, I had 10,000 employees, but now it is all corporate. I never took people to lunch, I never bought dinners, I never did any of that stuff. I just loved my business so much that I just worked. I would clean your house so well that you told both your neighbors and they told both theirs, and I built one of the best [cleaning companies] of its type in the country. And now we are corporate: we buy lunches, take people golfing, and do that sort of stuff for promotion. It is a different mentality.

You have to find a thing that people want. For example, I wrote a book called "How to Work Your Way Through College." You would think that book would be in the 40s, 50s, 60k sales range. I spent a lot of time on that book. And now I have 5 businesses I started and I run. And now I have that book all finished. It was going to be for college students.

Now I have that book all finished, and it was going to include how to build your life, your reputation, your spirituality, and how valuable it is to have passion. And I got a bunch of college kids, and asked them to find all the ways, and I was going to have on the back of the book, all the different jobs you can get. It was really going to be a neat book. You know what I have found, Kim? Hardly any kids work their way through college anymore, hardly anybody does that. Most people have rich parents or they think they deserve it or they get loans or scholarships. Someone else is paying their way through school. It's a whole different world. Kim, I shelved that book – I had all that money and time into it, but I just put it in a box and I didn't put it out. It wouldn't have sold anything.

My first three books were best-sellers. Then I said, 'One of the problems in the world is men not cleaning. It's not a woman's job to clean everything!' People say, 'Oh, I got my wife a washing machine!' or 'My wife loves her vacuum!' So I made a vow that instead of having my audience, instead of being 99% women, I would have half men. So I did a book called 'Who Says It is a Woman's Job to Clean?' I don't know if you have read it or seen it but it is a really good book. But it didn't sell! All of our other books sold like crazy. They sold only 25,000 but they printed 75,000. I couldn't figure it out. I had a guy in Chicago… he said, 'You pointed that book to women! No woman is going to buy that book and give it to her husband and say, 'Here Slob! Read this!' He said, 'You should have pointed the book to the men! You should have named it *How to Make Your Woman Love You* or *Be a Good Lover by Doing the Cleaning!'* It was brilliant!

So you guys saw the museum, and you saw the passion of it. And it's still there. I'm still putting in 14 hour days working on it.

People love movies, and they love a success story. They can't do it on their own, but if they find somebody who has done something, they can hang on psychologically and emotionally. They can hang onto that hero. They feel like they've done it! That's why we're psyched about people at ball games…we're too fat and lazy to get on the field ourselves, we're eating popcorn! Seriously …I think that's the bottom line of all business: having the passion and love for what you do. When your career is just a job, then all you are is a mechanic, and you can't wait to retire. But if you really love what you do, you never get tired. There's a whole bunch of philosophy.

A lot of people think they are entrepreneurs but they are not! They manage something. Their dad gives them money and suddenly they run the store. Entrepreneurs are a whole different breed! They are people…. exactly what you're doing…they're people who have a passion for what they do. But the best definition of it that I ever heard, Kim, and I've heard a thousand definitions for entrepreneurs. The best one I ever heard was when I was teaching up at Oregon State. Some woman came up to me and said, 'You know what an entrepreneur is? They think they are right!' I said, 'That is so phenomenal!'

Generally, we are not right…we are wrong half the time! But we love our stuff and what we do so much that we work the hours and we might make the wrong work! But you think you are right! You bring up someone who is a fanatic in their church or their family or their life or their diet…you watch people who really think they are right. Whether they are or not is immaterial! So if you're an entrepreneur, you think you're right and you think, 'Man, all these houses I have cleaned! And I am the best toilet cleaner in the world!' If you think it, then you have the passion, and then you put the time in and the energy…that's what makes things go. It isn't the talent or the hard work. It's just that 'I have a cause'!

There are a couple of great stories in the Bible. David and Goliath…everybody sees that story as the little guy knocking off the big guy. That isn't the story. The best part of the story is when David showed up to fight the first guy, one of the guys said to him, 'Why are you here?' And David said to him, and to me this sums up the whole testament, 'Is there not a cause?' And that is so prominent. It is a theme through anyone you interview and put in your book. We are all excited to have a cause. To me that is the whole bottom line of success is to ask if you have a cause. If there is a cause there, you don't get tired; you don't get hungry.

The second one is the apostle Paul. He had been beaten up, he was the worst guy in the world, and he was on the way to Damascus when he had a vision. Christ appeared to him, and he said, 'Who art thou?', and Christ said, 'I am Jesus Christ.' And the first thing Paul said back, the first thing which sums it all up, is 'Lord, what will you have me do?' He didn't say, 'I believe I am saved!', he didn't say 'Wow!', he just asked the question, 'What will thou have me do?' And that's the bottom line of all accomplishments in life is 'do'!

Right now I am working on a book on measuring. Everyone wonders where they rate or how they measure. [Everyone asks], 'Where am I? Where am I?' We all want to wonder where we are in comparison, how good we are, how efficient we are. We take tests. Everything is evaluated in our life.

'Do' is the magic word in your book! People can have philosophies and they can try things, they can have success stories to tell, but 'do' is a two letter word! It's everything! You don't have to analyze, you don't have to philosophize, you don't have to theorize, you don't have to say anything! You just say, 'What do you do?' That spells love, that spells appreciation, that spells support!

Once you get a theme going in your book, you can get collaboration. I use a lot of art in my books. [Describes *Clutter's Last Stand.*] That's a good book. I spent money on the art on that book. Instead of preaching to people, I said 'This is where you stand.' I taught them principles and let people govern themselves. A lot of people want you to say...instead of saying 'You ought to go on a diet', they want to know specifically what to eat and what not to eat, what time to eat.

I kept really good records when I started [with Varsity Cleaning]. I had 8,000 typed pages of how we did stuff and I edited it down to 2,000 pages. I took the bio out. I spent $150,000 on it. It was 600 pages called *How I Swept My Way to the Top*, and it is kind of the story of the creativity.

There is the average person in the world, and then there are management people, who work for people and manage and teach, and then there is a level above there called entrepreneurs, that think they are right and they actually run things. Then there is another level above them called pioneers.

Pioneers are people that pay for it, who come up with ideas – they don't do things like everybody else. They make their own notebook, they make their own toilet suitcase, they design their own houses, and they don't build like everybody else. They come up with something unique. They make their own mailbox; they have their own portfolio. Instead of making a bio like everyone else, they find one that fits them and they make it. There are very few pioneers.

Everything is cause. If you have a cause...you see people like the Tea Party people or some politicians or religious fanatics or people with a cause, you can't hold them back! They might be obnoxious but you can't hold them back! They don't know when to quit. Don't use the word 'try', don't use the word 'quit'. Just use the word 'do'. Come up with a unique way of that and I tell you, it will work for you.

One thing I noticed about *Clutter's Last Stand* is that you do a fantastic job of using humor. I think everybody can relate. You talk about how people find a piece of junk and they say, 'Oh, I can use that again' or 'Couldn't I use this at another time?' It just seemed to me to work its way in because everyone can relate to saying, 'I really should get rid of this but...'

D: Humor, even in my cleaning book, my first one called *Life After Housework*, which became a million seller...the first guy from the big publishing company said, 'Oh, you can't make cleaning funny! Nobody wants to clean!' And then the books sales were huge! If it goes past 10,000, it is huge...it went past a half million. I went back to him and said, 'You can't win 'em all, can you?'

When you go to the Museum, there is a lot of humor in that. People like to hear about other people's failures, and they like to hear about other people's successes. It makes people feel good…people like you. You've got a good subject matter if you find the right people who have really interesting…I learned as a janitor. A lot of people started IT companies, the Gates and them.

But I took the most hated subject in the world - we punish our kids with it - I took cleaning, toilet cleaning, the lowest end of the scale, and made it funny and appealing. I got on national TV and I made it work in books. People like that. If you take some obscure job that everyone else rejected…the more people you can find, to pick something that represents the public, like recycling old rubber tires, or some stupid little thing.

I met a lady 30 years ago named Sandra Phillips. Pull up Baby Banana Brush on your computer when you get time.   She has eight children, she's really sharp, and she invented a little banana toothbrush for her grandson. She's a woman, she's 64 years old, with eight kids, and she was a stay-at-home mom. Now she has invented these toothbrushes that sell all over the world. It is unbelievable…I just shake my head. We were in business together and we taught some seminars and worked on a couple of books together. And I see the letters, and all these national stores in Taiwan, and it is just this stupid toothbrush. So she's somebody who would be really good to feature. People love it – she wins awards and people love to read her story. I sit back and I am just amazed at what she has accomplished.

We were in business together for a while. We taught together and we wrote 3-4 books together. Now she's got 20 grandkids and a huge business. She and her husband live in California, and all her kids live there. I went with her and her husband to Hollywood, and they took me to the Home and Garden channel – she saw that going on. She said that was not good to have these young candy wrapper women that run these shows! She asked, 'Can you do better?' I said yes, and I introduced her to the producer and that's the last time they called me. They went out to her home and they did segments with her and the home ec person for that channel.

When I speak at conventions or anything, there are always 4 or 5 speakers at these big things. There's always an astronaut, there's always a famous politician, there's always a famous movie star, or singer, rock singer, and then there's me, the toilet cleaner. We have 4 sessions. By the last session, I have everybody…at the first session, I only have a few, but then the word gets out, 'Hey! This guy is funny!', and by the last session, I have them all. I am not smarter or better than the rest of them. Everybody knows when they go to listen that they can't be an astronaut or few can be a movie star, and people in the audience know that, but when they come to me, they know I am a janitor, everybody knows they can be a janitor! I am believable. The more you can take people who are believable, the better.

We made it fun. As you saw in the museum, which you can mention, we made all those games! There's a book called *How to Motivate your Cleaning Crew* and it mentions all the parties we had with cleaning to make cleaning fun. When we had dinners, we would get a toilet and put lemonade in it, a brand new toilet, and dipped lemonade out of it! We would make 'baby bean dip' and put it in a baby potty! And we would have corn chips so you could dip into it!

I loved the soapbox derby exhibit at the museum! [At the Museum of Clean, there is an exhibit where Don and other people working for Varsity Cleaning created soapbox cars out of janitorial supplies, including trash cans, brooms, etc.]

D: We had a janitor rodeo too! And we had a little music thing where we made a band out in Las Vegas! To find these people who are really real, who are unique, Sandra Phillips and me. I mean, a lot of people have invented a car or started a computer program or made stuff on Twitter. Everybody is doing that; it is commonplace. The more stuff you can take out of commonplace, the better your book will be. People will say, 'Look at this guy! He cleaned toilets and he made a million dollars! And he did Oprah! And he developed a toilet bowl brush!' Or they will read, 'Oh, this woman, her stupid baby toothbrush is selling all over the world! And she's got eight kids, and she is a stay-at-home mom, and she's over 60?' Women aren't old at 60…and people still want to do something great with their life! And they want to read about it!

When I did the books, I did it at the perfect time because they had all these talk shows. I would fly into Philadelphia and do the 6 o'clock TV show for a minute and a half. 'Oh, we have this toilet man on the show, and we have Kim Eley, she's talking all about the heroes…' You have a good subject, because they can ask, 'Who is your favorite? Tell us about these people.'

You have your favorite ones. 'I know this old toilet cleaner who carried around a toilet suitcase! He ended up hiring thousands of people and cleaned all over the United States!' You can use my story. You've got to find people that…in fact, I got a call yesterday, it is sitting right here in front of me. In Omaha, Nebraska, they are going to have a big convention and they want me to speak. They're at a college and they will have entrepreneurs, and half these kids are just dreamers. They just read Wall Street stories. And I tell these people, 'Wall Street is not Main Street. You can be from Podunk, Ohio or from Idaho. I'm from a high school of 42 people.'

I guess you will self-publish your book? Print it for a couple of bucks, sell it for $10. Wherever you speak, you will sell 10 or 15 books, 50 books. When you do that, you can make $500-600, when you make a free speech at the Rotary or someplace. The main thing is, you've gotta capture…everyone has to clean, and to find a manual to package it…to find these right people. There's lots of people starting to make little brooms.

People like the unique. We're so flooded in our market. Look at all the TV stations, all the things on, they explore every little angle. There's all kinds of shows about junk and clutter! It's hard…they've done it so well, it's hard to compete with it unless you come up with some guy who makes harmonicas or some guy who is a hillbilly…people really identify with that, Kim. They think, 'Man, I could do that!' When they read your thing, they should think, 'I can do that!' Then they will read it and do it. There's a lot of neat stuff.

Clutter's Last Stand is a neat book. It's well done. I paid $18,000 for the art but I really like the structure of the book. We are such a visual society and to have a bunch of pages…art really made a difference and all people have commented that they like it. I can get a piece of art and show what I could describe in 3 paragraphs. I can use the art.

It makes a big difference. I think that's one thing, along with the humorous way you were writing… the pictures really jump out at you. I think everybody…when I was growing up, we had what we called 'the Lost Closet' because that's where things went to disappear! And a lot of the illustrations brought that back to me!

D: Well, that's the big thing, when I started talking with people and started to listen, and have Sandra mail you a few things, and you can start getting paragraphs together which are interesting. You hook the reader, and tell how [the subjects] did it, tell some of the funny stories…Don did this…stories I called 'I Said Them But They are True' about all the screw-ups I did, and all the rugs I shrunk. I cleaned the Kennedys' place and movie stars and I worked for the Mafia! And you find all of these little things that people are really intrigued by. And when you are on TV, it really puts stuff well. They will film for 5 hours to get 2 minutes…people are just used to that now.

Commercials – some of them have 18 scenes! Kids are so used to the movies just flashing by. I hadn't been to the movies since 1985 and somebody took me to a movie the other night. It just about blew me away. It flashes – it's only like 3 seconds of flashes of things! In the old movies, you could zero in and enjoy them.

It's so true!

D: Then when you put your books out, some of them are on Kindle. I don't know how many people stole my stuff. I haven't paid much attention to it because I have got so many other things going on. So I just faced the facts…you can hardly give a book away now. But I still think people like writers, if they get a good subject going on in this day and age, everybody wants success! And everybody is going to school, studying, having dreams! Most people think they want their own business. You need one chapter on the perils of someone owning their own business.

The biggest question I get is, 'Don, are you still working on the job?' And I say, 'No, my bowl brush picks itself up, goes running down the hall, and puts itself away!' I journal every week, poetry and everything. I write in it a lot. I find people still like my stuff. I keep it short, and concise. Some people go on and on! Think about the cover, think about your title. 'They Did It, and You Can, Too!' Not too long ago, someone said they were writing a book about how they take little kids' coveralls and take rags and make coveralls!

I saw that on TV!

D: I thought of the title, 'From Rags to Britches'! [Laughs] It's really a good title! Some of my own books, I can't come up with a title at all. If I know what you're doing, sometimes a guy like me can come along and say, 'Hey, here's a great title!' You have to let people know what you're working on. Tell your husband, your friends. Writing a book…tell people and they will start finding those people like the one I told you about.

Find those unique people! There are seventeen tattoo parlors in Pocatello. To talk with someone about tattoos is not unique unless you can find an angle. Everybody is doing it. Everybody is taking courses at night for photography and computers and scrapbooks…hundreds of people are doing that so you are competing in a huge pool. Take yourself out of that pool. Come up with…here's the 100 most creative entrepreneurs and use it from that angle.

***

Don's ability to think differently completely defines his career. He took (using his words) the world's most hated career and made it entertaining and delightful. It's not that cleaning itself is exotic – I mean, few things are as universal – and as universally hated. What is exotic is turning cleaning on its head. Don makes it thought-provoking through the antiques (looking at old vacuum cleaners is really interesting!), the social aspects (cleaning and feminism), the current (the Museum of Clean is built to be "green", very topical in today's world of environmental responsibility), and the humorous (you have to love Don's "toilet briefcase" – talk about a conversation starter!). Certainly this different way of thinking that defines Don and other entrepreneurs like him mean that all entrepreneurs fall within the category of Tickers because of their passion, energy and innovation.

After I interviewed Don, I became really excited about my book. That's what a Ticker does…they pick you up and take you on a mental journey with them. With Don's help, I had great ideas for selecting additional Tickers, identifying entrepreneurs from pioneers, and many great tips for writing my own book.

Don's passion is contagious. He got me excited because he was so excited. I realized that people who are Tickers push past the boundaries that hold many people back. Boundaries like normal expectations, being afraid to look silly or out of the ordinary, or people telling them they can't do something doesn't stop a real Ticker from pursuing what they love.

While I had business connections with Bill Smith and James Hartle, I had never met Don except my one visit to the Museum of Clean. I was so surprised and excited to talk with Don…that I reached out to him and he actually was willing to talk with me! I had been afraid before of being rejected or even laughed at. After talking with Don, I made a list of people with whom I wanted to talk. I decided to reach out to them no matter what the reaction was.

Just like with Don, I sent emails to people whose careers interested me. I reached out to people I had admired from television. I sent emails, letters and even some small gifts to a number of people. Sending out the emails made me feel vulnerable. It took some courage to send them out. I received rejections but the strange thing was that even when I received rejections, I got a thrill just knowing I had tried.

I realized there are many Tickers who aren't on television but are just as passionate and out there with their love for what they do. I thought about people who have unusual careers and people who just love what they do. I kept branching out. I asked friends. I talked about Tickers. Tickers wasn't a reality at first – it was just an idea – but the more I talked about Tickers the more real it became. I decided to keep my "feelers" out – I would reach out to people whose careers I admired but I would also reach out to my friends and invite in Tickers. I was so glad I did. While I managed to find Tickers on my own, I also was inspired deeply by the Tickers whom my friends recommended. And I became more and more excited, and kept asking for interviews, and kept putting myself out there. And the stories I discovered!

Story 4: H – Owner of The Mansion on O Street: Everyday Magic

I hate business meetings with a white-hot passion. When I joined Zeta Phi Beta Sorority, Incorporated, in 2003, I was drawn to the community service, to the opportunity to join like-minded women in improving the lives of other people, and the fact that working together would mean we could do more for others than we can do as individuals. No one, however, told me that being a member of Zeta Phi Beta would instill in me an intense dislike for Robert and his rules of order, the recognized guide for running business meetings.

Having said that, I am extremely passionate about being a member of Zeta Phi Beta Sorority, Incorporated, and the amazing work that my Sorors do! In July 2014, I had been hyped up and excited about attending our bi-annual national conference called the Boulé. I was even more excited that the 2014 Boulé was going to be held in Washington, D.C. Living 2 ½ hours away from D.C. meant my sorority sisters and I could charter a bus to the Boulé hotel, a cheaper and easier option than flying. Having friends who live in Northern Virginia also meant I could socialize and stay with my friends, riding the metro to the Boulé hotel every day.

But the layoffs at my office occurred the week before I left home to catch the bus to Boulé, and I was still reeling. I was troubled knowing that soon some of my team members would be unemployed. I was freaking out because Jerry and I still had to pay off our two-week vacation, and now both of us would have to take some unpaid leave in the near future. I was confused about my career path and started doubting everything. I was smack in the middle of the depression stage of grief about my office and my future. This cloud of confusion and concern threatened to ruin my trip.

I tried to attend some of the business meetings at Boulé but I was bored out of my gourd. To my Sorors' credit, everything that was being discussed was important Sorority business. But my brain, and more importantly, my heart, was just not into it. I had to get out of the meetings and out of the hotel. I needed time by myself to think. It was odd because I was surrounded by my beloved Sorors and I was in one of the most populated cities in the U.S., but what I desperately needed was some alone time to process everything. So I took the opportunity while in D.C. to go on a walkabout by myself.

To save money and get some exercise, I decided to walk from my friend's house to the Metro station to the hotel, and I also walked to locations to eat. I wanted to explore

D.C. on foot. I searched my iPhone for places to go shopping. I found a consignment shop and a yarn store and walked to them…as an avid bargain hunter and knitter, normally these finds would excite me. But visiting these places just didn't do it for me. I still felt cocooned in a funk.

I'm a firm believer in retail therapy! Shopping feels good to me because it reminds me of many wonderful shopping trips I had with my Mom. I don't even have to buy anything on these trips to feel better. So I did another search for places to shop. And unbeknownst to me, my search would take me to the most magical place I have ever experienced.

I followed Trip Advisor which led me to the Mansion on O Street because they stated it was a place to shop. I was confused because when I walked to the address, it looked like I was in front of a row house, not a mansion. It also did not look like a storefront. And O Street is a residential neighborhood. I didn't want to walk up to someone's house and say, "Hi! May I shop here?"

I then noticed some signs in front that stated "Valet Parking for the Mansion on O Street" so I knew I was in the right place. I saw another sign stating to walk downstairs if you are there for the inn. I started guessing this was a bed and breakfast. There was another sign in front that stated the museum hours, and another that said the museum was open. I thought, so this is a B&B and a museum…interesting! I guessed that every museum must have a gift shop, and that must be where the promised shopping would be, so I decided to walk to the front door and hit the buzzer.

A woman's voice answered. I said I was there to see the Mansion. She opened the door and let me in. I think she could tell I was confused.

The first thing that caught my eye was a signed guitar at the front reception desk. There was music playing and there seemed to be a ton of knick-knacks around. Not a surprise - most B&B's have a lot of interesting items on display. I think I asked if I could shop. The woman asked if I had been there before and I said no. As I continued looking around, I noticed that some of the walls were painted in bright, sparkly paint. I looked over the woman's shoulder at the guitar, and noticed the signature. "Oh wow," I said, "Is that signed by Bob Dylan?" She nodded nonchalantly.

The woman then started explaining the Mansion. She said you can pay a fee to view the Mansion as a museum. She said 'everything without a heartbeat is for sale'. "OK," I thought, and I had to laugh. She looked serious. She said I was welcome to tour all of the rooms in the Mansion, but cautioned me that it is also a hotel. She said if there is a sign on any door in the Mansion stating "Do Not Disturb" to please not enter because it is a guest's room.

Then she said there are 70 hidden doors in the Mansion. She said on average, most people find about two. What? Did I mistake what she said? I had to ask her to repeat the info about the doors. She explained that there are so many hidden doors that even some of her children have not found all of them.

I looked at her, surprised. It was dawning on me that this was not the average B&B.

While the woman led me to the room to the right of the front entrance, I continued looking around. There were so many things to look at that I could not figure out where to focus first. I saw tables set for a tea service. I saw beautiful vases and pictures. Then I turned and over my shoulder I saw a shadow box with "Purple Rain," a picture of Prince and a signed guitar. Signed by Prince. Where am I? The walls glittered in the light of the chandeliers.

As I often do, I asked the woman her name so I could introduce myself. "My name is H," she said, casually. I thought, "Wow, even her name is amazing. It sounds like she is related to MI6 or some other secret organization." I shook her hand and thanked her before she left me to tour the house.

Fate had taken me around the corner into a magical place which felt like a cross between Willy Wonka's factory and the Addams Family house.

***

The Mansion on O Street in fact is not a traditional mansion but a series of five interconnected town houses. The Mansion has over 100 rooms and over 70 secret doors. Edward Clark, the same architect who designed the U.S. Capitol over two centuries ago, designed the Mansion. Mr. Clark, his brother James "Champ" Clark, Speaker of the House during Teddy Roosevelt's presidency, and his other brother, known as "the artist," lived there. Some of the leftover tiles and wood from the Capitol Building were used in the Mansion by Clark. It is believed to be the last, virtually intact, private residence in Washington, D.C.

In the 1930's the home was converted into three separate rooming houses for FBI Director J. Edgar Hoover's G-Men. And in the 1960's, the student leaders of the protest movement lived in the Mansion. Norman Mailer wrote about them and the house in his book, "Armies of the Night."[x]

On the Mansion on O Street's web site, it states: "The only museum of its kind, O Street Museum has always been dedicated to exploring the creative process. The collection rotates and changes daily. From the art, to the music, to the surroundings, no visit is ever the same. From artist's letters, to animation stills, to written manuscripts, to one of the largest "raw and exposed" music collections, our galleries are not limited to one genre. O Street Museum offers an immersive, tactile experience where you will hear rare studio cuts, leaf through manuscripts, touch sculpture and tour through a multitude of architectural styles. We offer a wide range of programs including artist-in-residence, live concerts, art-leasing, jammin', raw & exposed, songwriter's workshop and kids' programs. No matter where you look you will miss something. But it's not what you miss, rather what you're willing to see. Magic and miracles exist. Not just in the mind. It's the simple things, small steps, the goals we chose, the way of life we want to breathe. How easily everything changes when you choose to look at the same thing from a different angle, and do it."

***

The owner of the Mansion on O Street is an extraordinary person. H.H. Leonards, the founder and chairman of the Mansion on O Street™, is also the Chairman of PIR marketing, O Street Museum Foundation and Beauty Unites™. In addition, Ms. Leonards was also the executive director of a global computer foundation and was responsible for the distribution of more than $100 million of computer equipment and services. She has also been Chief Marketing Officer of several international corporations.

Ms. Leonards has focused on making it economically feasible for corporations to leverage their philanthropic contributions for their benefit and the benefit of society. She has been a member of several boards, including:

- Columbia Women's hospital, Washington, D.C.
- LV Enterprises, Scottsville, Arizona
- Mildred Alberg Trust, Miami, Florida
- Rock and Roll Hall of Fame & Museum, Cleveland, Ohio
- Rosa Parks Museum and Library, Montgomery, Alabama
- Sequoia Foundation, New York City

Ms. Leonards was adopted by the mother of the civil rights movement, Mrs. Rosa Parks. Mrs. Parks lived in the Mansion for a number of years. It was with Mrs.

Parks that Ms. Leonards met Pope John Paul II. Ms. Leonards has also met all of the United States presidents since President Reagan. From a chance meeting during a dinner at the Mansion, she was commissioned to redesign and be the general contractor on the first I.M. Pei building in Washington, D.C. despite never having studied design in college. She wrote the first million-dollar check to the Statue of Liberty restoration campaign for American Express. She was asked by the Rock & Roll Hall of Fame museum to raise money for a major exhibit to commemorate John Lennon's 60th birthday (and 20th anniversary of his passing).

On her web site, Ms. Leonards states that she succeeded with all of these amazing achievements despite nearly flunking out of grade school. She said, "I graduated from high school in the bottom ten of my class. Sadly today, we seem unwilling to measure creativity and spirituality and, therefore, fail to recognize untold numbers of children who have so much to give. But not here. At the Mansion, we never look at anyone's résumé; everyone has a clean slate, and gets an equal opportunity to work and thrive."

***

I spent a blissful three hours exploring the Mansion that day. It literally filled me with delight. I oohed and ahhed in every room. I am a huge classic rock fan, so the signed artifacts like guitars and photos would have been enough to get my motor running. There were Beatles nesting dolls, a Yellow Submarine jukebox.

I amazed myself by finding seven of the hidden doors. I found secret rooms, and also gazed at not so secret rooms that had amazing décor. I felt giddy, and I was tiptoeing around as though I would scare the secrets away if I stomped around. My mind had been interrupted from the track of gloom and doom I kept playing over and over since the layoffs. Instead I was wondering where I was, what kind of wonderful place this was, and oh my God, is that really an actual letter from John Lennon framed on the wall?

I was thrilled and the tour left me humming, like I was a beacon of energy. It was a complete turnaround from how I felt when I left the Metro station, wandering aimlessly. It was there that it hit me: I must write a book. I need to explain this amazing passion that I felt and the contact high of energy I received from the work of other passionate people who inspired me.

When I came home from Boulé, I kept going on and on about the Mansion to Jerry. I described it all and insisted that he had to experience the magic, too. Imagine my shock when I pulled up the website to show Jerry only to realize that H, whom I thought was just a volunteer with a spy-like name, was in fact H.H. Leonards, the owner and founder of the Mansion! She was so unassuming and had put on zero airs when I met her. I had to know more about her and her vision. There was a story here, and I had to know.

**

The most powerful part of your imagination is your visualization. Through visualization, your mind can imagine an idea, unconstrained, and also imagine how it will be received, and how it will look, feel, taste, behave. I liken it to testing for software. You can apply your idea in hundreds of different scenarios, analyzing it over and over to find new applications and uses, in the testing lab between your ears.

What you can also develop are the basic requirements of an idea. What started the idea in the first place? What makes the idea tick? Is it to make people feel better? To get people to connect? Go back to the basic requirements and expand. Ask yourself, what about trying this? Try it out, move it around, like Legos or building blocks. There is no limit. You have the power. You are the explorer.

Once you are ready to bring the dream into reality, prepare yourself. Your dream is perfect in your head. In your head, it is like the Platonic model of perfection.

To Plato, there was what he called the world of forms, which is a world of perfections or ideals. When you think of a chair, for example, the picture in your head is of what is to you the perfect chair with no imperfections. This is the "form" of the chair. And all objects, living or dead, work towards their perfect state, according to Plato. All of us are working in some way to meet our perfect nature. As Oscar Wilde said, (and Chrissy Hynde of the Pretenders paraphrased in "Message of Love,") "We are all in the gutter, but some of us are looking at the stars."

Life is not perfect. People are not perfect. The implementation of ideas will never be perfect, but despite that fact it can still be beautiful, amazing and wondrous. The transformation of an idea into form and reality can inspire wonder and has created the most amazing places and concepts from mankind.

It can be a slippery slope for some of us, the transformation of a dream or idea into reality. In the world of reality, there are always constraints. The office clock is ticking. There is a bill to pay. There's that exhausted, tired-to-your-bones ache you might feel at the end of the day. There's that nagging feeling when you tell yourself you could be doing better. All of these things are in finite quantities. That is a part of reality. You must steel yourself to face the challenges of the finite. You must hold onto your magic in a world that says magic cannot exist.

Time cannot be expanded. It can be spent. In transforming a dream or idea into reality, you must spend a quantity of time. The time you spend on your dream or idea will mean you will spend less time on other things, things that may also matter a great deal to you. Family, friends, earning a living, the everyday stuff of life like paying bills and taxes, etc. You have to consider how much the other things mean to you compared to what the dream or idea mean to you. You have to acknowledge your own mortality and identify that you will never have the time to spend on everything you would like to do. This can be a depressing realization.

But the flip side? The flip side is that you can decide what matters to you, and therefore choose where you spend your time. There are some basics. Do you want to eat? Well, of course. You have to eat in order to live. Then you will need to do something that enables you to feed yourself. Do you want to have shelter? Most people need shelter and therefore want shelter. Then you will need to figure out how to make this happen, and on what level. Everything else is gravy on the mashed potatoes, icing on the cake.

Do you want what you want because you want it, or because everyone says you should want it? Look deeper into this. It is perhaps your longing to fit into a group that makes you say you want the biggest house on the block or that shiny, gorgeous new car. Maybe it isn't the thing itself that you want, but the way you think it should make you feel, or how people will react to your having that thing, that really motivates you. ("My Ferrari makes me the coolest kid on the metaphorical block!! Look at me!") If it's not the basics (food and shelter), then do you really need it? What if your dream or idea gave you a better feeling than the things you supposedly want? ("I have a Ferrari but I still feel like a jerk. What happened?") What would you do?

In order to obtain our food and shelter, we need to figure out how to get them. For most of us, that means getting a job. A job pays you money, money you can use to pay for food and rent. If you want better food and a better, safer place to live, you will likely have to pay more for those. Tired of only eating Ramen noodles and Captain Crunch cereal? And scared to open the door in your affordable but slightly sketchy, low-rent apartment? In order to make decent money for better food and a better, safer place to live, you have to work in a job that pays a certain amount of money. The economics are another part of reality that dictates what we can and cannot do. In our imaginations, we can live off air and have it all. In reality, that may not be a possibility.

This reality is what drives many people to take jobs that don't support their ideas or dreams, but support someone else's idea or dream. It's a balancing act. For some people, all they want is a steady, secure life and they don't want to pursue their dream because it would be uncomfortable. They want to remain safe and secure.

For Tickers, safe and secure doesn't feel right to them because they so desperately desire to fulfill their dream. Their longing to create their own reality, to achieve the blueprint in their heads, makes them deal with some level of discomfort. Discomfort can include having to be a "starving artist" for a while. It might mean putting up with living in a not-so-great part of town where the rent is cheaper. It can mean taking a job where you earn less money but are doing something that allows you to get closer to your dream, instead of accepting a higher paying job which is unfulfilling. It means taking some risks, daring to leap where others might cower. It means sometimes facing failure, and rejection.

How do you make dream or ideas come to life in the real world? It's similar to investing. I think the first thing is to look inside yourself at your own level of comfort with risk. Would you rather play it safe? Or take a leap? How risk averse are you? People think about this in terms of financial investments, but it can apply to you and your dreams, too.

One of my very best friends, Tara, told me one of her dreams was to open a food truck selling doughnuts. She said it would be fun for her because she likes to bake, and she could wake up early, make the doughnuts, sell the doughnuts, and have the rest of the day off. She doesn't pursue this dream, however, and said she doesn't plan to pursue it, because she loves her wife and son too much to risk having them go without. She has a secure job. She has health insurance, a steady paycheck, and doesn't have to be concerned with the whims of a potentially fickle doughnut-eating public.

But Tara still experiences incredible delight in her life! She's a huge Disney fan and loves to go to the Magic Kingdom, dazzled by the fireworks. She's also a guitarist in a rockin' band! And most of all, she loves her family and spending time with them. She adores these interludes between her ordinary job. Her not-so-interesting job affords her the very interesting and fun life she has outside of work. She has done her own risk assessment with her life, and decided she feels more comfortable with the security of a secure job. She loves her dream of the doughnut truck, and speaks fondly of it. But that's not her. That life would make her uncomfortable. And she is perfectly happy baking with her son on the weekends, planning amazing Disney trips, rocking out with Tonic Jane, and she loves her life madly.

So I think everyone needs to do a risk assessment, which goes hand in hand with a list of priorities. So ask yourself: What's really most important to you now? Is it your family? Owning the "McMansion" you've had your eye on? Charting your own course, taking your life literally into your own hands? Is that too scary for you? What does that feel like in your gut? What does that feel like in your heart?

Of course, it is important to acknowledge we are never truly in control. Even if you decide you are completely risk averse and choose a stable and secure job, there is no guarantee these days that the company won't fold or that there will be layoffs. You must remain ever vigilant and aware of any changes that could happen.

So, if you do have a dream or idea, say to bake the world's best chocolate caramel cupcakes, and you have weighed the risks, and you decide to go for it? How do you make it happen? How do you go from dream to reality? What takes you from the weekend baker to a dedicate cupcake artist? What do you need to consider?

H is a woman who had a passion and pursued it. She followed her dream with blind faith and a determination but no real plan. For a pragmatist, this approach would seem like a road to failure. For her, it was the start of an incredible journey.

***

I wrote to H for months after I realized I wanted to write a book. I was thrilled, completely over the moon with joy, when she agreed to let me interview her. We coordinated for me to come and stay at the Mansion in January 2015 so I could interview H and also show this amazing place to Jerry.

Jerry and I had booked one of the least expensive rooms because we try to keep costs down. I was initially bummed when Ted, H's husband, had emailed and said the room we wanted was not available, but they would be sure to select a comparable room for us.

Jerry and I drove from Prince George to D.C. on a Saturday. I could not wait for Jerry to see the Mansion! We planned to spend Saturday night and leave Sunday after eating brunch at the Mansion. When we arrived, H greeted us and to my surprise, valet parked our car. To our even greater surprise, Ted told us that he had arranged for us to stay in the Penthouse. Wow! We had our own private elevator to one of the most lavish and spacious hotel rooms I have ever seen, let alone stayed in! Double wow! Among the many amazing items in the penthouse were guitars signed by Jeff "Skunk" Baxter from Steely Dan and the Doobie Brothers and by Sarah McLachlan. WOWWOWWOW!! Jerry and I were so excited! We walked around the Mansion a bit while I waited to speak with H. She's constantly taking care of the tourists and hotel guests at the Mansion. She was super busy and I was super nervous.

When H agreed to meet with me, it was the end of the day. Lots of visitors had been there at the Mansion…one of the volunteers, Michelle, said they had about 150-200 people coming in for tours! We had checked into our room and I didn't have my questions or recorder with me. Oops! I ran upstairs, took the incredibly cool private elevator, dug furiously through my bag for my recorder and printed sheet of questions, and had a momentary freak-out when I couldn't find either. Once I located them, I got lost on my way back to the second floor to meet with H.

H and I sat down on one of the sofas. It was in the same room where I had seen the tea set and picture of Prince the previous summer. However, I noticed that the room had been redecorated. H said we would be able to hear better in that room. She asked if Jerry and I had eaten dinner, and when I said no, she asked what we like to eat. Then she recommended a place around the corner, Asia 54, which serves sushi and Thai food. She gave us directions to get there. She said they have the best pad Thai she has ever had in the United States, and an amazing salad with avocado, raw tuna, and raspberries. "It's normal sushi but how they present it is different," she explained. "They have a really great and robust menu, and you're going to dream their food for the rest of your life."

While I was nervous initially, H has a calming demeanor. She also asked me questions about myself too. Her answers continually surprised me. I was like, "She wants to know about me?"

***

K: I'll tell you my plan. I'm writing a book about people who are really passionate about what they do. And I came here in July and just got such the amazing vibe when I came in here that I knew I wanted to write about it. I don't know if you remember me…. when I came here in July, I walked outside the back door! Ted had to open the door and let me back in. And now I am getting lost…

H: Good! Well, the purpose of the house is to understand that it is good to get lost because then you get found again. If you never get lost, you never have that experience.

Yeah, absolutely! I love that! I see that you are from Lafayette, Indiana. What was it like growing up there as a kid?

H: It was incredibly great. And anyway, when you are growing up, you don't know any different, so I assume most people think it is incredibly great. But now that I'm not there, what stayed with me is that everyone was the same. There were no people who were in or out. You were "out" if you had dirty clothes, and the people who were supposedly "in" helped the people with dirty clothes so they would have clean clothes. So it was a really warm…you didn't lock your doors, everyone said "Good Morning!", a deal was a deal, and if you shook a hand, that was it. Leaving that was exceedingly difficult, and even though now that I am 64, it's still difficult to deal with the fact that people aren't like that. And it's been all these years. But what a great environment! I was very blessed.

I read online that somewhere you said, "Positive energy is important and can come from being bad at something." What does that mean?

H: If you fail, it's good. If you make mistakes, it's good. If you don't try, it's not good. So it doesn't matter if you are great at everything. It matters that you are open to try anything.

Oh awesome! Thank you. Online it says that the Mansion combines art, architecture, literature, and imagination. What were your inspirations as you were growing up in Indiana?

H: God, God and God. Probably in that order. It's very strange to say but it is real.

I saw that you attended Purdue University. What did you like about Purdue?

H: I think that…from my experience, my favorite course was the psychology of literature. It taught me how to look at books not from a perspective of what happened, but how the author perceived what the psychology of the human being is, because everyone is so different. I'm glad I worked myself through college because it really helped me and created the basis for what I am doing today, but I don't think it is important to have a college education. And that's what going to college taught me. So I encouraged all of my children not to go to college, if they chose not to.

Did they follow your advice?

H: One did, and two did not. But really, and especially today, you don't need to go to college to learn. Because the internet is so extraordinary! It is at your fingertips, anything you want to learn. It's pretty exciting! What college does is that it gives you four extra years to mature and grow up. In that respect, it's important. But you can get that same experience through working, through writing, or just breathing.

After living in Indiana, you became drawn to Washington, D.C. to become a nurse. What drew you to DC?

H: I wanted to join the Marines, actually, because everyone in the Midwest is patriotic. It was during the Vietnamese War, and they didn't want women at the time. My best friend and I went down three times to become a nurse in the Marines. They kept losing pieces of our paperwork. So after the third time, I said to her, "God's telling me to do something else. I'll go to our nation's capital and see what I can do." She said, "I'm just going to go for my fourth time." And they didn't lose her paperwork after the fourth time, so she went on to Vietnam. She said that she was so glad that I didn't because I'd still be in a mental hospital. God does work in mysterious ways.

And then I came to Washington and I was so disillusioned when I got here because people weren't here to help their country or the world. They were here…it was all about them, and greed and power. It was very disillusioning. So I thought through music and art, that they would remember who they wanted to become and maybe do something positive with their lives. And that's really what's happening inside the house.

Where did you grow up?

I have to admit I was realized surprised at this point. I really didn't expect H to interview me!

I grew up a little bit north of Richmond. I lived in Texas for a little while, but mostly in Richmond. Now I live about 30 miles south of Richmond near Petersburg. Jerry's from Petersburg, and it's been really fun getting to know that area because the people are really warm. Not that they aren't warm in Richmond, but it's the kind of place where people just come up to you and say, "Hey, how are you doing?" And I forget that when I come here because I am used to saying that when I walk up to people. I don't know if you encounter that or not. I'll walk up and go, "Hi, how are you doing?" And people will look at me like, "She noticed me!" It always surprises me!

H: So what drove you to write this book?

Well, I went through, not an extremely tough time, other people have been through tougher. But we had layoffs at my job this summer. I had a team of four people and we had to lay off three of the four people. And it just really was upsetting, as any kind of layoff is. But we have an extremely small company, and a lot of people were good friends. And it just seemed very senseless to me, just seemed like a lot of corporate nonsense. I was really down. I came here because I belong to a sorority…I joined a predominantly African-American sorority and it has been the most fun! I was really looking forward to coming to our national convention. And I was feeling really bummed out about the people, you know, having to let them go. And I coincidentally ran into this place. I was looking to go shopping! I was going to do some "retail therapy" and I came in here. Actually you greeted me, and I walked in, and the positive energy and the creativity made me…it stuck with me. And I was like, "You know, I wish there was a really good book about people who do what makes them tick. People who just, dang it all, they love the creative and the music,

art, all those kinds of things. That just really stuck with me. And later on, I was like, "Well, why don't you write that book, Kim?" So that's where I am now.

H: That's nice. That's awesome! And you are still working full-time?

I am still working full-time.

H: So did you learn anything about what was real, after the initial shock of having people let go by the company?

I think I have…I have really done some soul-searching and looking into what I want to do, and sort of culling away, "OK, this is <u>not</u> what I want to do." I'm a project manager but I'm the sort of project manager who really cares about my people, or at least I think I do! I like to mentor them, I like to see them grow and explore and do better things. I've been thinking about becoming a life coach.

H: So the book will help you get there?

I think so! It is so much fun! And so revelatory already! It's opened my eyes to a lot of things.

H: Cool!

I know you have written two books. What inspired you to write them?

H: I always wrote. And my husband said, "You really should write a book." I went, "Well, OK. Why not?" So I am working on my third one right now. And it is called, "Lessons."

Fantastic! [I pause to write.] Sorry, I am jotting down notes. I know I have my recorder but I never trust it. I was doing an interview and it up and died on me in the middle of the interview! So I brought extra batteries with me; I am prepared!

H: So you know who George Carlin is [the comedian]?

Oh yes, I loved him!

H: Unbelievable wordsmith. So Ted's brother was interviewing him, and it didn't record the entire thing. And it was for a radio show! So he had to go through what he felt was the humiliation of going back to George and starting all over again! He said it was probably the worst time of his life. Because George just kind of looked at him like, "?"

[Laughs] I can imagine George Carlin's reaction!

H: [Laughs]

I'm sure it wasn't funny at the time!

H: No, it wasn't!

It's a great story! I've found that a lot of bad experiences are good stories.

H: Yeah, they are. And that's the way you have to look at it. So we had a bride who was thrown in the pool in the back [of the Mansion], which is a horrible, horrible thing. The groomsmen thought it was funny. Not to a bride! I don't know any bride who would think that is funny. But she can tell that story five years later and it is semi-OK. And that's the way to look at it.

I saw that you had worked with severely handicapped children. How did that affect your life?

H: I loved it. They were great kids, but I had nightmares at night. I kept my commitment to work with them for a year, but then I realized that's not something I could do as a full-time occupation. But here, we bring kids in here that blow their wheelchairs around the house. So I have pieces of that that happen today.

What's great about when they come in here is that their parents are usually always worried about their kids when they are out. They don't know what's going to happen, and they don't know how people are going to react to them. And here they just sit and relax, and they say things like, "This is the only place where I can bring my kid and not worry." And the kids will go off on their own, and blow around the house! It's very neat.

I bet they have a blast!

H: Yes, they do.

Online I read that you said people are afraid to be themselves in DC. Does that sort of go back to what you were talking about when you first moved here?

H: Washington is an odd un-city. It's not really a city. No matter where you come, the world is mostly government-related. People are afraid if they go out of their box, they will be beaten with a hammer, boom. I think there is a reason. But it doesn't make it a real city to live in. And it's sad.

That is sad.

H: It's sad that people come to this city with their own agenda. It's sad that that's what it is. But in this house, it is magic!

It is! Absolutely! I felt the energy the minute I walked in the door. I was like, so low, and it just knocked me over.

H: Yeah!

I also read that you purchased the Mansion in 1980 using credit cards. What kind of leap of faith was that?

H: It was a way to get the house. It was when they had just come out and they hadn't linked credit cards together. I applied for like, lots of them. They all came in at the same time with cash advances, because that's when it first came out. That's how I got the cash for the house. I still live on credit cards. We now have, oh my God, maybe 64 credit cards. That's how we go through and fund it, at huge interest rates. But it is better than not being here!

I always tell people, don't worry about where money's going to come from. If your focus is on money, you'll never live a rich life. But if you just do what you believe in, you'll always be…[gestures around to the Mansion surroundings.]

I read also that the Mansion supports Habitat for Humanity, and I know you have a special connection with Rosa Parks, and the Red Cross. What have those experiences meant to you?

H: All of them are an accumulation of what we live for. My book is Live Heaven, but it is really true. You need to live while you are alive, as if you're in heaven. That should be the model for everything. Because why wait? And if we are truly here to serve people, which is my mission, then that's what you do.

Were you always certain of your path when you bought the Mansion?

H: Yes. I didn't understand it but I was always certain. There have been times….I mean, it's just a miracle that we are still here. I never worried about the finances. Even if we are losing a ton of money, somehow I know it is going to be fine. So I don't worry about anything.

I'm upset by human nature a lot. But that's not my problem.

When you bought the Mansion, did you have the vision of expanding the way that you did?

H: Yes. But it really wasn't my vision. I say it was really God's pictures that He gave me. I'm not the idea person; I'm just the facilitator. I just make the pictures that are given real.

I loved this concept of being the facilitator. I believe that was the element I was missing when I tried to write stories prior to this book. My gift lies not in creating a story of my own but in sharing the stories of others and being a channel for which to deliver their messages.

That's amazing! That is resonating with me! Do you consider yourself a story teller?

H: No. If I was, I would be much more verbal. I create a stage for other people to have their stories in. I create a stage, and I'm in the corner cleaning the stage. I'm not in the center; it's not about me. Other people can create…they can write their books, they can write their music, they can just be themselves, they can meet a new friend. They are front and center, not me.

Michelle [one of the Mansion volunteers] was telling us about, and forgive me if I get it wrong, but she was telling us that Arlo Guthrie's daughter performed here?

H: She's one of the people, yeah.

And Michelle talked about how she told all these wonderful stories. And that would literally would be a stage for storytelling.

H: But your stories too. People will be sitting here and you will see something, and it will remind you of something, and then you tell your family story, and then someone else tells a story. I'll never forget it…two guys in their fifties were sitting upstairs in the Mediterranean. They were not sure why they sat down. And they turned to each other and started talking. And then they started crying. And someone came downstairs and said, "These guys are crying upstairs. I hope they are OK!"

So we ran upstairs, and they said, "No, no, everything is great! We grew up together on the same block. When we were four, my parents left. Moved – and they didn't tell me I was moving. They just stuck me in the car and were down the road, and then said, 'Oh, by the way, we are moving to a different state.' And I never had the time to say goodbye to my friend." And it was before Facebook and all that stuff. So he said, "I don't know how many times we might have passed each other…" They didn't live in Washington; they were just traveling. They sat down and started talking, and it was unbelievable.

Stuff like that. People open up and talk, and in another hotel, no one talks to each other. And in a restaurant, no one says hello. Like you were talking about. Here, people just feel comfortable with each other and they just start talking.

How do you connect with your inner passion?

H: I don't even know what that means. [Laughs]

What inspires you on a daily basis? Because there's bound to be good days and bad days. What keeps you ticking, so to speak?

H: The people that come in the house. Music. Books. God.

How did you guys create the 25th anniversary album, "Realize your Vision?" How did that come together?

H: I wanted to do something special; I love music. And I wrote some songs. So it started with writing the songs,

We're in the process now of going for our 35th year, and we are back in the studio. But we can't afford it. Before I had the money to do it right. Now because of the tools and stuff, we can afford to do it because it is so inexpensive now, thanks to Apple! So right now, we are working on the song, "Live Heaven." Paul Williams, who is the president of ASCAP [American Society of Composers, Authors and Publishers], and also he just won the Grammy last year for Best Album of the Year along with Daft Punk, wrote the lyrics. Felix Cavaliere of the Rascals is doing the music.

What do you like best about your path?

H: I'm not sure what that means. But I can't wait to get up in the morning. My body hurts at night because what we do is physical. I mean, it really hurts. But I can't wait… at 2, 3 in the morning, I can't wait to get up. Because it's an adventure. Every day is different, but it's not. Because it's different people, it's different stories that they're telling me. The house is physically changing. Like tomorrow night, this whole room is going to change.

When are you guys leaving?

We're leaving tomorrow afternoon, after brunch.

H: And you have to go back?

Yeah.

H: It would be great if you stayed another night – Sunday night – and went in the middle of the night, because you'll see this room, how it magically just transforms to another world. But it looks different from when you were here in July.

It does! I asked Michelle, I asked, "Where's J. Edgar Hoover?" And she said, "He's dead!" And I said, "No! The wax figure!" [When I visited in 2014 there was a wax figure of J. Edgar Hoover in one of the front rooms. When I returned in 2015, wax J. Edgar was nowhere in sight.]

H: Actually we were just talking because the person I was sitting with is an agent in the FBI, and I was telling him the story of when J. Edgar Hoover [the wax figure] was here. And how interesting it was that some people came in, and they were adults, and they would say things like, they would see the name Hoover and say, "That's the guy who invented the vacuum cleaner!"

[Laughs]

Seriously! And I said to him, "It wasn't just a one-time thing." And then other people would say, "That's the guy who built the Hoover Dam!" And then sometimes it was the President! And it's incredible how history is just disappearing. We're in Washington DC; you would think that people would know who J. Edgar Hoover is! And it wasn't kids, it was the adults. But the best one was…"Is this the guy who invented the vacuum cleaner?" [Laughs]

It puts reality, or what the world is, in history, because it's really "his story". So everyone has a different story, and everything is real. And I'm not going to tell the guy who told his kid that this was the vacuum cleaner inventor that he's wrong in front of his kid. I went, "Yeah, that's right!" [Laughs]

What kind of weird or unusual comments have you gotten? Have you gotten anything similar to Mr. Hoover?

H: Yeah. Consistently, constantly. The house was really built because I couldn't leave the world the way it was, and I wanted to build a world that could be. So it's just always interesting to see who people are. And sometimes sad.

We were also talking with the FBI agent that some people are born bad. They just come out, and there's nothing in their environment that will change that. It's DNA. It's how you get a family where two brothers who are a year apart, and one is good, and one is evil. And it's the same parents, same environment. It's just they're born that way. And how I used to raise boxers, and the litters would pop out. Every dog from the same litter had the same parents, same environment, was different. And the moment the dog popped out, their nature was set. You can teach a dog to sit and heel, but you can't change who the dog is. So that's interesting.
But you can help people along the way. Let's just say if you're lost, spiritually, you can redirect that to who you can become. Not necessarily who you are. That's possible.

So if somebody is born bad, they could potentially...

H: I'm not sure...people who are born evil, I'm not sure if they can change, to tell you the truth. But people who have lost themselves along the way...you talked about wanting to become a life coach. You can help them find themselves again. It's just like someone that is a battered woman giving them belief in themselves again, they can go off and do something tremendous. If they were an evil person, they wouldn't be able to, if that makes sense. There's a difference.

Do you have a motto or words that you live by?

H: I have a pretty strong foundation...yes. I don't know if they are words but they are a strong foundation.

Is it true that you are a board member of the Rock and Roll Hall of Fame?

H: Yes!

How did that come about? You're passionate about music...

H: I love music. How it came about is really about the foundation of life. My son was in school, and he's a baseball fanatic. Actually he's an all-sport fanatic. We won an auction to see the Cleveland Indians, and a three game series, and then we could meet the president of the Rock and Roll Hall of Fame for a personal tour. My son did not want to go to the Rock and Roll Hall of Fame, but…three days before we were supposed to leave, I was supposed to give a speech in London, to Parliament, but Zeke came to me and said, "Mama, I want to go to the series." And I was like, "Oh my God." But then I looked at him, and I said, "We're going!" So someone else went to Parliament, and I went to Cleveland. So I always tell people, "You have to do what you believe in, not what you think is the right," so he came first. So we went and had a fantastic weekend going to the baseball game! It was incredible! It was so much fun! The baseball field is amazing.

And then the last thing we did was to go to the Rock and Roll Hall. And coming down the stairs was the president, and I burst out laughing. He said, "What are you laughing about?" And I said, "Because you come to the Mansion all the time! I don't know what you do, and now I can't believe I'm paying to meet you, because I already know you!" Because I never ask people what they do, ever! Because it doesn't matter.

So we started going through the museum, and he started giving me a tour about the music, and I wasn't really interested. And my son was <u>definitely</u> not interested. I was on the board of the Rosa Parks Museum being built in Montgomery, Alabama. As we went around to different exhibits, I was asking questions that would help Mrs. Parks. So I'd say, "How much did this cost?", "How did you decide who designed it?", "Where are the designers from?" Those were questions like that. And he said, "I don't know, I don't know. You'll have to talk to my curators." And halfway through, he said, "I can't believe you are asking me questions that I don't know. And it's not about the music, which I do know!" And later he turned to me and said, "I get what you're asking me. I get the reasons why. I'll give you an example of how these exhibits come about. Yoko Ono just called me yesterday, and she's getting ready to show John's bloody glasses. And things that no one has seen. It's taken her 20 years to do this. It's the anniversary of the 20 years of his death, and his 60th birthday is within 2 weeks of each other. She asked if I could do an exhibit, and I had to say yes. It's John Lennon! It's Yoko! When I hung up, I said, 'Oh my God, how am I going to come up with a half a million dollars?'

And the rest of the tour, we're talking about his dilemma. So at the end of the tour, I said, "Could you do me a favor? Could you give me 48 hours? I think I can raise the money for you. Because I do marketing for companies." He looked at me and said, "Sure!"

And I got back to the hotel room and I made two phone calls. I called the president of the company I do marketing for, and I called the chief marketing officer of a company I did work for, and I said, "You have this opportunity; you're going public. You get the rights to John Lennon's name for one year, and you get the rights to the word 'Imagine.' This is what the deal is." And they both said yes.

But I didn't tell them that I called the other one because I didn't think they'd come right away. So I asked both of them, and both called me back and said, "We're coming." And they were flying in...one from the West Coast, and one from Europe, within a half hour of each other. I know them, and they hated each other! So the president thought he was a better marketing guy, and the marketing guy was making too much money, and he didn't need him. The marketing guy thought he would make a better president and the president was a piece of shh, which happens a lot in companies! So I was afraid to pick them up at the airport.

So I asked the president of the Rock Hall if he had a board member who could give them a tour of the city, that could be a little bit intimidating so they weren't fighting. And then bring them to the Rock Hall for a tour. So they did that. And they were so pumped up, seeing Cleveland and getting the tour. Then at the end of the tour I was in the meeting. The marketing guy said, "I like this deal, I think it's great. For these reasons, I'll commit a half a million dollars." But the president said, "I think that's wrong, I think that we're not giving you enough money for the value of what you're offering. I'd like to make it a million." Then the marketing guy said, "Well, what is your equipment like? Do you need an upgrade?" They said yes, and then they talked about that for a while, for about 45 minutes. So the marketing guy said, "I'll commit to a half million dollars of networking equipment." So it was one guy trying to make the other guy...so instead of getting a half million dollars in 24 hours, it wasn't 48, he got 1.5 million dollars, so they asked me to be on the board! Which was <u>incredible</u>! But if I had gone to London, none of that would have happened! And my life would have been irrevocably different! Maybe good, but not as much fun.

So I always tell people, "Make your decisions based on who you want to become, and what your priorities are." The kid came first...it wasn't about me; it was about him. It just happened, like, "Oh my God!" So that's how that happened.

Now everybody else comes and goes on the Board and I'm still there. Which is even more
amazing.

We went there a few years ago!

H: It's fun! I love Cleveland, I love what they're doing there!

Yes! They have some fantastic restaurants, and great places.

H: I could retire there! My husband's from Cleveland. But he said, "No way I'm going through the winter!" But it is interesting too that while I'm on the board, there's a guy I sat next to all the time, and every time I went to a board meeting, he said to me, "It's too bad my brother is married. You two are soul mates." I do a lot of different things, but I did a concert on Wall Street for a company. And somehow, I called because one of the star entertainers died the night before, and I called the guy and said, "What am I supposed to do? So and so just died!" And he said, "I'm at my brother's wife's funeral, I will have to call you back." And then two years later, we met, and that was it. And he was right! So again, if I had gone to London, I would never have been on the board, and I never would have met Ted. So there's a sequence of things for a reason. And if I had met when he was married, I don't know if it would have been the same.

I also read that you're an executive director of a computer foundation and you've donated PC equipment. That's so awesome! I bet that's a lot of fun! I guess that wasn't really a question! [Laughs] I literally wrote, "How fun is that?" and put a little smiley face. That must be amazing.

H: It is. Yes.

When I visited before, I had seen that you don't like snakes or showers. Because I saw the shower curtain [signed by Janet Leigh]...

H: I don't like bats at all! We have someone upstairs doing our books who loves bats and snakes! I just found out three days ago, and I just looked at her, going, '*Are you nuts?*' But she said you have to look at what bats do for the world, and so it's not a bad thing. But I do not like bats!

And why not shower curtains?

H: Because I saw "Psycho" when I was a little kid, and it just like, freaked me out. And what was interesting when I met Janet Leigh is, we became close friends, because she said she never saw another movie she was in after that because she was so scared from the movie. Even though you're in it, she didn't know what was happening because you do snippets. When she saw it, with the music and everything else, she never took a shower again after that!

But it's very difficult now not taking a shower! Because a lot of hotels don't have bathtubs anymore. So...oh my goodness! I can't tell you how many times I've "sinked" it! [Laughs] It's not as good!

[We discussed my recent experience with the layoffs at my job and my book. I expressed excitement about my current journey.] It's been a fantastic experience the last six months...

H: So it's a good thing in a way that you got knocked in the teeth?

I think it is! I think it's one of the best things that ever happened.

H: And most people don't understand. They're hysterical. And it's like, all you have to do is stand up. And smile. Keep on going. It's all good.

And had this not happened, kinda similar to what you said about you not going to London, I wouldn't be writing a book right now.

H: That's awesome.

I'm really excited about it. Thank you so much for taking the time, and thank you for letting us stay in the penthouse! As soon as I saw it, I did a little happy dance! I was like, "This is awesome!"

H: Well it was perfect timing. Because it's our most booked suite. Because you just disappear…you forget what year it is and you forget what time it is, and you forget what city you're in.

I just thought of something. Do you have a favorite room in the house?

H: No, it depends on my mood. I love…I'm a "little space" person. I didn't realize why but I think in a past life, I lived in a really small little nun's room. Seriously. It's interesting because I have so much stuff here. But for me, I like the little spaces where life is stripped down and life is just really simple. It's about praying to God.

You kind of disappear into yourself which is a good thing because you spiritually rejuvenate that way. And you also understand that there is something bigger than yourself in that rejuvenation.

***

After our interview, H gave me a hug. She emanates such a wonderful energy that I couldn't stop smiling. Jerry and I ate at the restaurant she recommended, which was absolutely delicious. The avocado and raspberry dish was enchanting – the creamy pulp of the avocado contrasted against the tart, tingly raspberry.

When we returned from dinner, Jerry and I went to the Mansion's Amnesia Room on the first floor of the Mansion. In addition to a number of sofas and chairs, and lots of books (like stacks and stacks of books and tchotchkes), the room has speakers playing music all day and night. After Jer and I sat down for a while, H, her husband Ted, and their friend and Mansion volunteer Laurie came and joined us.

H asked us about the music we like. When Jer mentioned the Beatles, Ted hooked up his iPod and started playing some incredible tracks. He collects cuts from studio and home recordings from artists. These cuts cannot be played anywhere else. The fact that these are "forgotten" tracks, along with the hypnotic quality of the room and the music, is why this room is called the Amnesia Room. Ted's collection is like the origins of the creative process for a number of familiar classic rock artists and songs. He has a track of John Lennon and Paul McCartney, stoned and giggling, trying to work on a song together. His recording of Bruce Springsteen and several iterations of "Pink Cadillac" and "Born in the USA" were so different from the originals that they made me appreciate the songs all over again. H pointed out that the rawness of the tracks was amazing. And it was true. We listened and laughed and jammed for almost two hours, getting lost in the music.

And that echoed what H said early in our interview. Being at the Mansion is about getting lost and finding something new. We are so used to hearing polished versions of our favorite songs that we forget that these gems had to start somewhere. They were rough and raw until they were tried on and tried out by the artists. And that made me love these artists all over again.

I found it very interesting when H said during our interview, "…I never ask people what they do, ever! Because it doesn't matter." To so many people, what someone does is the opposite to them – it is the most important thing. I think the magic of the Mansion is that the whimsical nature of the place brings out an energy that resonates deeper than the superficial titles we give ourselves. When you walk into the Mansion, they protect your identity. Unless you expressly give permission, they will not confirm if someone is staying with them. But the identity protection goes to a deeper place. Not only will they protect your identity from others on the outside, but they also protect you by not challenging who you are. Instead of asking, "What do you do?", within the walls of the Mansion you are asked, "What do you love?"

A truly lovely thing came from our experience while we were at the Mansion. On Saturday night, H offered to let us stay another night with them in their incredible penthouse at no cost. I was sad that I had to turn it down. I felt awful saying no because I had had such a connection with her, and Jer and I had an amazing time with Ted. What I didn't say to H was that I couldn't stay another night because my Dad was having surgery very early Monday morning and I promised to take him to the hospital. I didn't want to say anything to H because I was worried about my Dad and I was afraid I would burst into tears which would have embarrassed me. We drove home Sunday so I could be there for my Dad.

On Monday, in the wee hours of the morning, I was at the hospital in Richmond waiting on Dad while he was in surgery. I received a form letter email from the Mansion asking about our stay. In my reply, I wrote to H, Ted and the staff telling them in detail how wonderful our stay was. Knowing that I could safely explain why we couldn't stay another night without getting emotional, I told them that Dad was having surgery. While at the Mansion, I bought a copy of H's book *Like Heaven,* and I was reading it in the hospital lobby as I waited to hear the results of Dad's operation. In the anxious hospital waiting room, I was feeling about as far away from magic and wonder as I had the summer before.

As I was reading, my phone made the "bing" noise announcing a new email. H wrote back from her personal email saying I was in their prayers and said we were welcome to stay again, and then she said, "Bring Dad!" I had tears in my eyes. I was reminded once again that there is magic in the everyday. It's up to us to choose to see it.

And then the following week, I received another email from H asking how my Dad was doing. I happily shared that Dad's surgery was successful. I got tears in my eyes again. With all the amazing and wonderful people she knows, with all the responsibilities she has, H thought about me. This was real, her love and passion. This was from a deep place.

Story 4: Mr. Bradshaw – Teacher, Coach, Survivor: Do you practice what you preach?

I was a miserable kid. I absolutely hated high school, and couldn't wait to leave. I don't think my classmates were any meaner or worse than any other high school classmates. I was a sensitive kid and took everything to heart. And high school kids generally have the sensitivity of a hyena in heat. I'm happy to say I have reconnected with a few people with whom I was friends in high school, but overall, I left and haven't looked back. To quote Steely Dan, "And I'm never going back to my old school."

Mr. Bradshaw is a teacher at my former high school. I had known of him but never took classes from him because at the time I attended the school was divided into a girl's school and a boy's school. And Mr. Bradshaw taught the boys.

I have become good friends with one of my former high school classmates, Anne. She's my "soul sister" and was very supportive while I was writing. We were having a good talk about "Tickers" and she suggested that I speak with Mr. Bradshaw. Honestly, I initially asked, "Why?" Mr. Bradshaw is a teacher and a coach, and has taught at Collegiate School in Richmond, Virginia, for over 40 years. I knew he was a good teacher and coach by reputation, but I was trying to be discerning in whom I chose for this book. As I stated before, I admire teachers. My mom was a Home Economics teacher for over 30 years, and my aunt was a kindergarten teacher, so teaching is in my blood. But I was focusing on people who have a passion for what they do and have built an unusual career from it. Teaching and coaching didn't seem to me to fit at first because I didn't feel they were "unusual" career choices.

Then my friend sent me an article from the Richmond Times Dispatch opinion section written by Mr. Bradshaw. It was then I saw the passion that he has for life. My initial dismissal to talk with him changed into a revelation. It is not the unusual nature of a career choice that makes someone a Ticker but instead it is the overwhelming amount of passion that person has that makes them stand out. I knew had to talk with Mr. Bradshaw.

    ***

There is a Warner Brothers cartoon of a dog and a wolf who work together at a sheep farm. Every day, they punch the clock to start their jobs. During the day, the wolf is at work being a wolf, and is constantly trying to steal sheep. The dog works hard as a dedicated sheep dog whose job consists of foiling the wolf's plans to steal sheep. The best part of the cartoon is that before work, during lunch and after work, whenever they have punched out of the clock and are living their "real" lives, the dog and wolf are great friends, laughing and talking like old chums. During the workday, however, they battle against one another as sworn enemies. It's funny because of the cartoon's focus on the artificial boundaries of our "work life" and our "real life".

Do we have a "work" life and a "real" life? How much of our work is reflected in our lives? In the United States, we tend to define ourselves by our work. You are asked, "What do you do?" at a party. And the expected answer is to identify your occupation. "I'm a lawyer/doctor/programmer..." Though our work is only part of our lives, as we are members of families, non-work organizations, and participants in hobbies or sports, we self-identify first as our occupation. We say, "I am a lawyer" instead of saying, "I practice law."

But are we really made of what we do? Are we truly defined by our jobs? Or are we separate from what we do?

In some cases, having a specific job alters the course of your personal life. If you have a job that requires you to uphold the law, for example, then you are expected to obey the laws in your personal life. A person who becomes a police officer is expected to obey the law not just during their workday but all of the time, every day, no matter the situation. You are not supposed to obey the law during your working hours and then go home and snort coke.

If you are a professional athlete, you may be expected to stay in a certain physical condition. You can't "clock out" and gorge yourself on foods that will make you gain weight or you will impact your physical condition and therefore jeopardize your job.

How else does your job impact your life? There can be physical effects. I think most people know that if you are unhappy with your job, it can cause some detrimental effects. Stress can cause you to suffer physically. If you have a job with odd hours, it can impact your sleep patterns and Circadian rhythm. If you have a hazardous job, you can risk injury or permanent damage. If you have a mentally taxing job, it too can impact your energy level. You may be drained when you come home, and not have energy to do other things you want to do, or interact with your family.

If you have a time-consuming job, that too can impact your life. People who are on-call have to plan their lives around their on-call time. If you get called in the middle of the night, or have to work weekends, that affects the amount of down time that you have. If you have a job that is emotionally demanding, that too can affect your life. A doctor in a cancer ward may have to create emotional barriers between themselves and their patients in order to cope on a daily basis. If you work for a creditor and have to discuss sad financial situations and their impacts, that too can wear on you.

How much can what you do on your job apply to your life? And can it improve your life? If you are keeping yourself physically fit for your job, then the benefits may spill over. You may meet co-workers who become life-long friends. You may even meet your soul mate at work and fall in love! You can form relationships with clients that become very profitable, financially or emotionally. Nurses may help someone become healthy again. Financial advisors can help someone save for retirement. Even if your job just allows you to make someone smile, it can be an emotional benefit and brighten your life.

Can your job actually help save your life? There are people whose monetary gain from their job enables them to have a better life than they would have before. Some people get a degree that opens doors and allows them to come out of a bad situation into a good one. But what if your career, one you selected just because you like it, ends up saving your very life, and making you into a better person than you thought you could be? Even if you were a really good person to begin with?

***

For Weldon Bradshaw, being a coach was "cool". He admired his coaches and because he liked them, he wanted to be one. For years, he used his skills as a teacher and a coach at Collegiate to help young men become better people. He helped them to think about how they interacted with their fellow students as teammates. He helped them see that being a member of the team meant being there for others, organizing a plan of action, and then seeing that plan through. He became part of the Collegiate family. Through his job, he met his wife and became a member of his own family.

Little did he know that in his toughest hour, all the lessons he shared with his students would end up helping Mr. Bradshaw to coach himself. An ordeal with liver disease made him look inward at all of the lessons he taught his students.

Raised in Norfolk, Virginia, Mr. Bradshaw attended Norfolk Academy and graduated in 1966. He had been a runner for more than 30 years. Mr. Bradshaw started working at Collegiate when he started coaching there part-time in the afternoon. In 1971, he came onboard full-time as a teacher and a coach. Later he became an administrator. Now his job involves coaching cross-country and track, teaching, administration, and work for the Collegiate online web site. He writes a weekly column called "Reflections" for the web site, and has done so for 14 years. He also has been a reporter for the Richmond News Leader and Times Dispatch, mostly covering sports. He worked for the

News Leader for two years full-time after graduating college from the University of Richmond and has written articles for them ever since. At the time when we spoke, he had just finished his 46th basketball season and his 45th football season. And he had been married for 28 ½ years to his wife, Emily. They have four children and four grandchildren. Mrs. Bradshaw spent 30 years teaching at Collegiate before retiring.

In 2014, Mr. Bradshaw wrote a book in 2014 called, "My Dance with Grace: Reflections on Death and Life" where he chronicled his battle with primary sclerosing cholangitis. Primary sclerosing cholangitis is an autoimmune liver disease which causes bile ducts to constrict and ultimately poisons you. Some people never know they have it, and some outlive it. For Mr. Bradshaw, it progressed pretty quickly. His first appointment was in December 2009 when the bloodwork was done. In February 2010, his doctor performed a liver biopsy, and figured out what he had. It was an autoimmune disease related to ulcerative colitis. Mr. Bradshaw had a liver transplant in 2012 at the Medical College of Virginia.

I didn't know what to expect when I called Mr. Bradshaw. My friend, Anne, and her brother, Todd, had spoken so highly of him. But would it be awkward to talk with someone about having a disease? Similar to the other people with whom I interviewed, I knew Mr. Bradshaw was pursuing what he loved to do. But how would have a disease factor into his passion? What was it that made him keep going despite the illness? I was excited but honestly a little nervous, like somehow I had time traveled back to high school.

***

K: I'm really excited to talk with you today. I'll tell you a little bit about my project. My book is about people who are really passionate about what they do. So you have worked for Collegiate for over 40 years?

W: Correct.

And it sounds like you are really passionate about coaching and counseling, and then of course having been through this health challenge.

W: Right.

So I wanted to ask you about your career, and your health challenge, and how that's impacted your work and also your life.

W: OK.

I divided the questions into before illness and after illness.

W: That's kind of the way I look at life, to be honest with you.

That's what I was going to ask you about. You do see your own life that way?

W: Things are so different now than they were before. The illness was really the transcendent moment. Well, a transcendent time, not a moment. It was over a couple of years, which culminated in the transplant. It is ongoing. Even now, I'll never be back where I was before, but I don't know that I want to be.

You told me about your book, so I went out on Amazon and took a look at it. It's called "My Dance with Grace: Reflections on Death and Life"…you were diagnosed with, and forgive me because I will probably mispronounce it, primary sclerosing cholangitis?

W: Yes, primary sclerosing cholangitis, and I'm still not sure I know how to spell it. Some people have it and outlive it because it progresses slowly enough. Mine progressed pretty fast once it got a head of steam up. I had the first appointment with the liver specialist in December of 2009. I had had some routine bloodwork which showed some elevated liver numbers. One thing led to another, and in February 2010, five years ago, I had a liver biopsy. That's where they came up with what they call the diagnosis of primary sclerosing cholangitis (PSC) …they really weren't sure what it was then, but that's what they figured it was. It's about as nasty a liver disease as you can get. It's completely an autoimmune issue; it's nothing I did to cause it. Eighty percent of the people that have PSC also have ulcerative colitis (UC). It's a fairly nasty disease that tears up your colon, and I was one of the lucky ones who had that, so…it was kind of a whammy of PSC and UC.

Goodness gracious. Wow. I wanted to confirm all that info, so now I am going to jump into my questions.

You attended Norfolk Academy and graduated from NA in 1966. Did you grow up in Norfolk?

W: I did, yes.

Who were you as a kid? What were you like?

W: I just liked sports. I wasn't very good at it. I went when I was in the 6th grade…Norfolk Academy was small enough at the time that I could make the teams that I went out for. That didn't mean I played a lot! But I liked teamwork and the coaches. I got to be pretty good at track, but I wasn't very good at most of the rest of it.

Did you try out for football and baseball?

W: I never played baseball because I ran track. I played basketball, I played football, I ran cross country. I wasn't very good at any of it.

The thing back then was that the school was pretty small, and it was all boys back then. They didn't have the luxury of being able to cut people. We all played.

**At least y'all all made the team! How did learning how to be part of the team shape your
career path?**

W: I had several coaches, three coaches, what they did as coaches…I just thought it was cool to be a coach and a teacher, but mainly a coach. Because I always really enjoyed sports and athletics, and I had the idea when I went to college that I wanted to be a sports writer; that's what I really kind of got hooked on. But along the way in college, at the University of Richmond, I worked at Collegiate a couple of years in the afternoon. I had to decide whether I wanted to be a teacher, a coach or a sports writer. And I ended up being all of them.

Oh, that's cool! So along with the three coaches whom you mentioned, what were your inspirations as you were growing up, and figuring out that you wanted to do sports writing and counseling and coaching?

W: Well counseling is not exactly – I mean, I'm not a counselor, I'm not a certified counselor. But as far as having been around long enough to have some institutional memory, I mean, there's a lot of informal counseling. But every teacher or coach does that. That's nothing unique to me. But I'm not a certified counselor.

There was no one thing. There was just the idea. I mean, teaching and coaching and sports writing just all made sense to me. There wasn't any particular inspiration. As a sports writer, I just read Sports Illustrated or read the sports page. I was excited by the prospect of writing. Writing involved painting a picture for the reader of what I was seeing or what that reader would have been there seeing.

It's interesting to note that Mr. Bradshaw didn't state that he felt passionate about teaching and coaching and sports. He said they all made sense to him. People can feel "passion" without being "jumping on the sofa, shouting it from the rooftops" passionate. "Passion" in this case made sense, or resonated, with Mr. Bradshaw. Different people experience their calling in different ways. To borrow from "Star Trek," maybe the way Mr. Bradshaw experienced his passion was more Mr. Spock than Captain Kirk, but he knew it was a calling nonetheless.

Right! So it would be from your perspective explaining to the reader, "This is what happened." And just giving them a sense of the spirit of the game?

W: Yeah. It's not so much what happened; that's part of it. But it's more what I'm seeing that I can convey to them in words that the picture can come in their mind. "Oh my gosh, I can see exactly what he's describing!"

So, what – and again, this falls under the "before the illness" – what did you like best about your path as a teacher and a coach. I guess it still applies now, but what did you like about it before your illness?

W: As time went on….when I started out teaching, I was teaching middle school guys and I still do that, seventh grade guys. I was coaching middle school teams. I was eventually involved in coaching at the varsity level. I was always kind of a bench warmer along the way. And I think I identified with them on a couple of things.

What always lit me up back then was taking somebody who didn't have confidence in their ability as a student or as an athlete and try to give them confidence in some way, give them opportunities to succeed. When I was coaching cross-country and track…it's not like cross-country gets a whole lot of spectators. Most people don't even see what we do. It's providing an athletic home to people who may not have any other sport that they do. It's giving them a chance to succeed where they may not think they can. A lot of times we end up with kids who have tried other sports and haven't been successful.

Sometimes we have people and all they want to do is be runners, and that's really great. But it's taking the kid who needs a team experience – whether it's a team that can help him, where his presence can help the team – and it's not so much in how fast a kid is, is does he learn the concept of being a part of the team. It's not about the individual, it's about the team. That always lit me up from day one, and all these years later, it really does.

I had a question that was, "How do you connect with your inner passion?", but honestly I think you kind of just identified that. It's the concept that you, having

been a bench warmer in school, could identify that quality in other kids and bring out the confidence that they didn't have in other areas.

W: You know, I had a couple of teachers along the way, coaches that….I was pretty good at track, I wasn't a benchwarmer there, I was good at that. But when I started - you couldn't be on teams until you were in 9th grade at Norfolk Academy back in those days, it's different now – but the first year in track in the events that I did, I was never in a place but last place. And the coach, who I had all four years, took me to every meet, he brought me to meets. I rode on the bus with the older kids and go, and I'd go and finish last in the meet. But he always gave me a chance.

And I learned from that that it was really important to give every kid a chance. We're all unfinished products! If he expected me to be a superstar from day one, it wouldn't have worked. He gave me a chance. And as time evolved, and I developed and got stronger, and a little bit bigger and a little bit quicker, I hope he felt – he's been deceased for 20 years now – but I hope he felt like his commitment to me was worthwhile. We weren't all that good in track, but I found a place to excel because he gave me a chance to excel.

That's awesome!

Now my questions are for you from after your illness. How did you initially get your diagnosis about your liver condition?

W: I can remember very well about this time [of year] being down at the VCU Medical Center. The doctor sat me down and told me what it was. And I said, "What am I facing?" He said you may outlive it. I said, "Don't sugar coat it. Tell me exactly what I'm dealing with. Because I'm putting together a game plan."

So much of when I speak out there publicly and I write, I talk about how I was able to deal with this because I know how to compete, I know how to prepare. And basically when I knew what I was working with, I put together a game plan. Just as teachers put together lesson plans, kids put together plans to study for exams, and coaches put together game plans. I had a plan. And a lot of the plan was…there was a lot of unknown. What I was going to do….I couldn't control how fast the disease progressed. I couldn't control how my doctors were. I just had to have a tremendous amount of trust that they were as good as they could be, and they were. I think I got expert, compassionate care. But what I had to control was how I dealt with it. And it was no excuses, no complaining, no "why me." I knew I had given a lot of advice to students, to athletes, to my own children throughout the years, about dealing with adversity, about dealing with challenges, and how when you fall, you get back up. And I knew that I had to deliver.

As a couple of years went on and my health began to deteriorate. Things were moving very fast in the summer and fall of 2012. I never wavered. Things got really challenging with a lot of symptoms and side effects from the medication, I just kept saying, "Tomorrow will be better. If this disease beats me across the finish line, it absolutely will not beat me." And we were going at it just like we were playing another team. You respect your opponent, you respect the weather, you respect the terrain, but in the sport I coach, cross-country, you don't ever fear them. And I just convinced myself (1) I was going to be all right whether I lived or died, (2) I wasn't going to be intimidated by something that can scare the heck out of people, and (3) I would just never give up. I admit it was uncomfortable but I was never going to acknowledge it was bigger than I was, even though it was pretty big.

And I assume something like this was unanticipated. And – I don't mean to put words in your mouth – but you probably didn't anticipate that the lessons you had been learning as a coach, as part of your career would be applied to your health.

W: Oh, that is absolutely true. And that's one of the things I talk to folks about. All along I thought I was learning how to beat St Christopher's [one of Collegiate's rival teams in Richmond]! I thought it was all about getting people to run fast or write better. It never occurred to me that I was preparing myself for kind of the ultimate race, the ultimate challenge. If it's not [the ultimate challenge], I don't know that I want to see it!

But I just…when the game was on with the liver disease, I just said, "This is another competition. Everything I've learned in all my years of competing and coaching and everything, I have to apply now." And I did. And it worked. It didn't save my life, but it enabled me to deal with it in a way that I don't think I could have otherwise.

After you received the diagnosis, were you still able to work for a while? I assume once it got really bad at the end you were hospitalized.

W: It's funny…I started school and practice in 2012. I was very jaundiced. The whites of my eyes were yellow which is a sign of pretty significant liver disease. On October 4, 2012, I went on the liver transplant registry. I was still working full-time, coaching full-time and writing for the paper during that time. And it was like trudging through about six feet of snow. But I was still doing it. If I laid around and thought, "I feel bad"…it wasn't like it was painful, your liver doesn't hurt, the side effects are uncomfortable, but it's not like, "Oh my gosh, my liver is killing me!" You don't feel the pain in your liver.

But the fatigue and jaundice were overwhelming. I know that I went on the list on October 4th and it was October 21st – by this time, I was checking in at the VCU Medical

Center pretty regularly, and things were moving pretty fast. But it was October 21st, a Sunday, when I told my wife, "It's time. Let's go to the emergency room."

They admitted me and ran a battery of tests over the next six days to determine if my body could withstand the transplant. Obviously it did.

Oh my goodness.

W: It's all right; it's really all right. You know, the thing that this liver disease is, I use the term "luck of the draw." I have always from the get-go considered it to be good luck. I'm not making this stuff up now! I documented everything, you know, when I wrote the book, and I kept every email I sent. It's just kind of chronology of it. So I know I'm not making this stuff up, and I can be honest with myself. But I just really looked at the disease as a God-given gift that challenged me to do what I wanted to do. I respected people who had dealt with challenges. It never occurred to me that I would actually have to do it. But I did. Runners don't quit when things get tough.

Wow. Of course, the good news, you had the transplant. How has your health been since then?

W: It's fine. I will never have a clean bill of health in the sense that I won't have to go to MCV and take pills because I will always have to do that. The thing with the transplant was the days that I was hospitalized – that was six days – they sent me home and by this time I was number one on the transplant list for people with O type blood. So the next compatible liver that came available would be mine. The problem is there aren't enough organs out there for people who need them. The odds of a liver becoming available were pretty slim, to be honest with you. I was home for nine days, and I went back, they admitted me to the ICU on November 8th. I saw the doctor, who [would do] the surgery, came in and said, I'll never forget it, "If I can't transplant in a week, you'll be dead." Well, you know, he told me much later that he meant by the end of the week, and the 8th was Thursday.

Making a long story short, I got to Day 6, and the surgery was on Wednesday, November 14th. It took seven hours which is fairly short for that type of surgery. I came out of la-la-land from the medication four days later, very weak, very debilitated. It took me a very long time to get my strength back. And there were setbacks along the way. The liver came from an 84-year-old stroke victim, and it was the oldest liver ever to go into a patient. A lot of things were transpiring to make it challenging. I just kind of kicked into that competition mode. So I would say I was perfectly patient through the whole thing! I always had my eye on the goal that I was going to come back to school full time. I was going to be doing what I wanted to do, of course, being careful. I didn't do anything foolhardy with my health that would compromise my health.

Right! After the surgery, when did you end up coming back to school? Did you work part-time?

W: Yeah, I was just coming in...I came back full-time in May. It's a short year, of course. I was coming in and out of there...I was in there most days when I felt like it, and when I didn't have to go in for treatment at MCV. It could be a fairly long day. Probably 3-4 days a week, I was going in for an hour or two or three. It was just trying to get my feet in the water again, and not go stir-crazy sitting around the house.

Understandable! I can imagine after you had such a busy schedule, it was hard to make yourself sit still once you started feeling better.

W: I learned to be by myself really well. I always try to find the positive in it. I really valued what I call my alone time. My wife was on medical leave with me to take care of me, and she went back in January. By that time, I was able to drive again, so I was fairly mobile. I just got to the point where I was looking forward to going back to school full-time and kind of getting back into the swing of things, but I also came to really value my alone time. That's when I did most of the writing of my book, and did a lot of reading. It was a good experience. I just don't want to do it again.

Oh yeah, I can understand that! My goodness! So did you...when you had that time to sit back and reflect on everything you were going through, because it sounds like everything happened in a quick amount of time, was there anything you learned upon reflection that didn't hit you during the time?

W: That's a really good question. I continue to learn, and it's one of the reasons I wish I had waited a year to write the book because there is so much I know now. I was very aware that the odds of my survival were slim to none. I knew statistically that the odds of me getting this disease, which is very rare, were like .0008, like 8 out of every 10,000 people in the population. And I know from conversations with my doctors, whom I've gotten to be very good friends with, the odds of my survival...well, neither one of them thought I was going to survive it. I was very grateful and appreciate life. But it was more...even when I was still in the hospital, I thought, "What do I do with this now?" It was never, "Why did I get sick?" It was, "What did this very flawed, imperfect person do to get this second chance?" What do I do with it now?

It's what I've spent the last 27 months reflecting on and trying to put into practice. I feel like I'm just scratching the surface of it. How do I take these experiences I've had and help people who maybe don't have the support system I had, or don't understand the competitive process like I think I do? A lot of people have strength of faith, strength of character and all that. It's, "What can I take from this experience that many people may look at as a negative and use as a positive?" I never looked at it as a negative. I didn't particularly like going through it but it's not like I had a choice. I didn't want to waste energy worrying about something I could not control.

Now you mentioned something about your support system. Who were your main supporters, and how did they help you?

W: My wife was my primary caregiver; there's no question about that. We have four children, they are in four different time zones now, but they were all at home, and the grandchildren were in the ICU and then at home. And they are rarely ever together. They were all at home because they wanted to say goodbye to me, basically. The crew at school…Collegiate does a lot of things really well, but what they do really well is take care of each other. The care and support from the community, from the community of graduates, the letters, the notes, the emails, the texts, every way to communicate came to me. I know I was on prayer groups in more states than I can imagine.

The work that I do at the Times Dispatch, I know a lot of people at a lot of schools around that I know from what I heard along the way…not just people who were contacting me directly. People were calling Charlie McFall [a fellow coach at Collegiate] to find out how I was doing, and people contacted the newspaper to find out how I was doing. I felt very much the love and support, care from the Collegiate community, the Richmond community, the Tuckahoe YMCA where I work out pretty regularly. It was pretty incredible. I felt like, "I'm not going to let these people down."

Right! That's awesome. What would you say was the most surprising or positive part that came from facing your illness? I know you said you faced it as a positive, and "What am I going to take from this?" Was there something that took you by surprise?

W: Well, every day when you have PCS is a surprise because you kind of have a game plan together. But part of the game plan is making adjustments when something gets thrown in your way that challenges you. I guess the thing – and I'm probably repeating myself now – I just learned how to compete, I'm not a tremendously religious person but spiritual, I am, yes, and I stayed strong. We all know we are going to die sometime. It never occurred to me that I would have a chance to lie in bed on the 9th floor of what they call the Critical Care hospital at the VCU Medical Center, and have a chance to think deeply about my own death. I did. I've read enough about near-death experiences and the aftermath to know what I saw, what I felt, and it was never bad. It was always, "If I die, if

I don't survive this, I will be all right." I'm not in physical pain – of course, they have drugs to take care of that – but I'm not in spiritual pain, I'm not in emotional distress. I'm worried about what how everybody else will be affected –

Oh, of course!

W: –But what a gift to have that opportunity, and to have survived that opportunity! And that was…when I got the diagnosis, and did enough research, and knew what I was facing, I had the idea that I might die from this, but until you are right there, how do you know? But it's all part of the progression of, I guess…in sports, you talk about peaking at the right moment. I peaked at the right moment in the toughest competition I've ever had. When I say that, it's being mentally and spiritually prepared for some challenges that were pretty incredible but never intimidating.

Some of the questions I asked for before your illness were about how you had passion for being a coach and a teacher before your illness. How did your role as a coach and teacher change after your illness?

W: Really good question. Preparing kids to compete still meant as much. Winning or losing probably wasn't as important, to be honest with you. It didn't mean I didn't want to win. I just kind of learned the bigger picture. I always preach the gospel, especially in running or track, where you can't control your opponent, do the best you can and let rest take care of themselves. It doesn't mean that I don't want to win. It just means that I see life differently; that if you do everything that you can to be a champion, you're a champion, whether or not you get your name on the record or the banner in the gym or the trophy.

While I knew that intellectually, I have lived that. I find much of what I've said to kids in class in regards to stories I teach, or on the track, or on the cross-country course, hasn't changed. It's just that my life experience has changed. So when I talk about dealing with adversity, don't fear your opponent or the weather, you know, always respect them, I'm saying it and I've lived it, just in a non-athletic context. I've really been cognizant of that over the past couple of years. I'm really not saying much different. Life experiences have made everything I say different.

Right! If I can paraphrase, what you've experienced is true to the stories and the experience you've had with sports. I guess it was, to an even higher…what am I trying to say?

W: It's to a much, much higher level than what's…I mean, I always thought it was about beating Woodberry or the Saints!

[Laughs] Right!

W: And it really was. And I always wanted to do that, not because I didn't like them, it was just competition. You compete to be the best you can. And the coaches have all become really good friends of mine. To be honest, beating Woodberry or beating the Saints or beating Benedictine or Trinity or any of them really pales in comparison. Not to beating liver disease, because I don't feel like I beat it, I just dealt with it the best I could. A footrace is nothing compared to lying in bed in the middle of the night reflecting on your own mortality. "Bring it on! Give it your best shot. I'm not scared of you."

You come out of all this with what seems like a real contradiction of emotions. There is a tremendous amount of confidence that nothing is going to scare or intimidate me, but a tremendous amount of humility knowing that I didn't get here talking with you on the phone today without a tremendous amount of help.

So much of this is just what you learn as a teacher or coach, and what you try to convey to kids. It's really…I have had the chance to be a teacher and coach on a level I never could have imagined. I was coaching people who were watching me, and I was coaching myself.

What kind of advice would you give to other people who have had their life changed by illness or some other misfortune?

W: This is what I do – when I speak to groups or volunteer at the VCU Medical Center. I talk to people. I've had plenty of people over the last couple of years call me and say, "Hey, I've got this cousin that has just been diagnosed with this or that, could you talk to me?" And I'll always do that. What I tell them is, "Don't feel sorry for yourself. Don't quit, don't cut corners, do what the doctors tell you to do. Rely on your faith and your family, your friends. Whatever you do, don't quit."

Being a survivor is one of the greatest compliments I could ever give anybody. In the world I live in, we're on one level the recipients of those who have given their organs. On the other level, we're survivors because we survived our experiences. What I talk with people about who are wading into this new world, they're just kind of sticking their toe into the water, so to speak, is you do everything you can to be a survivor, to set the example for people, your children or your colleagues or your neighbors who are watching you deal with something because you never know the ripple effect you're going to have on people. And always honor the people who got you there. The woman who died at 84 with a pristine liver – what a life she must have led! It's pretty incredible. Always look at challenges and opportunities and let the toughest challenges be your finest hour, so to speak.

Do you have a motto or words that you live by?

W: The license plate on my Mustang says DNTKWT which is about as simple a "Don't Quit" as I can get it. It's funny…when I speak, I talk about several things I said along the way. When I was diagnosed, I emailed all of our children so they'd all read the same thing at pretty much the same time. I promised them I would dance at Grace's wedding. Out of four grandchildren, only one is a girl, and she [Grace] was six years old at the time. So that was pretty bold talk when you're facing a potentially catastrophic illness.

But you know, I've relied on a lot of quotes. "The only way around is through," that's Robert Frost. There's a tremendous amount of that. There's a lot of scripture that has spoken to me very, very loudly. A couple of things I've said…I mentioned odds. I remember hearing the odds, and asking the doctor, "If I check out of here, what are my odds of getting home and at least spending my last days there?" And I remember the doctor saying that since I was on life support, if they unhooked me, I wouldn't even make it to the car downstairs. I came to the understanding that if there are odds, there's always hope. We all go to dark places in our minds, but always keep your eye on that candle glowing in the distance. I've always believed that. I'm sure that's nothing creative or original from me. I'm sure it's from scripture. But the bottom line is don't quit when things get tough. Tomorrow will always be better. I have given you lots of mantras! [Laughs]

You know, the cold I've been working on for the last couple of weeks…when you have a weakened immune system, it's hard to shake these things. Your head gets congested, and your sinuses get clogged up. Every night, I say to my wife, "Tomorrow will be better," and I was saying that when I was dying of liver disease. Liver disease is more easily treatable than the common cold!

I've always tried to find the humor in it and the positives in it. But isn't that what we try to teach our children? Isn't that what we as teachers and coaches should be conveying? I put to use everything I learned as a teacher and coach and I put to use everything I learned as a student and athlete. That's kind of getting off the subject of the passion you have for life. But if I hadn't been passionate about coaching and competing, I doubt I would have been the same.

Whose paths do you admire? Do you have a hero or role model?

W: There are a lot of people, and I will give you two in specific in a second. People have faced challenges that seemed intimidating or seemed daunting to some people, but they refused to be intimidated by them. Two in particular, both of them have died within about a year and a half, but one of them is John Chewning whom I talked with for years. When he was young, he battled with cancer, he had heart trouble, he had MS. He was, you know, his body just gave out a couple of years ago. I never heard him complain. I worked with him closely, and he was…if he never complained, how could I complain?

The other was a guy named John Waddell. John was a fraternity brother of mine at [the University of] Richmond. We were the same age. The summer when he was 27, he was injured in a diving accident, broke his neck, and was a quadriplegic for 39 years. He passed away this past September 12th. But John was one…we had been friends all these years, and talked many, many times. When I was sick, he never once said, "Hey, if I made it through what I did, you can make it too." He didn't need to. I just always drew strength from him. He never had a bad day. If he was ever down about what happened to him, I didn't know about it, and I knew him about as well as anybody other than his wife. When you spend all the time I did in the ICU, you have a lot of indignities done to your body. And to be frank about it, I thought along the way, "If John Waddell could have a catheter in him for 30 plus years, then who am I to complain?" I never did complain. But I think…I just came to respect people like John Waddell or John Chewning and I had a game plan, and their inspiration was probably part of the game plan.

You sort of touched on this, but what inspired you to write your book?

W: I've written stuff for years, and I've had the question many times, "Are you ever going to write a book?" And my answer was, "If I ever have anything to say." And I remember in the ICU, maybe the day I came out of la-la land, telling my wife, "I think I've got something to say now."

It had been such an incredible journey, before we knew the liver became available, I remember saying to her, "If I don't survive this," and I mentioned four of my former runners, "you get these guys together, tell them the story, and have them put something together about this." I think it can be helpful to people.

In my adult life, writing is how I express myself. The focus of the book was short and to the point. It's about a hundred-page pep talk, no medical jargon or anything that would have people thinking I was feeling sorry for myself.

I read some of the feedback on Amazon to your book, and people really responded to it!

W: I hope it is worth the read. I've seen the feedback and it is very nice. I'm sure most of them are friends and relatives! [Laughs] I know some of them are my children.

When you write, you kind of put yourself out there for the world to see. Sometimes people agree with you, and sometimes they don't. And sometimes when they do, they write very nice things. And sometimes when they don't, they write very ugly things. You just have to have confidence that you've done the best you can.

My last question is: As I was preparing for my interview with you, I read some of the "Reflections" columns[xi]. Of course, one was about the recent Superbowl (2015), and Russell Wilson [quarterback for the Seattle Seahawks NFL team] having gone to Collegiate. I read a couple of your posts early on in the season when it looked like the Seahawks were doing well, and then afterwards, when of course I think it was tough for everybody when the SuperBowl went the other way. [There was a last-minute play in that Superbowl game when a call was made by the Seahawks to throw the ball, a move that some call one of the worst play calls in NFL history and one that caused the Seahawks to lose to the Patriots.] I was going to ask you, what inspired you to write that about Russell Wilson?

W: The one the day after the SuperBowl?

Yes.

W: That got a lot of response. I watched the game, and as soon as the end happened, I hit the off button, and I said, "I can't stand this. Gosh, I can't believe this happened." And I went upstairs, and somewhere around 2 o'clock, I woke up, wide awake, and said, "I'm going to write something." And I pulled out a couple of old envelopes from the trashcan, and scribbled some notes on it. I went to school, did carpool, went to the back of the library, put my fingers on the keyboard, and what came out is what's there. And sometimes, I spend way too much time on these things and overthink them. And I probably put less time and thought into that one, it was just what flowed.

I think what I wanted to convey was that Russell gets it. He knows there are ups and downs. Don't feel sorry for him; things happen. He'll be all right. From what I gather, he is. It's one of those things: how do you deal with adversity when it happens in front of millions and millions of people?

Russell Wilson – I've written more about Russell than I have written about anybody in the column. I've seen an incredible amount of stuff about him. It was probably December of 2012 or January 2013, it was his rookie year. I get this email from him. And it was a Sunday, and the Seahawks were playing the Arizona Cardinals on national TV that night.

And it was, "Hey Coach," and I never even coached him. "Hey Coach, I've heard you've been sick." It was a very encouraging email to me, wishing me well, and saying he had just heard about it. In typical Russell, "I know God will take care of you," this kind of stuff. And then he ended it with, "Well, I've got a big game. Go Hawks!"

With all the demands on Russell Wilson's time, he really didn't need to do that. But he did because he saw a need. I see the guy who's probably going to be in the NFL Hall of Fame one day, but my main takeaway is that when I was struggling….he said something about thanks for always believing in me. That's some insight I have into Russ that I have, and a lot of people have other stories.

It was fun writing that column. I had no idea it would get the response it did!

I appreciated reading it because I was really bummed the next day.

W: When you've been there, and I go into MCV and see these incredible caregivers, they have some great success stories, like me. And they have some people that they can't save, even with all their medical know-how, machines and skills they have. I've seen both ends of it. It makes a football game pretty insignificant, even the SuperBowl. That's really…I think I had that figured out before. I just have the street cred to say it now.

I wouldn't trade where I am for anything. I wouldn't trade these experiences for anything. I was able to deal with it all because I followed the models and mentors I had, I knew how to compete, and I knew I'd better set the example for people who were watching me. And that's probably it in a nutshell. I just would prefer not to do this one again.

    ***

Never complain, always face your problems head on, and stay focused. While Mr. Bradshaw probably never imagined he would need these lessons himself, throughout his career he was teaching himself as well as teaching others. Learning what would motivate him would make him push forwards when all of the signs were negative and it seemed like the end.

In Mr. Bradshaw's case, his career is a mirror of his life. And he honestly lives by his words. Life is unfair, and good people get horrible diseases. If Mr. Bradshaw had just decided that the diagnosis was too awful, and just decided to give up, he could have done that. And no one would blame him. We all have to face our own mortality at some point. But why not fight? Why not try as hard as you can to be one of the people who fights the odds, and tries to do the difficult, if not impossible? The result may be the same

– not everyone wins their battle against disease to continue this existence for another day. But what a way to go!

"Do not go gentle into that good night/Fight, fight against the dying of the light," wrote Dylan Thomas. It may be that in the fight itself, we defend our right to be here. We get a chance to choose life, to choose the beautiful over the tragic. We get a chance to be our best selves. Our best self is not us at our prettiest or smartest. It is us taking our will to live and using it as a weapon to our advantage. It is us making the decision to draw another breath as long as we can.
What can we learn from Mr. Bradshaw? Don't take things at face value. A doctor telling you the odds are bad is not the same as saying, "Give up. It is hopeless." People will tell you the odds and they may advise you against fighting them. But everyone wants you to overcome those odds.

So your dream career may be a long shot. So? It is still your dream career, and while there is a chance it may not come true, you don't have to just shrug your shoulders and say, "OK, screw it. I give up." You have the choice to make. Do you want to just give up? What would it do if you decided to keep trying? What would that be like? In both your career and your life?

Many people seek wisdom in quotes. We crave words that will help propel us in the right direction, like a sign saying, "Turn right." We have thousands of decisions that we make every day. It can run the gambit from "What shall I have for breakfast?" to "What should I wear today?" all the way to, "Do I want to spend time with this person or not?" and "Where am I going in my career path?" These decisions are ours to make and they control where we take our lives. In a way, every decision you make determines what kind of person you will be. And what kind of words or quotes you say to yourself provides the controls over how you confront the thousands, if not millions, of big and little decisions you make every day. Ultimately all those little decisions and big decisions and ways of viewing your world and dealing with it make up who you are and where you plan to be.

Most of us tend not to think in this manner all of the time because it can be daunting. Putting that much weight into decisions could make something like deciding whether or not to eat the cookie or wear this shirt or the other a paralyzing event! ("If I wear the red shirt, it could alter my destiny!" LOL). But when we start paying attention to the decisions we make, and to the words we tell ourselves, we start to take control.

One of my favorite quotes is from Charles Swindoll: "Life is 10% what happens to us and 90% how we deal with it." When you apply this quote to something like a bad day, you can perhaps say to yourself, "OK, today really sucked. I got in a car accident. But at least I survived."

It's harder to apply this quote to a situation like Mr. Bradshaw's. How many of us could receive the news, "You're dying from a liver disease, and if you don't have a transplant, you will die." That's a lot harder to spin into good news, right? But what Mr. Bradshaw shows us is that as hard as it might be to hear news like that, you still have control. Not to be trite, but you could say he faced the ultimate bad day and controlled his reaction to it. He didn't sugar coat it and say, "Hey, I'm going to be fine, doggone it!" That's not what it means to control how we deal with something. He faced it, looked at the odds square in the face, assessed what's important to him, drew on the words he told his students, and applied them to himself. He couldn't control whether he would receive a new liver or not. And thankfully he did. He did control how he faced the situation and the possibility of dying, in a way that exemplifies courage and grace.

Story 5: Samantha Martin – Animal Trainer: The truth about cats and dogs

When my husband and I were on our two-week vacation in 2014 (right before we came back to work to find co-workers were being laid off- that two-week vacation!) we were driving to Seattle. Our friend Will texted and said, "There's a cat circus coming to Seattle. Would you like to go?" Being cat lovers ourselves, and always up for something fun, we said, "Hell yes!" And that's how we were introduced to the Acro-Cats.

We were totally charmed with the show. Will had brought some fresh catnip from his garden with him, and when one of the "purrformers," Jax, left the stage, she made a beeline right for Will. In fact, she sat with us in the stands until after the show. We loved it!

Samantha Martin, the animal trainer, announced to the audience, "You know the meaning of humility when you work with trained cats!" Everyone laughed knowingly. The audience, like Jerry and me, knew from our experiences with cats what Samantha was saying. We had years of saying, "Max! Get off the table!" only to have Max the cat back on the table shortly afterwards. So we wondered how Samantha and her fellow trainers were going to get the cats to jump through hoops (literally)?

You may wonder what happens at the cat circus. Normal domestic cats are trained to do a number of tricks. For the Acro-Cats' show, the cats will jump from one perch to another, climb up and pull down a flag from a flag pole, and walk a tight rope.

The Acro-Cats have two claims to fame. The first is one of the Acro-Cats, Alley, who broke the Guinness World Record in 2014 for the longest jump by a domestic cat at six feet or 182.88 cm. Their second is that they are featured in Ripley's Believe It or Not for being the world's only cat rock band! The cats play a guitar, a piano, the drums, chimes, and cowbell. Also pitching in on drums is a chicken, Cluck Norris. The star of the show, a confident white kitty named Tuna, also challenges Cluck Norris to a game of bowling during the show. With the humor from Samantha and the other trainers, who warned that the performers sometimes ran into the audience, but stated, "Don't be alarmed! They are just cats!", and the feats by the cats, the audience stayed engaged and delighted.

***

Tasks that are difficult are often compared to herding cats. That's because cats are notorious for not obeying orders. Are the cats onto something? In the animal world, cats are truly Tickers. They are motivated by whatever makes them excited. And what makes them excited varies from cat to cat. There is an internet joke where they compare what dogs love versus what cats love:

***

DOG DIARY

8:00 AM - Dog food! My favorite thing!
9:30 AM - A car ride! My favorite thing!
9:40 AM - A walk in the park! My favorite thing!
10:30 AM - Got rubbed and petted! My favorite thing!
12:00 PM - Lunch! My favorite thing!
1:00 PM - Played in the yard! My favorite thing!
3:00 PM - Wagged my tail! My favorite thing!
5:00 PM - Milk bones! My favorite thing!
7:00 PM - Got to play ball! My favorite thing!
8:00 PM - Wow! Watched TV with the people! My favorite thing!
11:00 PM - Sleeping on the bed! My favorite thing!

CAT DIARY

Day 983 of my captivity!
My captors continue to taunt me with bizarre little dangling objects. They dine lavishly on fresh meat, while the other inmates and I are fed hash or some sort of dry nuggets. Although I make my contempt for the rations perfectly clear, I nevertheless must eat something in order to keep up my strength. The only thing that keeps me going is my dream of escape.

In an attempt to disgust them, I once again vomit on the carpet. Today I decapitated a mouse and dropped its headless body at their feet. I had hoped this would strike fear into their hearts, since it clearly demonstrates what I am capable of. However, they merely made condescending comments about what a 'good little hunter' I am. The sick bastards!

Today I was almost successful in an attempt to assassinate one of my tormentors by weaving around his feet as he was walking. I must try this again tomorrow - but at the top of the stairs.

I am convinced that the other prisoners here are flunkies and snitches. The dog

receives special privileges. He is regularly released - and seems to be more than willing to return. He obviously has issues.

***

The joke is funny because the cat sees the world and constantly asks, "What's in it for me?" whereas the dog just aims to please.

I imagine in our pursuit of getting what we want – following our passion – we are a combination of the stereotypical dog and cat approach to life. Like dogs, we care what others think and we behave in a way that will win us praise. But like cats, deep down we want to do what we really want to do. If the boss asks us to work late, we'll say sure – to please the boss. But in our inner monologue, we may be thinking like the cat – "surely he can't be serious – what do I have to do to get a break?".

Trouble can happen when people in your life have expectations of you…they want you to be obedient like a dog, but you have seen your path. And your path is not what the people in your life expect. It takes courage to lead your own way – confidence in your convictions, and a clear vision. Some Tickers have that vision and that leads them to their path, come hell or high water.

Almost a year had passed and I was in the midst of writing this book. Our friend Will came in town from Seattle. He asked, "What about talking to the lady who runs the cat circus?" Great idea! And then, as fate would have it, on the Acro-Cats web page, it stated that Samantha and her cats were traveling to Richmond to do several shows the following month. Taking my cue from serendipity, and our wonderful friend Will, I contacted Samantha and coordinated an interview.

Samantha Martin is someone who seems somewhat uncomfortable talking with people one on one until she starts talking about animals. She reminded me of myself when I was much younger. I always felt awkward with people and gravitated towards animals. Still to this day, if I am at a party where I don't know many people and feel slightly insecure, I have been known to seek out the host's dog or cat and hang out with a furry friend.

After we delighted in the Acro-Cats show in Richmond, I met with Samantha. Oddly enough, I found she acted a bit like a skittish cat at first. She was busy with the stage items, and then ran back to the green room for a while. I was worried that she had disappeared! Turns out she and her fellow Acro-Cats team were having major issues with their bus. It needed transmission fluid. Jerry, who wasn't sure what to do with himself during our interview, kindly volunteered to buy Samantha and the Acro-Cats crew some transmission fluid. And two of the cats, Nola and Dakota, made a break for it and hid under the seats in the auditorium.

Samantha returned, and when she and I found a place to sit, she started talking about the show and seemed more at ease. She started talking about her busy schedule and things that had happened right before the Richmond show, and caught me while I was still turning on my recorder! I turned it on mid-conversation.

***

S: …We just went to a bunch of things, and you know, this place, that place, just traveling all around for three and a half weeks. And then I had a week back in Chicago, and it was like, Rush! Rush! Rush!

K: Yeah!

S: And then it was like, "Fly to Pigeon Forge, Tennessee!" You know, the bus was in the repair shop, and I have to pick up the bus, and they're like, "You know, your tires are going to fall off, and we really need to get blah-blah-blah taken care of," and they ended up being able to take care of it. We ended up having to spend the night there. So they got that done. Then we drove back and I stayed up all night long getting the bus clean and getting the cats loaded. And then we drove here and just started. So it's been "Blah!"

[Laughs]

S: But it's never boring! I'm never bored. I'm always over-stimulated.

I can imagine! Well, thank you for taking the time to do an interview with me. We actually went and saw your show in Seattle last year, it was about this time, and I was talking with a friend of mine. He said, "You're always talking about the Acro-Cats! You love them! Why don't you see if you can interview her for your book?" Then I looked online and y'all were coming to Richmond. I'm like, "Ahh! The stars aligned!" It was perfect. So thank you.

S: It's great when the stars align! When they start to align a lot, in a weird way, people can think, "You have the worst luck!" But I think, "No, I have the best worst luck!" It's just the way that the stars align, and with my bad luck ways, we always end up with better luck than bad luck!

Oh that's cool! In my research online, and thank goodness for the Internet, because I can find out all kinds of wonderful articles and other things people have written, I read that you grew up with dogs. Is that correct?

S: I grew up in a household – it's not that my parents weren't animal lovers – it's just that, I could have a cat and a dog and no other – one cat, one dog, or two cats, "As long as you live in our house, you live by our rules! When you have a house of your own, you can own as many animals as you want!" I grew up with that in my ear. I always hated that – "Our house, our rules!" So now it's my house and my rules! And I opened up a zoo! So I had like a hundred animals in my house for quite some time period.

Oh my goodness!

S: I ran an educational zoo for about 20 years.

That's awesome! Is that the Brookfield Zoo?

S: No, no, no, I ran my own. It was called Samantha's Amazing Animals. But it started out as the Rat Company.

Because you started with a rat, is that right?

S: I started out with rats, and then I said, "I'm going to open up my own company training rats, and have a rat company! Trained rats for all occasions! Film! Television! Do live shows!" And I trained them to do stuff like this [pointing to the props on stage like hoops and a tight rope]. Imagine this set condensed to much smaller with rats doing it. And so rats kind of gave me my start. And that's why I include the rats in the show today to pay homage to my humble beginnings. [Samantha starts the Acro-Cats shows with a rat walking across a tight rope before the cats come out to perform.]

There we go! Oh that's cool! I also read that you were in a boarding school when you were a teen and you were –

S: Military school. I went to military school for a year and smuggled in a rat. I had a rat keep me company. I just really wasn't getting along with humans at that point.

Oh no. What was your rat's name?

S: Ramsey.

Cool! And what attracted you about the rat?

S: Well, I was reading a book about different kinds of animals as pets. And there was a little chapter about rats that said glowing things about rats. "Oh rats this, rats that!" So then we had little outings at this military school. And it was near Christmas time and they put us all on a bus and took us to a mall for Christmas shopping, and there's a pet store that happened to have pet rats for sale. So I bought one and smuggled it into the military school. And I was really impressed – I mean, this rat was really like my best friend throughout my time there. He would sit on the edge of the tub when I took a bath, and he would follow me around, and I'd talk to him and say cute little things. So it was really one of those – you know - moments where the stars aligned and it put me in the direction – rats entered my life! And I've had rats ever since!

How did you hide the rat?

S: I managed to hide it for only like a month, and I got caught. So they made me take it to the science lab, and it had to live in the science lab. So I would just hang out there and spend a lot of time studying in the science lab so I could hang out with my rat there. And then I would go home, and I could have my rats back in Princeton where I lived where I finished my last of high school there. Then I went to college, went to the University of Iowa, and had rats and kind of put the whole career on the back burner. I was in college trying to figure out what I was going to do, and what I didn't want to do. I started out as a psychology major, and I was like, "Well, I don't really even like people. This doesn't seem like a good career choice!" [Laughs]

So then I worked into music, and they made you learn, like, Latin, and I'm like, "I don't want to learn Latin!" So I switched to open major, and then I switched to general studies, and then I dropped out for a year because I was like, "Nothing interests me really. I just want to have a good time!" So then I waitressed here and there, did all these odds and ends jobs, and I was like, "Well, this sucks!" [Laughs] "I'd better go back to school. I don't like this either!" So I found an ad in the local paper for an animal behavior course at Kirkwood Community College. So I called to find out about this course, and I found out they had a whole series, which meant I could get a degree in animal services. I enrolled back in college at Kirkwood Community College for a two-year program and that was like, the thing! I was like, "This is it!" It was animal-based, all the subjects were ones I was interested in, and I found it useful. We did internships, hands-on learning. I'm more about learning on the job as opposed to being in a classroom reading about it. I'd much rather go and spend time. So that was the beginning of it all.

I had one more internship to do, and I was coming to Chicago on a regular basis to visit just because Chicago is a fun city. And one night, I was coming home from this particular club that I liked, and we passed a pet store called Animal Kingdom. And I was like,

"What's that? That looks really cool." They had wild animals painted on the outside. So I wrote down the cross streets, and the next day, I found my way back to this pet store. I went in and I said, "I really want to work with exotic animals and I need one more internship. You get 120 hours of free work from me because I really want to work with exotic animals." And they're like, "You should really talk to my brother Bill. He has this animal rental company, here's the number, address." So I found the address on Graham Street and walked into his building, and as soon as I walked in the door, I was like, "This is what I want to do for the rest of my life!" It was animal rental, training animals for commercial and films, basically, and for live shows. Ever since I was seven years old I knew I wanted to train animals. I wasn't sure in what capacity and how. I walked in the door and knew this is what I wanted to do for the rest of my life.

I did my internship there and was hired some time period after that. And then, I started my own company with the rats. I thought, "I'm going to train rats for horror movies! That's going to be my career choice!" My parents were thrilled. They're like [sarcastically], "This seems like a great idea. Glad we sent you to college!"

So they objected to it?

S: Very strongly.

So Samantha's Amazing Animals, I saw that you have a website for that.

S: It was initially The Rat Company, and then it became The Rat Company and Friends. And then somebody said, "People think that you're just rats." Because I couldn't make a living on just rats, I expanded the company and I added more animals. I had like eight different animals – a snake, a kinkajou, a chinchilla, and a ferret – a small group of animals – so I did educational shows. And people were like, "You should probably change your name because people still think you are just rats. You should change to Samantha's Amazing Animals." And I was like, "NO! I'm The Rat Company!" Because I was very punk rock back then. But then I thought about it, and I was like, "Do I want to be a success? Or do I want to be cool?" [Laughs] So I decided I wanted to be a success and cool, so I changed it to Samantha's Amazing Animals. And then I changed it to Amazing Animals by Samantha because that came first in the listing in the yellow pages!

At that point, when the whole transition was going on, I had my business cards made out when I was The Rat Company, and I was working part-time in a pet shop and I was also cocktail waitressing at that time. But I told everybody, "Someday, some guys are going to walk in and they are going to need a rat for a movie, and I'm going to be ready for them!" I had my cards printed out, the rats were trained, all we needed was that big break. And of course, people think it sounds crazy, that it is never going to happen. Then one day, these two guys walk into this pet store, New Town Aquarium, and they needed a rat for a movie. And I'm like, "I've got rats. I can train them to go into a box and answer a telephone." I said all I wanted was the movie credit. I got hired; my price was right.

The pet shop I worked for, they were kind of dream squashers. They didn't want to give me the day off for my dream job. So I quit! I quit my full-time job for this one time, non-paying movie job. And never regretted it. I didn't think twice about it. I was like, "OK, I quit!" And I never looked back. It turned out to be a great move because a TV station showed up and covered it, WGN, and they called me "Chicago's very own Rat Lady!"

Cool!

S: The next thing you know, it was rebroadcast on CNN, and I got press all over the country. A guy in Italy saw it, and I am flying over to Italy for Christmas to film a TV show! It just snowballed. I got all this attention, and became infamous a little bit. And my shows started getting booked. And I started getting more movie gigs. But then, that's when I realized I couldn't make a living on just rats so then I expanded to the other animals, and that's when Amazing Animals by Samantha came into play.

I did that for like 20 years. I kept adding animals. The largest animal I had was a binturong, which is like 60 pounds or so, so 60 pounds or less, small exotics. I turned my house literally into a zoo.

What is a binturong?

S: It's a Chinese bear/cat. For 20 years I did that. One day I woke up, and I was like, "I'm not doing what I really set out to do. I really wanted to train animals for film and television." I was doing more educational programs, going to schools and libraries, and kid's parties. And I don't really like kids.

[Laughs]

S: So it became a real dreaded thing for me. I was like, "I am hating my job."

Take note, potential Tickers! It's interesting to observe that even though Samantha was following her dream, at this point in her story she wasn't on her true path. Sure, she was working with animals, but she realized she didn't like it if it meant she had to interact with children. She got a bit side tracked at this point. But she kept working to find her direction.

117

I had just come off a contract where I was traveling with this group called the Festival of Cultures. I had a small group of animals, and I was the Wildlife of the World portion of a bigger production where they had representatives from Mexico and Europe and Africa and Polynesia. We would go to campuses and we would put on four programs a day for school buses full of kids. Once again there were kids, but it was 20 minute shows and it was kind of exciting because it was travelling.

I really got the travel bug! I was like, "I love travelling! Being on the road!" Staying at the Red Roof Inn, pets stay for free.

That's perfect!

S: Every year it increased, so by the fourth year, I was on the road for four months, and I loved every second of it. And then that came to an end because they weren't going to do it anymore. So I came back and that was the year I started the cat circus. But the final year that I did that [Festival of Cultures] I had graduated to an RV, because before that I had an ambulance, and then I moved to a 27 foot RV. I turned the RV's kitchen table into the stage for the band.

I had started training cats at that point. I was rehearsing the band and trained these cats to play the instruments. And I would be like, "Hey!" to random people here and there. "You want to see something really cool?" And I'd open up the RV door and they are like, "I don't know, this is starting to sound weird." [Laughs] I'd open up the RV door and the cat band would play! And they were just blown away! They were like, "There's this cat band playing in this girl's RV! It's kind of weird but it's really cool!" And it got really great reception. I was like, "I think I'm onto something here."

So then when I came back [to Chicago], and [the Festival of Cultures] ended, I decided to shift to cats. And kind of fade out the exotic animal thing. At that time, the economy tanked as well. People were not going to be shelling out 400 bucks for their kid's birthday party. So I made the shift to cats, and Tuna was a brilliant cat so I started training her to do these tricks. I would bring her along to schools and libraries. The economy crunch didn't hit the schools and libraries right away. At the end of this very educational show with the exotic animals, I would be like, "Hey! Here's a cat doing a trick!" So I kept bringing the cats along to do something at the very end and see how people reacted to it. I slowly started to expand on that. I decided to put a show together.

My goal was of course to train cats and get them movie jobs and television, that sort of thing. I didn't really have a name as a cat trainer at that point. And my cats didn't have a résumé. One of the big problems with cats is that if they are not working consistently, then they lose their edge and they get issues. They're like, "Whoa! What's this? New thing!" So I had to figure out a way to keep them working while building a reputation as a cat trainer. So I put this show [Acro-Cats] together but I didn't have any place to book the show, because it wasn't even a show yet. I found an ad in the paper for an art gallery looking for an opening, like "We need some entertainment!" And I'm like, "I can bring these cats and they can do stuff!" [Laughs] So they're like, "OK!"

I had these props that I found at the hardware store, like some ladders and rope, and I was experimenting at this point. I brought them to the gallery and set things up. And the cats were pretty terrible.

[Laughs]

S: Except for Tuna – Tuna was a rock star. And the band – the band worked! I had been working with the band for a while. The Acro-Cat portion was just terrible. People laughed, because we would say funny things, and then the band would play, and it would be like, "Yeah!" So then I learned as I went on what worked and what didn't work.

Cats really don't like a theater in the round. They need to have a solid back wall because when people are behind them, they are like this [imitates looking around]. So I'm like, "OK, we need a solid back wall." And they are sniffing the floor constantly. So I laid out a flooring for them so they have their own – so I made a portable stage that I can take places. And we started finding art galleries that we could come to and bring the show, and we would just pass the hat [to collect money for the performance]. I would be very excited and tell my good friend, "I got another place for the cats to perform! What are you doing Thursday night? Do you want to be my assistant?" They're like, "[reluctantly] OK." They would kind of hang their head. After the show, they would say, "[whispering] I've got your money!" The cats were terrible. They're still terrible! Sometimes I'm like, "Why are you so terrible?" [Laughs]

So I just kind of built it from there. We finally booked a theater in Chicago, Gorilla Tango, because they were a low rent theater. They took a split at the door. We got a great article in the Tribune and the show ended up selling out for weeks.

Awesome!

S: People just showed up in droves to see the cats. It was a contained theater so the cats really didn't have many places to go. Things were really moving along. But then there was Branson. That was a bad incident. It was a bit of a setback.

Branson, Missouri?

S: Yes. We got hired, because there is a guy, Gregory Popovich, who does a cat act. He used to work in Branson for many years, and he had billboards. I mean, "Popovich's Amazing House Cats!" [In looking up the act online, it came up as "The World Famous Popovich Comedy Pet Theater". They currently perform in Las Vegas at the Planet Hollywood Casino.] He had up and quit on them because he had a season-to-season contract and he said, "I've got a gig in Vegas! See ya!" So he just bailed on them. So they hired a guy to bring in somebody. This guy put together a variety show with a bird act, a dog act, and some cats. Well, there was a Russian woman who had some trained house cats, so they were going to be doing this gig, but they weren't available for the first week or ten days, so I got the job.

We were very excited! We packed up our stuff, and went to Branson. It was a disaster! Our props were terrible, we had no stage presence, our costuming was like "Eh," and the dog people hated us because they had been doing it for years. They were very professional. We were all over the place. They did not like our professionalism. The bird people hated us because our cats wanted to eat their birds.

[Laughs]

S: In the first rehearsal, Tuna ran offstage. And I was just mortified. I wanted to sneak off in the middle of the night and not even bother to collect the paycheck. People are showing up from miles around to see the Amazing Popovich and his amazing cats, and they are getting Samantha's not-so-amazing Acro-Cats! [Laughs] It was traumatizing to realize how much you suck.

But then the guy, Ed Finland, who put the thing together, he pulled us aside, and he got our props organized, and he told us tips on showmanship, and how to play it off when the cats screw up. He said, "Just go out there and own it! 'Look at this cat doing absolutely nothing!'" We drove back to Chicago, took a couple of weeks off and regrouped. And we started putting the show together again and got a little bit better. We added music, and started slowly turning it into what it is now. It's still a little bit – people always describe it as "Do It Yourself – DIY." And I'm always like, "Really? Is it that obvious? I thought we were doing pretty good. I'm sparkly!"

And it is not a slick act, and it is still not as good as Popovich. And I don't think it ever will be because my show is compromised by the relationship I have with the cats. Russian animals – they obviously don't abuse their animals, because you would be able to tell, the cats would be cringing – but they maintain a very professional relationship with their cats. Their cats live in kennels, they come out, they do their job, and then they go back to their kennels. That's why they're so good because that's all they know. Work, eat, work, eat. My cats are pets. They hang out, we watch television, I pet them and love them. And I forgive them when they slack off, and when they screw up on stage, which reinforces them screwing up onstage. I have to just fumble along sometimes with the cats and their moods, and what they feel like doing. It's still not at that level like the Russian cat circus.

But it seems like people love that aspect of it because they can see their own cat in the show. And they see the cats coming out off the stage, wandering around, rubbing up against them, so it actually seems to be a win-win. Some people, I'm sure there are some people who are like, "It's a cat" [acting annoyed] but more people enjoy the show, and come see it again and again, which makes me feel like the show doesn't suck that bad because these people come and see it every year.

Personally, my opinion, we really enjoyed [the show] when we saw it in Seattle. A lot of times you will see a trained animal show and it feels like, "Oh that's amazing! Whatever," like you don't have that connection. You kind of connect with the [Acro-Cats] show because you're like, "I have a cat. I could not make my cat do anything. My cat would probably roll and show its belly and be like, 'Pet me!' and then when I go to pick it up, it's like, woo hoo! [imitates cat running away.]

S: And they do that sometimes too! Jax is like the worst. She's like the biggest jerk. And then she comes out and just lays on the stage. And she'll go up there, and throw off Asti who is trying to do her encore. And then just comes back and sits on her skull. [Samantha has a prop that looks like a large skull upon which Jax sits.] She's just kind of the wild card these days. Her popularity has really grown. She does some of the best tricks - when she does her tricks, she's the best. When she gets more reinforcement when she goes out into the audience, so when I ask her to do tricks, she's like, "I'm going to go out there because I feel more gratified coming out here! Everyone's loving on me and petting me, and you're just giving me a piece of chicken! That's a no-brainer! I'm outta here! Later, loser!" She's really become quite popular.

So it sounds like social media is a big part of what you're doing now. The cats have their own Twitter accounts?

S: Yes, they're tweeting. Ally is on Pinterest. Who knows what they'll come up with next? Yes, they have quite a few followers and they have their Twitter wars. It's between Tuna and Buggles mainly, and Oz is kind of clueless. And Jax is definitely involved in the following as well. They have their Facebook pages. It definitely turned into this craziness!

It's great because we are really living the dream. Even though it is stressful when the bus breaks down all the time! But I get to be around animals I love, and I get to travel. The scary thing is, as I get older, I realize, "I need to take care of myself. I don't want to break a hip!" I sprained my ankle six weeks ago, and it put a damper on things. No one else can do this show. Before, with the zoo I was running, other people could go out and do the show, because they could explain what an alligator is and do the demonstrations. But this is a glimpse into my world! I'm not lying when I say, "This is my living room furniture and kitchen table" [pointing to the props and Rock Cats set on stage] because I'm a little lazy. I don't want to go to a separate facility and train the animals. I want to roll out of bed and be reminded that my work is right here! So I don't have to get in the car and drive to go to work. If it's raining, snowing, whatever is going on, I roll out of bed and my work is right there reminding me. So I'm not going to blow it off! I will blow it off a little bit…I'll wake up at noon, have some breakfast and then lunch at the same time, and then make some phone calls. But then the animals will kind of start reminding me, "Are we going to work today? Are we going to do something today?" It's like right there.

I like it – I like being surrounded because the cats are living with me. They're letting me know what they can do and I'm watching them, and going, "Wow, look at the way that cat is jumping!" A lot of training is just observation. Just watching them be my cats and then I think, "You know, I bet that would be really cute. I bet there's something I can do with that." So I go to Toys R Us and I'll walk down the aisles, and I'll be like, "Oh, I think that would work," and I match the item with the cat, and try to put the ability together. And if it works, I might hire someone to make it a little more pretty, but I do the initial prototype. It really just came from the inside of my head and working with the cats.

In a way, it's like it all worked out. The cats started getting production work, like Tidy Cats and Cat's Pride, and all the Pet Stages products, my cats are modeling on them.

Oh cool!

S: It all worked out in the end so far. Knock on wood! [Laughs] I mean, at any time we could have the zombie apocalypse! My cats would throw me under the bus. "She's hiding under there!" [Laughs] "There she is! I don't care what you do with the girl – leave us alone!" But that's what I respect about cats. Dogs are like, "I'll lay down my life for you!" Cats are like, "I'll eat you as soon as you stop breathing!"

So with training, you were saying even with the little kittens that are five weeks old, they can start that early?

S: Oh yeah. I just started clicker training them two days ago, just kind of clicking the clicker and giving them a piece of chicken. Then they got really excited about the chicken! I showed just the basics. I'm just planting the seeds so there is a part of their brain that will get it, that this click means something, that treats will follow. With clicker training, the sound of the click is like a promise. "The treat's on its way!" So that's how all the training ends up. Because you could say, "Good cat!" but the cat doesn't know exactly what it did that was good, because it may have done several things.

When I was training Tuna, when she was doing the movie "Zeke", she had to pull a trigger on a gun. She's very adept at tapping. If you touch anything, she will touch whatever it is. But she had to touch the trigger, which is a very specific spot. So with the clicker, I was able to tell her exactly what moment she was doing it right. We used a little tiny feather target. She's didn't hear the click when she touched here, she didn't hear the click when she touched there, but she heard the click when she touched right there [on the trigger] so she knew that was the spot. So that's how the clicker works for getting that exact behavior at the exact time. That's what's so great about it.

It sounds like some cats are more receptive to it than others.

S: Some of them are lazy. Some would rather be a lap cat. Some of those cats I end up retiring, and they stay back in Chicago. Like Nola is really great at sitting at her mark, just having her picture taken. She may end up being a production cat rather than an actor cat. And Oz, I've had him since he was two days old. I keep him around because I love him so much, but he's not the sharpest. He tries, but he's really not the sharpest. Some of the cats definitely are slower.

So how did you get Tuna?

S: I had a neighbor down the street who was going back to Poland to visit and she asked if I would take care of her cat while she was gone. And that cat ended up being pregnant. So she went to Poland and she never came back – we never heard from her again! So the cat gave birth to these white kittens. I never thought of myself as a white cat person. "I like black – I'm Goth! I've got lots of black clothes!" This white cat was born, and I was like, "That's really, really cute." She looked like a little fluffy cotton ball.

There was something about her that just seemed to be special. I found homes for the other kittens and I kept, and I started training her. She just had such an aptitude for training. She's not very affectionate, but she was ready to work, on the ball. She really inspired me. I thought, "This cat training is easy!" With the other cats, not so much, but she is an alpha female and very focused on training. She was really the inspiration and why I started with the cats. I had her mother for many years before she passed. And Tuna had a couple of litters herself before I spayed her. I thought her bloodline was so amazing I didn't want it to die. This was before I started fostering.

In 2009, I put the show together and we were starting to book theater gigs, and I decided to add another cat to the show. I wanted it to be a rescue, but I thought, what if I picked the wrong cat? It's hard to tell sometimes. So then I thought, what if I foster a litter, and then I can cherry pick the good one. I ended up pairing up with a group in Chicago, and they sent me to pick up my first litter of kittens. And it was an animal welfare league, which happens to be a kill shelter. So when I walked in the door, they said, "Here's your group to pick from. Whatever you don't pick is scheduled to be euthanized today." I was like, "What? WHAT? Well, then I will take them all!" I took eleven.

Oh my goodness!

S: They all had respiratory problems. So I brought them home and they gave all of my cats respiratory problems! I was medicating thirty cats.

Oh no!

S: That's when I learned something very important about keeping them separate. So then I got everybody well!

I ended up finding homes for all eleven because none of them really stuck out. But then I went back and got another group. And that's when the fostering started. Because you don't really know the fight until you are thrown into it. And you realize all these kittens are dying every year because they don't have a home to go to. Immediately everybody got spayed in my household because I found out about low cost spay. Before I was spaying one cat a year because it was $500 a cat! I didn't know about low cost spay – that you can get it done for $35.

Once I found low cost spay and neuter, I realized, "Wow! This is going on! I should not be reproducing kittens when there are so many that are being born and disposed of and need homes." So everybody got spayed at that point. I've been fostering ever since. Now I put them in the show, and they travel with me. Every once in a while, I become a foster failure because I'm like, "This cat is amazing!" and end up keeping them. And then there's some, like Nola, which really aren't that amazing [Laughs]– I was really hoping she would turn out better! I'm really starting to rethink her position in the company! Did we get her – did she ever come back?

Yes, actually I was able to help – I got her and I got Dakota. She was OK at first but she got a little cranky!

S: She's like that. She's all like [pretends to be friendly] and then she's got this ugly side to her.

Is it different working for yourself versus working for someone else?

S: I hardly ever worked for anyone else. I had that pet shop job and I did a lot of part-time jobs in college.

It is different – you can set your own hours. And I thought if I work for myself –

[My husband comes in with a big container of transmission fluid.] Hi!

S: Oh you found a big one! Yeah!

[We chat with my husband about the transmission fluid, then continue.]

S: Yes, I worked for myself for so long that I don't even know how I would work for someone else. It would be hard to go back at this point. "Get up at a certain time – what?"

Were you ever afraid when you broke out on your own?

S: No! I never was. I was one of those, dive right into the pool without looking to see if there's water in it. I never had that fear of, "What if it doesn't work out?" I believed that someone was going to walk through that door and ask for trained rats for a movie! I really was just out there – I never had fear like that, I just had belief. The power of belief is very powerful. And then you get that reinforcement, and it's like, "It worked! I told you it would work! I told you it would happen!"

I think you kind of answered this, but did you have an outline for your path?

S: A business plan? No! I'm always…I always keep charging ahead until I hit that brick wall, and then I'm like, "Oh, I didn't anticipate this!" And then I figure out how to fix that problem, and then I move ahead. I just never…my parents sent me to school to get my "Mrs." – they wanted me to get married and have kids. They really didn't anticipate me being a business person. They had different plans for me. But I didn't want to get married! It's never really been a dream of mine to get married.

My parents were married – they were married for 54 years! It was like "Leave it to Beaver" – "Honey, I'm home!" My mother was a stay-at-home housewife who raised us kids. Mom read and did arts and crafts, a very devoted mother and housewife. Father brought home the money and like you see in the movies, it was really idyllic. But it really kind of seemed boring to me. I just didn't want that.

Plus the rules! "My house, my rules!" If I get married, that means there's their rules and some sort of compromise? So neither person gets what they want? And that didn't seem really cool either. I mean, "You don't get what you want, and I don't get what I want" – really? I just do my own thing, and I'm happy. And then you're not happy, and we'll break up, and I'll just get another cat. [Laughs]

There we go! [Laughs]

S: And then I become the stereotype of single woman with multiple cats! Which is the butt of every movie now! I'm like, "I'M DOOMED!" [Laughs] "I couldn't get married if I wanted to!"
One thing is I'm inflexible about the décor in my apartment. I don't want to go somewhere else to work. It's "my house, my rules!" Everything has to be purple.

It all has to match!

S: Yes, it all has to match! My way of compromising would be, "Everything in the house will be purple, but if you want a pool table in the living room, I'm fine with that!" Or a Jacuzzi off the back porch, whatever! But the house needs to be purple, and all the cat props must be there. We divide the house in half and make it like a duplex. You can have that half, and that would be the best I could do.

That would work! So, what's the most unusual comments or reactions that you've gotten from what you do?

S: Just that people love the show as much as they do! I'm like, "Really?" Sometimes it's like the worst show ever, and I'm like, "Oh my God, that was the worst show ever!" And I want to crawl in a hole and die. And people will say, "That was the best show I've ever seen!" And I'm like, "Are you kidding me? You've never seen the Russian cats! They're just really…" [Laughs] So like that to me is just the craziest thing I've ever heard. Or they say, "This is the best Saturday night ever!", "Now I can die 'cause I've seen everything!", "This is the best night of my life!" I'm like, "Really? Wow, you must not get out much!" [Laughs]

What's the most unusual animal that you've ever worked with?

S: Probably the binturong. It looks like a big bear and cat rolled into one. Nobody knows what it is. "Is it a bear? No. Is it a cat? No, it's a bear-cat!" Or "It looks like a big ferret!" Oh, OK! We'll just go with that! [Laughs] Then people will say, "It's pretty big for a ferret," and I'll say, "Yes! Yes, it is!" And now both of our lives can just move on!

Do you still have a serval?

S: Yes, I still have the serval. He lives in Chicago. It would be cruel to out him on the road because he's a 50-pound wild cat. They need a lot of space to run back and forth. It's problematic if he's everywhere. They make terrible pets.

But my house is just barren. It's made for animals. I have a room that's mine, and the rest is for the animals so it is easy to clean.

That's cool.

S: It's like living in a big kennel. The kitchen has a cage as the door, an actual cage door, separating the kitchen from the rest of the house. So if I'm feeding, I can feed things separately.
It is not like a normal house at all! All the knick-knacks go into the hallway. That way nothing can get broken. So you can't really have the typical comforts of home. When I go into a normal person's house, I'm like, [stage whispering] "Wow! I've almost forgotten – this is how it's supposed to look! And how would I ever adjust?" And I think, "Isn't this nice? Look how comfortable this is!" And there are knick-knacks around, and I can set my glass of wine down! And I don't have to do this [pretends to lift up things] with my food! That's why I guzzle champagne, because the second you set down a glass, the cats are like, "Ooh! What's that?" and knock it over! And it breaks…you don't want to be holding this glass forever. So I take two sips and then glug-glug-glug and put it in the dishwasher. So then I go out to eat with somebody and they're like, "You chugged that glass fast!" [Laughs] I'm like, "It's a long story!"

Occupational hazard!

S: Right!

I read on your Amazing Animals website that one of the groups you worked with – did you do a music video for Megadeth?

S: Oh yeah! That was back in the early days when I was the Rat Company. We supplied rats. I could send you a link – there's a video of it. You see rats crawling on a piano, and I think there might have been some pigeons flying – although that might have been another job we did.
I started getting all the rat jobs, like in horror movies and music videos, because music videos and rats sort of go hand-in-hand. So I started getting rats for several things like that.

Is it hard getting animals to do things on cue with cameras? Is it ever like, "We're waiting!"

S: Oh, it's like a lot of "Hurry up and wait". And they have no patience at all. Because they want the shot now. They don't give you a lot of prep time. And they lie to you when they book you to do the job. They'll say, "Oh, it's really easy! We want this blah-blah-blah," and you get there, and they want something completely different. They want back flips, or you know! And all these people involved. And they want the cats to weave in between people's legs as they party down with loud music coming from speakers! And when they booked it, they said, "Oh, this cat's just going to be sitting by a fireplace." And it's like, "NO! It's a club scene, not a fireplace scene! It's a nightclub!" So you really learn how to extract information. "Will there be other people? Will there be other animals? Is there going to be a disco ball and noise?"

That's why I do this [waves her arms towards the Acro-Cats stage and props] because this prepares them for anything. And that's why my cats are the best in the business. When they go on set, people who hire us for production stuff, and if they've worked with cats before, they are so thrilled when my cats come on the set. They are used to distractions - nothing really fazes them. So this [performing in the Acro-Cats show] is like prep for film production. But then it evolved into this which I also love. So it's like I have two different jobs. And then with the fostering too, so it's like three different jobs.

Is there anybody in particular who is like a hero to you?

S: This guy Moe DiSesso was like my mentor. He was the rat trainer for "Ben" and "Willard." I don't know if you saw those movies back in the day.

I remember those!

S: He was like my mentor. When I was in California, working on one of the rat documentaries, I ended up getting stranded there because there was a heat embargo, and you couldn't ship animals back and forth because of the temperature. I ended up hunting him down and stayed at his place for a couple of weeks. He became my mentor and taught me a lot of different things. He was an amazing man. He's passed away since. He definitely was kind of a hero, an inspiration. He'd say, "WHAT THE HELL ARE YOU DOING?" He was very vocal! He'd come in and I'd have the rats everywhere. "Work with those rats one at a time!" he'd say.

And I am still to this day a multi-tasker. I'll be clicker training a cat over here like this while I do this…mixing up my signals, and the cats are all confused! Especially now because I am training more on the road. It's hard to find those times when I can just sit and focus and train the cats properly. My training is definitely a little bit sloppy. So the cats do end up getting some mixed signals when they are onstage.

Do you have a motto or something you live by?

S: It changes every year! One year it was like, "Let's just give it a try!" And then this year, [because of their bus troubles] it's "Turn on the flashers!" [Laughs]

So it varies depending on what's going on?

S: Yes! "I don't know - Let's just give it a try" definitely was it one year!

What advice would you give other people who want to follow their passion?

S: I'm a big believer in…this is what you're going to do every day for the rest of your life, for like, how many hours a day? How can you not?

It's…with the financial thing, I guess you really have to be motivated because you have to work some sort of job to make the money and then still do what you want on the side. So you end up working insane hours. Something has to give, really. That's the thing. I've wanted to be an animal trainer since I was seven years old, so it was never…some people just don't know what they want to do. I was lucky to know what I wanted to do at seven and persevered.
And then I had parents to rebel against, so that was helpful.

[Laughs]

S: If you have something to rebel against, that really feeds the fire!

For instance, if you are in a job you don't love, that too can inspire you to change!

And when people say, "That can't be done! That's crazy!" I say, "Oh, yeah?" "You can't train cats!" "Oh, yeah?"

So it's just the…it's all about choices. It is hard to….you can't do it all. You have to make a decision in life. Which is why [during the show] I always make the joke about being single. The truth is that I am single by choice because these animals really require a lot of my love, time and attention. And I am very passionate about what I do. So to try to share my life with someone else and do that whole compromise thing…I believe marriage is something that you have to work at. So I feel like I've chosen my work path. I am single by choice because I am very happy with what I'm doing, and I don't feel guilty about ripping some other human off. Being like, not meeting up to my end of things in a marriage. But I chose not to do that. I'm not letting someone down. Except for my parents, a little bit, because they didn't get to have grandchildren, so I feel bad for them about that. But then I'd be stuck with them now if I had had kids for them!

Maybe there's a way to do both, but it's easier if you don't have to divide your time. And there are people who do it together, and I think, "That's insane! I would kill them!" [Laughs] I have a lot of friends in the animal business who are in a relationship, and they work together and raise animals together, and I'm like, "I just don't know how you do it without killing each other!"

What do you think about potty training cats? I've seen it done on the Internet. Can it be done?

S: Oh yeah, I have a friend who lives in Seattle and she's actually the person to talk to about that. She has actually done it, and she recommends not to do it because some of the cats get really particular. If you're not there to flush the toilet, then the next cat will be like, "Oh, I'm not going to use this!"

I haven't done it because there would always be a line! I'd be waiting my turn, and there would always be six cats in front of me, and I'd be like, "I've really gotta go, guys!" And they would be like, "Wait in line like the rest of us!" [Laughs] So it really wouldn't work.

Have you heard of the "Paw Project" with people not declawing cats?

S: That's been a thing for a while. I've never declawed my cats. I mean, they are Acro-Cats – they need them to jump, climb and catch. I know it is a big controversy these days. I always felt like if the cat is kept in a home, it would be better to have the cat declawed than have it tossed out on the street. But if that's the kind of person who's going to get rid of their cat for some x, y and z, they are probably going to find a reason to get rid of the cat. A lot of times, if there is a behavioral problem because of scratching, if you remove the claws, another behavioral problem will occur that's worse than the scratching. Declawed cats end up getting put out on the streets or in a shelter then have a worse behavioral problem. So I definitely will not end up declawing any of my cats.

So what do you like best about your job? What gets you out of bed in the morning?

S: Well, the cats actually keep me in bed.

[Laughs]

S: I would lay there all day with them. They are furry and….that's the cool thing about them. People will complain that their cats will wake them up at five in the morning wanting to be fed. My cats already know that's not going to happen. They're all about, "Ooh, she's not moving." Because I am usually moving around, doing x, y and z, so when I'm down and lying in bed, they don't want me to go anywhere so they trap me in the bed! So some other commitment will get me up, like, "Oh, I have to do a show in an hour! Get out of bed!"

I love the cats. It's fun watching them learn when I am training them to do something new, and add that new challenge. When they get that light bulb moment, it's an exciting moment for me and for the cat. And for the audience, to add something new. Because I'm never done! It's never like, "OK, that's it! I'm done! It's perfect!" There's always going to be new goals, new ideas and new things to do. And new cats. Although I am kind of at the max – we have fourteen right now. It's really…a lot of people probably would not find this a dream job. You're living on the road and sleeping on a bus full of cats, and they set off "bombs," and you have to use a lot of incense.

That was all I had. Thank you so much!

S: Thank you for your help!

***

It was funny…after our interview was over, Samantha became quiet again. I followed her around a bit, dork that I am, and later Polly Smith who works with Samantha's Acro-Cats team came over. Polly and Samantha have a great rapport which was fun to watch. I asked Samantha to show Jerry the kittens she was fostering. I helped them carry the cats out to the cat bus. Then I said farewell and thanked them again.

After doing the interview in June 2015, I continued to follow Samantha, Polly, Tuna and the Acro-Cats on Facebook. I was thrilled when Bill Geist interviewed Samantha for the CBS Sunday Morning News program. And then the coolest thing happened! In November 2015, I learned Samantha and her Acro-Cats would be featured on the Late Show with Stephen Colbert. They were booked for the first show after the tragic attacks in Paris on November 13, 2015. But Stephen Colbert had them on anyway, saying that they were silly and fun, all the things the terrorists hate.

Samantha and her crew actively tour. Right before Christmas 2015, they had a successful Kickstarter campaign. Thanks to over 1400 backers, they raised more than $150k to buy a new, more reliable bus for their traveling show. At the time of publishing, Samantha and her crew had picked out a new bus but were in the process of making modifications. They posted some terrible pictures of the cat bus being towed when they were on tour in the Southwest. In Phoenix, the bus broke down but they had to keep it running to keep the air conditioning on for the cats' well-being. Once again, social media came to their rescue! Acro-Cat fans donated money so Samantha and her crew could purchase gas to keep the bus running.

As someone who always considered myself part of the "Misfit Toys," I really connected with Samantha and her story. Many of us can identify with how she must have felt as a young girl, lonely and unhappy at military school, and in need of a friend. That love she felt from Ramsey the rat must have made a world of difference in her life. She trusted that feeling she had from being with and working with animals. Even when the rest of the people in her life- her parents and people at school - were encouraging her to get married or study something "serious" at school, she had the guts to continue to trust that feeling and seek out a life working with animals. And even when Samantha found a career with animals but hit a roadblock when it meant working with kids which she hated, she didn't stop. She refocused and continued exploring what she loves and what she wants. She kept circling back, examining, "Why didn't this show work in Branson?" Some less brave souls would have hung it up after a humiliating show, but she didn't. She sought advice and guidance. She ensured there is humor in the show. It's not just a show about performing animals. It's a show about loving animals and all their quirks and flaws. And in that, we can also learn to love ourselves and all our quirks and flaws.

Samantha's journey also shows how important it is to be willing to learn, adapt and be flexible. In the beginning, she wanted to be the "Rat Lady" and didn't want to change her focus. But then when she realized she couldn't just make a living from rats, she expanded her animals to include many other species. She learned she didn't like working with kids, and that she did like being on the road. She learned that the cats get restless and forget their training during commercials when they are not practicing all the time, so she realized having a traveling circus would be a great fit. She keeps trying new things, keeping what works and ditching what doesn't. I'm sure for someone who was a rebellious young woman that this was tough to do! But she not only listened to her heart but also learned what works and what doesn't, and found her perfect path that way.

I was absolutely charmed both times I saw the Acro-Cats perform. I know now it is because of the authentic love of Samantha and her crew. They truly celebrate cats, not by turning them into something they are not (professionally trained Russian cats!) but by delighting in their unique personalities. And also, by celebrating the people who share the love of cats by watching them perform and adopting the foster kitties.

Story 6: Danielle Fernandez – Juicer: Squeezing the good stuff out of life

Shimmying and shaking, in 2005, I became a belly dancer. One of my dearest friends, Evelyn, started taking classes and she had become friends with Heather, a belly dance instructor. I had to try it out! Belly dancing was a great deal of fun. I loved learning how to shimmy and getting to practice the dance routines.

In 2005, I was also passionate about cooking. My friend Jen and I decided to start our own catering company, and we called it Food for Thought. Our first official gig was making food for a hafla, which is a belly dance recital, for Heather's dance group. Jen and I had a blast! We made Mediterranean cuisine – hummus, tabbouleh, and grilled chicken. Part of the way through the hafla, I ditched my chef's hat for my belly dancing dress and shimmied on stage! It was a successful evening for both cooking and dancing.

During this time, Jen and I started looking at books on how to start your own business. I bought tons of advice books and checked with my Dad, a tax attorney, on the best way to set up a business from a legal perspective. (We went with an LLC – limited liability corporation – which Dad said is the best way to protect yourself from being sued). Every book I read said the same thing – write a business plan! I read up about business plans. I compared the sample plans from the books, looked at all of the advice, and ultimately wrote a half-assed draft. Ugh.

I really didn't want to work on a stupid plan. I wanted to cook! Of course, planning played a large part of our business. When Jen and I booked a catering gig, we would prepare for the number of people attending, what the host liked or didn't like, how much food to buy, whether to rent glasses or use our own, blah blah blah. But we really lived for the actual cooking, slicing and dicing to our heart's content in the kitchen. It was so much fun!

Eventually, Food for Thought ceased to be. Jen became busy raising her two sons, and I was overwhelmed with my full-time job. I tried for a while to continue on my own but without Jen, I did not have as much fun. Instead being a little busy I felt totally exhausted after each catering gig.

After dabbling in small business ownership with Food for Thought, I am hardly an expert. I do have some idea about the trials facing entrepreneurs. In an article in the Houston Chronical called, "What Makes Being an Entrepreneur Challenging?" Tanya Robertson writes, "While being an entrepreneur does have its benefits, it also has its challenges. When entrepreneurs first start out, they're often considered a one-man show, meaning they're responsible for doing everything on their own. This usually equates to working really long hours, juggling numerous projects and having to constantly come up with new ideas." [xii] So I always wonder how entrepreneurs handle getting over the initial hurdles. How do they get through the tough times at the beginning? There is a lot of trial and error. What do they do to keep going?

Fast forward to July 2015. I had happily reconnected with one of my best friends from when I was growing up. Tracy was always – and continues to be - amazing. She and I share a wickedly fun sense of humor and a desire to help others. I went through some ups and downs while growing up, but Tracy always helped me see that life was so much more than the narrow focus that I had back in middle school.

Tracy and I had lost touch after she moved to the West Coast. Thanks to Facebook, we were able to reconnect. She came to Richmond a few times to visit family and I was so happy I got to meet with her. One morning over coffee, we had an incredible conversation. It was after the layoffs that had shaken my world. I talked with Tracy and asked her about what makes her passionate.

Just as it was when we were kids, Tracy had remarkable vision. She told me about her life, how she has become a yoga instructor, and how she and her husband live and work on a ranch in Colorado. She told me about how she has discovered painting, and now loves to create new canvases. I told her my dreams about helping other people to discover their full potential. I think part of why I want to do that was because Tracy and other talented friends in my life have helped guide me to where I want to be, and helped me understand that just because I dance to the beat of a different drum doesn't make me a bad person. Instead I am my own person! Tracy encouraged me to pursue helping other people pursue their passions and talked with me about becoming a life coach, author and speaker.

So I was absolutely over the moon when Tracy and her husband Thom invited us to visit them in Minturn, Colorado. Seeing the beautiful ranch where Tracy and Thom work and live was incredible. Thom and Tracy grilled dinner for us and we ate outside of their barn turned house (a real "loft" apartment!), looking at the mountains, and watching the stars. It was heavenly. Tracy and Thom are just the coolest, and we adored meeting their friends and walking in their footsteps during our visit.

It was while I was in this wonderful head and heart space that Jerry and I went with Tracy and Thom to the Farmers' Market and Art Show in Vail. We tasted the food, drank the wine, and gazed at the amazing art. Jerry even accidentally ate a dog treat! (To his defense, they were set out at a booth like samples…but it was still hilarious!)

While we were at the Farmers' Market, we ran into a young woman whom Tracy knew. Her name is Danielle Fernandez and she was selling fresh juice at the market. Tracy stopped to chat with her friend while I looked at the yummy selections that Danielle had to offer: Dandelion Wine (kale, spinach, dandelion greens, celery, apple, cucumber, ginger), Roots (carrot, kale, ginger, beet, lemon), Bloody (tomato, jalapeño, celery, cilantro) and Cosmic Charlie (carrot, apple, cinnamon, honey, orange). Tracy bought a Cosmic Charlie and offered me a sip. I had never been into juicing, so honestly I didn't know what to expect. Delicious!

Then I noticed the name of her company – Main Squeeze – and the eye-catching logo. I could tell that Danielle was young but she was very confident. She really was really excited about juicing! She answered Tracy's questions about the juices and her business while I stood back listening. I was really impressed with Danielle so I found her business card and called her when I got home. Danielle graciously agreed to interview with me.

I was super excited because I knew that Danielle had just started her business. I wanted to talk with her about the initial kick-off, and how she tackled the challenges. I also wanted to know how she was balancing having another job while starting Main Squeeze at the same time.

***

K: So first of all, thank you so much! I really was excited to talk with you. With my book, I am meeting with people who are really passionate about what they do. I wanted to talk with you because you are just getting started with your business. Part of my goal with writing this book is that I want to inspire other people to branch out. So I wanted to talk with you while you're kind of gaining a following, but still have some things to figure out for your plan.

D: Yeah, thank you! I was really excited when I got your email. Like you said, I'm really new. So I thought, I don't know too much, so it's funny you wanted to interview me, but I'm really excited!

Well, wonderful! Thank you! And I tell you what I do when I'm researching folks for my book. I go out on the Internet and I try to find everything I can. I found your Facebook entry so I "liked" it.

D: Thank you! Yeah, I don't have a web site or anything. Everything is so new. A web site would be a great thing to have! But I have my Facebook page now.

Excellent! One thing at a time! Facebook is a good start.

D: Yes, it's crazy how much free marketing you can do with Facebook, so it's pretty awesome.

Definitely! When I did do a little bit of research online, I found something called CouchSurfing. Which I had never heard of! But I saw…I think it's your site on there. And I saw that you've been to Spain, oh gosh, you've been to a bunch of countries, but you lived in Spain, and Switzerland – is that correct?

D: Yes, that is correct. So I just graduated college in December, and in Spring 2013 I did a semester abroad in Spain which was really amazing! After that, I was a nanny in Switzerland which was supposed to be the whole summer but ended up being just a month because of my visa.

Couchsurfing is really cool, actually. When you're travelling, people will allow you to stay, even on their couch. You get to know the area, and the local feel, so yeah! It's really cool.

Oh, that sounds amazing! My husband and I love to travel, but when I saw Couchsurfing, I was like, "I've never heard of that!"

D: It's definitely not like – I wouldn't travel with my mom using Couchsurfing! My mom would be like, "What the heck is this?" [Laughs] I traveled with a friend.

I bet that was a blast! And then I read that you're a Django Reihnhart fan, so I was like, "I know I like her already!"

D: Yeah, that's awesome! He's really great. They had a tribute concert in Vail but I was out of town, unfortunately. Of course, it was on the one day I was out of town, which is like, never!

I wanted to talk with you because when I visited Tracy, and we walked around the Vail Farmers' Market, she bought a bottle of your carrot juice, and it was really delicious!

D: Thank you!

When did you start getting into juicing personally? Like, before you decided to have a business?

D: Well, I bought my juicer about a year and a half ago. When I was around 18, my mom started juicing at home. So I had moved out already but I would come by and visit at home.

So basically, the whole story on why I started by business is, because my mother was diagnosed with multiple sclerosis when I was 14. The doctors had her on pretty much every pill known to man. And she took a shot of Copaxone every day. She injected herself with that every day and it would leave abrasions on her skin. She took other medicines as well, went to the hospital twice a year, and when I was 18, she [accidentally] overdosed. She almost died.

And that was a huge turnaround for my mom. She realized that that's not the life she wants to live. She didn't want to be dependent on pharmaceutical drugs. So she started researching alternative therapies and medicines. She started eating super clean, and exercising, and juicing a ton. And eventually she became independent from all her medicines! She doesn't go to the hospital. In part of a year, she was off all her medicines. That was four or five years ago, and she hasn't been to the hospital since.

Danielle's mother provided a good role model to Danielle about taking control of your life and your decisions. She decided her prescribed path of medications wasn't working for her so she changed her approach.

Wow, that's amazing!

D: Yeah! That inspired me to want to work with food and work with proper nutrition. I think down the line, I might want to do something more medical or nutrition based. Seeing my mom, her whole life change, pretty much through juicing a ton. She lost weight and she gained energy. I have a 9-year-old brother who was about 5 at the time – and she just became an all-around better mother, better person, because she was getting so many nutrients at once. That's how juicing came into my life, and I was really inspired by my mom.

WOW! That is awesome! Oh my goodness!

D: She's actually coming out in a week so she'll be able to see the Farmers' Market. I'm super excited!

Cool! So where are you from originally?

D: I'm from Tampa, Florida.

So you're from the East Coast, too? [Laughs]

D: Yes! It's so different, it is crazy, between Florida and here!

I can imagine! When I was visiting Tracy, I was like, "This place is amazing! My hair! My hair dries in two seconds – and it stays straight!"

D: Yeah! In Florida, my hair is crazy! Here my hair is great, and I don't have to use products or anything! It's amazing! I'm really excited for my mom to experience this humidity.

Especially this time of year when it's so hot in Florida! So when did you start thinking about creating your own business doing juicing?

D: It was April of last year. A buddy and I were having lunch in Denver. There's another juice shop in Vail now but at that time it wasn't there. We were like, "There's no juice in Vail! This needs to happen! We should do this!"

We had a super slow start. We were in contact with this music festival, the YarmonyGrass Festival, at this place called Rancho in Bond, Colorado, which is about 45 minutes away from Vail. And they said, "We would love to have you guys come out and vend juice, if you want to!" And we said, "OK, sounds good!" So me and my friend Pat did that. We got our license for that event.

After that, I was like, "We should try to do the Vail Farmers' Market! It's really hard to get into, but let's just try!" So we got into the Farmers' Market, which is super exciting! We found out in October or November. In May or June, my partner at the time decided he didn't want to do it anymore. He has a Monday through Friday job; he's really serious about his career, and said with this there would be too much on his plate. So at first I was pretty bummed out. Then I was talking to some people, and they said, "You need to just do this for yourself!" I never really thought about that because Pat and I were partners in the whole thing. Then I was like, "OK, I will do this by myself." So I took his name off all of our licenses. It was a partnership and now it's an LLC. So then I started it myself.

When he and I did it together, we only did that one festival, and the licensing and stuff. I say I didn't really start doing much until the Farmers' Market because the festival was making a little tiny piece of what it is now, because it is so much work! June 21st was the first Farmers' Market, and that's when the ball got rolling!

I had no idea what to expect! I remember the first market; I was so nervous. People had been there for years, and they were all set up, and knew what they were doing. And I was like, "OK, I'm super nervous, but here it goes!" And I lucked out! My neighbors next to me – I don't know if you saw them, the goat cheese farmers? They are fantastic! They helped me set up my tent; my tent was confusing! It's really fun! Every week I feel more comfortable. I feel really comfortable at this point.

This summer has been the beginning and it's really fun! You emailing me – it was amazing to see that someone else wanted to talk about it. And then, actually, a couple of days ago I was contacted by a woman about Peak Women's Wellness, this big event with Women's health in Vail. And I'm going to be sampling juice there on Sunday. So that's really cool! And then today, Vail Daily emailed me about writing an article, so it was really crazy! Within three days, I heard from you, and the other people! That's just like really motivating for me. We're about halfway through market season.

I also have another job. I do a kids' camp and I'm a nanny. I babysit for kids whose parents are on vacation. It's really fun! In the winter, I ski with the kids a lot, and in the summer, we'll go hiking, or whatever the case may be. For instance, today at camp we went rafting. We try to do a lot of active babysitting so it is a lot of fun. Sometimes I need to tell myself, "Danielle, take a day off because you need one!" So Friday is my birthday, so I will take the whole day off.

I work with kids and it is nice because I can adjust my schedule how I want. Which is good because it leaves me a lot of time to do stuff with the juicing. If things get busy with the juicing, which I hope they do, I can cut back on babysitting because it is so flexible. That's one really nice thing about having the two. Of course, the juice is going to be first priority so I have room for that, which is great.

Danielle's ability to adjust her schedule is a great way for her to "tick"! If you can find a job that allows you some flexibility, it can be a good way to start pursuing what you want to do – what makes you tick - while still ensuring you have some stability and steady income.

So I'm really pushing it with kids and juice. So you know, I'm really worn down. So to have three people really interested in what I'm doing and giving me these opportunities, I'm like super motivated! It's always nice to hear from other people too.

You're going to be at Peak Women's Wellness?

D: Yes, I will email you a link. On Sunday, I'm going to be at a breakfast, and I will be talking about the juice, why juice is good for you, how it started, and giving samples out Sunday morning at the event before I go to the Farmers' Market. I've been excited about that because I get to attend the whole conference which normally would cost about $500 and I get to be a part of that! And then there was a Farm to Table Dinner on July 22nd that is hosted by the Farmers' Market to get local produce and meat, and I sampled juice there. And that's where I met the lady from the newspaper.

And I think networking is one of my favorite things. Vail, as you probably noticed, is very small and tight-knit. Unlike New York City, it is small, and it is easy to get out there, meet people, and talk with them.

Have you had any issues so far? I know you have just gotten started. Did you have to juggle anything in order to make the commitment to do the Farmers' Market?

D: Definitely. In fact, I cancelled a month-long trip to Europe. We had a climbing, hiking, and biking trip planned around Mont Blanc. And when I thought I had a partner at the time [for Main Squeeze], he was going to do the market while I was gone. No problem! And then he bailed on me. I was like, "OK, this is a lot! I have this trip that I've paid a lot for, what do I do?" It was a really crazy time for me…this was in June.

So my friend Susanna said she would take the market over for the month I'm gone. Perfect! And then I went and talked…there's a lady named Rayla [Kundolf]. She manages the Matches Gallery here in Vail. She's kind of like my mentor. She said, "Danielle, I don't think that going on the trip will be beneficial for your business. Even if your friend takes it over for a month. People want to see you, and you don't know what's going to happen." And I said, "OK, I think you're right."

So I cancelled the trip. And I was really glad. Well, when I did cancel, I had all these emotions; I felt like, "Did I do the right thing?" But at the end of the day, I'm really glad I did it because I think it would have been too much work for my friend to take on, because I have to make juice for 6 hours on Saturday night, then work at the market. At the end of the day, I'm glad I cancelled it. It was a really hard decision, but you have to make sacrifices sometimes.

On the weekends, a lot of my friends are going camping, on camping trips, and I just can't go. And that's fine with me, because I'm doing something I'm really passionate about. If it was just because I was working at Starbuck's and I couldn't go hiking with my friends, I would probably be pissed off about it. But I'm not because it's something that I'm excited to do!

One thing that's hard is finding employees who are reliable. It's harder than I ever imagined! At first, I had a friend helping me, and that was great. Then I talked with her a week later and I said, "It's Fourth of July next weekend and I just want to make sure that you are fully committed to juicing with me. Let's juice during the daytime so we can go watch fireworks that night." "OK, no problem, I'll be there!" So when July 4th rolls around, she texts me at 9 AM and said, "Hey, I'm not going to come! I'm going to go rafting!" And I was like, "Oh my gosh!" Because she's my friend, I'm not going to yell at anyone! So I ended up doing it myself that day!

So I put an ad on Craig's List. I said I needed someone to help me for a few hours on Saturdays. And then someone responded, but it was funny because it was someone I know. She works at Big Bear Bistro in Vail, which is a really good shop to go to. And she's like, "Hey Danielle! I got your number. Are you looking for someone to juice?" And I said, "Yeah, I am!" So it worked out perfectly because the owner of Big Bear, her name is Vidette, she's helping me because I am using her kitchen as a commissary for no charge, which is amazing, because they are [$400 per month] at other places. The only catch is that she needs to have an employee there with me when I'm juicing. I was thinking, "Hmm, I don't think any of your employees want to just sit there for 5 hours while I'm juicing and just watch me!" [Laughs] But it worked out to be really good because Anna, who is my employee, works at Big Bear. So we're juicing together at Big Bear, and she works there, so all the angles are covered! It is super stress relieving to have someone I can rely on. And she's always there at 6:30.

That was the hardest part was finding employees. It was pretty stressful until she came along! Because at the end of the day, I have to do it, whether someone is there or not!

Oh yeah! You're able to go to Big Bear – is that a grocery store?

D: No, it's a sandwich shop. It's right near the gondolas. It's a great place to grab a sandwich and salads, the whole nine! They close at 6 and we go there at 6:30 and we're there until about midnight. It's really funny because it is next door to a bar. So around 10, we start seeing all these people, all the drunk people, and we're like, "OK! It must be Saturday night!" [Laughs] So that's really funny!

Did you have an outline for your path? Or did you just take things as they went along?

D: Honestly no, I didn't really have any outline. When I got to the Farmers' Market…so, when I told you I was either going to cancel Europe or cancel the Farmers' Market, and my friend was like, "Danielle, you can't cancel the Farmers' Market, it is a really huge deal! It's so much exposure! It's awesome!" and I was like, "You're right." So then when I was accepted at the Farmers' Market, I just rolled with the punches.

I got licenses, which was another pain. You have to have labels…the labels have to say something specific on them. I got the bottles. Right now in my room, there are about 1,000 glass bottles!

[Laughs]

D: I know about juice, but I don't really know a lot about business. So I was a little bit intimidated. But at the end of the day, the guy who works at the health department was super nice. He was emailing me and helping me out. Everyone is really friendly and open, and no one is trying…no one wants you to fail, basically. My step-dad helped me. I had one of my friends draw the logo, another friend digitized it, and then my step-dad put it on my business cards and my labels.

Nice!

D: So it was really cool that they helped out. It's a huge thing. In Vail, people are really drawn to things looking good. So that was huge, their help was amazing!

I kind of just went with it. I made a plan for the juices. I knew which juices I liked. Then I realized I needed to write the recipes down for my employees! I can't just tell her, "Whip it up!" So one night I made the juices, got the menu, got them perfect, and then wrote that down. So I have that in my notebook. I could definitely be more organized! I have an Excel sheet and I have a lot of stuff just in a paper notebook.

It's all a learning process! There's so much to business; it's really crazy. It's really fun, learning. There are a lot of people who have advice for me and want to talk about it, especially since I am young. People really like that, and they are really nice and helpful. That is a huge thing.

That's awesome! So how did you come up with the name, Main Squeeze?

D: We were just brainstorming ideas, me and my buddy Pat who I started it with. I don't even really…we would just text back and forth all these different names. And then we said Main Squeeze, and then we said, yeah, that sounds right. And we asked a bunch of our friends, and a lot of our friends were like, "Yeah, we like that! That sounds good!" Because it is like you are squeezing an orange, and also "main squeeze" is the one you like the most.

The logo was hard. We played around with lots of different logos until we actually found the one we liked. My friend who designed it, he doesn't even like it! He said it's too crazy for a logo, but I like it, and everyone else likes it!

I like it!

D: Thanks! I think he's thinking of the bigger…like [for] a big company you would need a little cute logo, but for this, it is what it is. So we kind of just played around and brainstormed a lot. Our friends have been a big help. I have a really creative bunch of friends and they are helping with ideas. I'll go to my neighbor's house…Pat, my ex-partner, lives two doors down from me. I would say, "Come over and try the juice!" He's super great – there's no bad feelings about anything that happened. He comes and tries juices, which is really nice. He helps me try stuff, and we try to make new flavors. That's the really fun part. Playing with juices!

Do you have a favorite juice that you're not sure if people would like or not? Like you would say, "I love this, but I don't know if the public would be ready for this!"

D: Yeah! I love, love, love putting cilantro and jalapeno in my green juice, but it's a bit strong, so I haven't really put that one out. Also, I have one now, it's watermelon, lemon, mint, cucumber, and jalapeno. At first, I was like, "I don't know if people are going to like this." But people love it!

I feel like with the crazier ones people just need to try them and they will like it. There are definitely some…like if I am making juice for me, or say my friends who drink juice a lot, I will put garlic in it, and a bunch of ginger, and watercress. That's going more for health than for tasting good. But if I'm juicing for some of my friends who never juice, I'll push it back.

My boyfriend was sick with a sinus infection so I made him a juice that was carrot, horseradish, orange, lemon and cayenne. I was like, "This is not going to taste good at all!" But horseradish is so good for you when you are sick with a sinus infection. He was like, "All right, fine!" And he drank a bunch of it for a week, and he wasn't sick anymore! So that was good! But I warned him, "This is not for taste! This isn't how it is going to taste at the Market!"

[Laughs]

D: When you drink more juice, your taste buds start to adapt. When I make green juice for the market, I put about a third of an apple in each bottle. When I do green juice for myself, I don't add any apple. I try to eliminate as much sugar as I can. Not that it's a bad thing, but it's not the best thing. I'll notice a lot that people who are more into juice, they are all about the drink. The green one is my best seller, which, I was kind of surprised! A lot of people come up and say, "Which is the healthiest one? If I'm going to drink juice, I want to drink the healthiest one!" And that's the green one!

And then when I deliver…. that's what I'm working on for this winter. Right now, I'm trying to think of how I can keep the business going in the wintertime when the market season is over, which is October 4th. So I'm thinking of delivering to hotels and spas…I'm putting everything out there so I can think about it. When I do deliveries, because we delivered to this one lady who wanted ten a week, which was awesome, and she would tell me, "OK, I like it really spicy, I don't like celery," whatever, I can customize it more for deliveries. But when it comes to the market, I just want to do four general ones that I think aren't too strong. A lot of people love ginger, and I do too, but a lot of people don't want a huge ginger bite, so I have to keep it a nice medium.

Another hard thing is knowing how much to make because the shelf life is only 3 days. So that is the toughest thing for this business is the shelf life. I've been really lucky in almost selling out, and when I don't sell I just drink them because they are good until Tuesday. For July 4th, I sold 70, but last week, I sold 45. So I have to really gauge how much. Now that school has started, it's going to go down. I will probably make only 50 this week. And my first market, I had no idea! I said, "Let's make 100" because I had no idea. And then, it's amazing how each week gets easier. I can imagine people who have done this for five years probably have it done to a T!

It's huge market, and it's every Saturday, every Sunday. Saturday rolls around, and I'm like, "All right! This is a big work day!" But once I'm there juicing, it goes by really quick. You don't realize you're there for so long because you're talking and it just goes really fast.

I know you were inspired to do juicing. Was there anything you read in college, a book, a dream or idea, that was sort of a guideline?

D: Not really! I've actually been reading this one book. It wasn't what inspired me to do it, but it's really cool! It's called "Juice Alive," and it's full of all this information. On Sunday, I have to talk about juice, so I'm going to pull a lot from that book.

I really do wish in college I had studied nutrition. I studied international affairs which is not really anything I want to do anymore, but I feel like a lot of people are like that. I want to keep learning more about it. I would love to one day….if someone has cancer, I would love to design meals, meal plans for people who are sick and try to get them healthy. I remember when my Mom had MS, not one time did the doctor ask her, "What do you eat? What is your life like outside of the hospital?" The disconnect between the medical profession and nutrition is terrible. A lot of places, there is a connection, but it's not mainstream, and I feel like, "Why isn't this mainstream?" It's so evident that eating right makes you healthier.

If I ate a pizza or a Big Mac right now, I would feel terrible. I love ice cream, and whenever I eat ice cream, before I eat it, I'm like, "I know I'm going to have a stomachache in 10 minutes!" And then I eat the ice cream and I have a stomachache. And then I say, "OK, why am I doing this?" [Laughs] It's being aware. I feel like it is worth the little stomachache I know I will have, but I feel like a lot of people just aren't aware of our bodies. And we're disconnected to what we put inside. It's just common sense; what you put inside will determine if you feel good or bad. Who knows? Maybe one day my juice business can coincide with that.

There's some wellness centers in Edwards and in Vail. I want to connect with them and maybe see about going in there one day a week and shadowing someone. And I could see if they ever want to have me bring juice to their clients. So getting on the wellness side would be cool!
In about a week, my Mom comes, so the week after that, my schedule is going to be more relaxed, which is exciting. So that's when I'm going to start contacting all these wellness centers and really putting it out there. So when market season does end, I have some other things going. And it's kind of fun! I don't have a plan, and I don't really know what's next, but I know something is going to be next!

Yeah! That's awesome! So when you're talking about the disconnect between medicine and nutrition, how do you select what type of produce that you use for your juicing?

D: I did these based on what types of juices tasted the best and which ones I liked, and whether my friends like it or not. For example, the beet one is filled with antioxidants, so if someone comes to the juice stand…like this guy from Texas came a couple of days ago and asked what would be a good one for altitude [sickness]. Beets are full of antioxidants as well as beet greens so that would be the one for them [to counteract altitude sickness]. If someone comes to me feeling sick, or sometimes hungover since it is Sunday morning, the green one is the best. It's full of chlorophyll and full of all the vitamins that are in kale or spinach. If they tell me they are trying to lose weight and they are trying to speed up their metabolism, I recommend putting cayenne in the juice, or having the watermelon one with jalapeno.

I just try to read a lot about the different foods and how they can help you. If I'm making a juice for myself, like one I made yesterday…I felt like I had a cold coming on, but it's not going to come because I am going to fight it! I put [in] watercress, which is the most nutrient dense vegetable, but it is really little and bitter. So I put watercress and garlic in my drink which are amazing immune boosters. What I would also like to do is to get more knowledge of that because there's always more knowledge to have! And if someone came to the juice stand and asked, I would be able to tell them which one would be best for them. I kind of do that, but I want to be more of an expert. Or like when my boyfriend was sick, and I made him the horseradish juice, it was really cool because I wanted to help him fight a sinus infection off, so I did a bunch of research and figured out what's the best juice to make. So it's kind of like a science experiment, and you have all this stuff to play with! It's cool.

That is very cool! So you mentioned a lot of things that you like. Is there something that you like the best about what you do? Is it the people, or the things that you discover? Or is it something else?

D: I really think it's the people I'm meeting along this journey. I've been meeting some really incredible people who come by the market. Like at the Farm to Table dinner, I met really fantastic people who are so supportive.

And learning! I'm learning so much every week, and it is really cool. And I'm getting the opportunity to do events like the Women's wellness that I will do on Sunday. It's exciting when I do these events because I know in my head I am about to meet 100 people who all live in Vail. There's something positive that's going to come out of this, even if it is just good advice. Something will come out of me meeting all these people in my town. I think just people, I just love the people I've been meeting, and networking, and everyone's positivity has been really cool.

That's awesome! Now in hindsight, since you've been doing this for a few months, is there anything you would do differently?

D: That's a good question. I think maybe I would have hired another employee from day one, because at first, my first day, I said, "I'm going to make all the juice in the morning, because I really want the juice to be made fresh this morning." So that's a terrible idea because it takes so long to make! Having an employee to start with would have been a good thing. But other than that, I feel like I've been doing everything pretty well as far as I can see.

Oh yeah! Excellent! I know you have kind of addressed this, but I wanted to ask how you plan to keep your business running after growing season. You had mentioned doing deliveries. Is it your thought you will do deliveries in the winter, and then start selling at the Farmers' Market again in the spring?

D: Yes! So the Farmers' Market starts June 21st. I would like to do…if I can do some kind of delivery, that's why I want to figure it out and see if it is worth my time. I don't want to drive somewhere to drop off one bottle of juice, you know what I mean? So making deliveries…meet at the gondola…say I always deliver on Tuesdays and Thursdays, and if they have an 8 AM gondola meeting time, and ten people who are going to do that, that's the kind of thing I need to figure out. And the people I've been meeting for the Peak Women's Wellness, I have been talking with them on the phone, and I will talk with them this weekend. Once or twice a month, they have ladies come out for trips, and the trips focus on health and nutrition, so I want to get incorporated into that. So if I can get incorporated into events, into trips and things like that, I feel like pre-bought juice may be the best. If someone says, "We want to have 100 juices for our event," I think that would be the best. I'm going to figure out how I'm going to do that, and I'm really excited to brainstorm about that. Because there are a ton of possibilities out there, so I just have to find what I want to do.

And I think the really great thing, with the Market, I came in really open to anything, and I really didn't have too many expectations. I just wanted it to be positive. And it exceeded my expectations, which is awesome! And I didn't have crazy high hopes, because I didn't want to get my hopes shot down. But everything that I thought would happen is happening and even more, so that's really exciting.

And everything is so new, and sometimes overwhelming! For example, my produce order wasn't ready two weeks ago, and so I had to wait 30 minutes for them to get it together, and…it wasn't that frustrating, but I'm used to going in and out in like 5 minutes so that 30 minutes pushed everything behind! So it's just like little things. It's been really fun and a good learning experience. I definitely hope to do the Market again next year.

Oh awesome! So you said you go from 6:30 PM until midnight with the juicing…how much time do you spend each week working on Main Squeeze? That can include creating recipes, marketing, juicing, all that good stuff?

D: Let's see…I would say the recipes are already done and set so I don't have to worry about that too much. Twenty to twenty-five, I would say? We do five hours for the juicing – well, really, it can vary between five and seven hours making the juice, and with picking up the produce and cleaning the stuff, it can be about eight. And then the Farmers' Market, another 8-9 hours, so 17, and just like various things. Some weeks it will be more. Like this week, I'm going to be networking a lot this weekend at the event and speaking at the event. Maybe like 18-23 hours?

I feel like being in Vail, living here, gives me this energy I didn't have in Florida. If I have 4 hours, I'm going to go on a run or on a hike. There's not that much down time for me, which is OK. But it's worth it. And the biggest thing is balance with all the things in my life. And I'm getting a good hang of that. It takes time, but it's happening!

Oh good! As far as marketing is considered, I know you have your business card because I picked one up at the Market! And you have Facebook. You said you will be doing networking and talking about your company. Are there other ways that you are going to market or reach out to people?

D: I also have Instagram! Once the summer dies down, I'm going to go talk to people, like concierges at hotels, and have a lot of word of mouth. I think that's really huge in our valley is word of mouth. At the end of the day, everyone knows everyone; it's really crazy how that works!

The marketing…I don't have too much. With social media, I actually have a friend who is teaching a class at the library called Social Media for Small Business, so I'm going to go to that class. She's one of my best friends and I'm really excited that she's teaching this class because it could be really cool! I feel like, in this day and age, we have something that people didn't have five or ten years ago. People are on Facebook and Instagram, and people are on it…it's a bit of a concern, maybe a little bit too much. It's a free tool, so why not take advantage of it? I'm going to try to focus on being more active on Facebook and Instagram with the business. I've done a little but I could definitely do a lot more.

I'm excited about the newspaper article! They're going to come take pictures of me on Sunday, and then we're going to have the interview Monday afternoon. And then they're going to write the article on me. So I'm really excited about that! And that's what's cool about a small town. Everyone reads it every day. And the newspaper wants to write about you because everything is so small. That's what's been really encouraging about people contacting me to do all these things.

I really found throughout Danielle's comments that she had a real sense of community. Her friends and family and even the whole community in Vail provided help to her and a platform for her to be successful.

That's wonderful! Have you gotten any unusual comments while working at the Farmers' Market, or has anyone asked you a question where you said, "I have no idea!"

D: People have asked me how much sugar is in each bottle, and honestly I don't know. I guess I could measure it if I see how much sugar is in each carrot, and in kale. It would take a long time. People ask how many calories are in the juice and I don't know – it doesn't matter – it's all calories of pure goodness! I had someone ask me if the juice is gluten-free, which is really funny. I'm like, "No, um, there's no gluten in juice! If you have a gluten allergy, you'd know that!"

My first market, I was really nervous. I was like, "People are going to ask me all these questions!" And people really haven't been asking me crazy questions, which is cool. On Sunday, I'm a little nervous since I'll be speaking in front of 100 or so women! So I'm going to get a lot of questions. So I'm going to study tonight and get ready with a rough draft. I'm sure there will be many questions that I don't know. So I'll email you Monday and let you know if anything weird or different came up on Sunday after my speech!

That is kind of hard because you're trying to anticipate what they're going to ask, so it's good you have the juicing book as a reference. Yeah, that would be interesting to know where they go with their questions!

So who has been your best supporter as you started the business?

D: That's a really good question. My friends have all been really great. Not one specifically, but I have had a few different ones who have been great. There have been times…for example, about 3 weeks ago, I was invited on a rafting trip so I went. To my workers, I said, "Can you guys make juice tonight? Here's the full email. I'm going to go on this rafting trip; I'll be back Sunday morning." So I get back Sunday morning, and there were only 20 juices made! I was like, "Oh my God!" So there was some kind of miscommunication with them. So I was kind of freaking out! One of my friends came over, and she went to the Market, and took care of the Market while I made juice that morning! One of my other friends, we were on a road trip to California, and we stopped over in Salt Lake so I could pick up the bottles. And as I told you, one of my friends helped design the label.

A lot of my friends have ended up doing small things, and they probably don't realize how much they have helped me out. But it really does! And people buying juice, that's been huge. And Rayla, she really helped me out a lot when she told me I should stay, and I probably would have gone on my trip if she hadn't said that. I was thinking that a lot, but once you hear it out loud it is a little different, so I decided to stay.

Also my stepdad. From the beginning, he was helping me with the labels and the business cards. I had all these questions…I think my stepdad has really been the biggest help because in the beginning, I was a mess! There was so much stuff going on. He doesn't help me anymore because I don't need his help anymore, but definitely all of May and June we were emailing back and forth. I was emailing him the designs, and he was helping me get my labels to be approved, so he was definitely a huge help! Without him, it would have been pretty tricky.

I'm happy I have had a really great network of people around me and in my life to help me with this.

That's excellent! Whose paths do you admire? Do you have anyone who is your hero or role model?

D: I think that my Mom inspires me so much. She had me when she was 21, and I'm 22 on Friday. Seeing how much she's done, and in just such a short amount of time [after her MS diagnosis], how much she's improved herself and bettered herself. She was so sick, and now she is inspiring women in her church. Women come up to her all the time and say, "Rosie, I want to be healthier! Can you help me?" And sometimes she'll call me and she says, "I'm so overwhelmed! These ladies want me to help them – I'm not a doctor!"

And I think at the end of the day, my Mom is such a huge role model to me and I really wouldn't be doing anything I'm doing – juicing, even beyond the juice – without her. She's given me the independence all through my life that I feel like it really helps me do this. If all through college and in school if I had been babied and handed everything, I don't know if I would have been able and had the courage to take such a big risk with starting my own business. And it's really nice that I had her as someone to look up to as, "You can literally do anything you want. You just have to want to do it." That's the main thing.

Oh that's awesome! I have two more questions. First, what advice would you give to other people who want to follow their passion?

D: Find exactly what it is in that passion that you want to do. Say your passion is the outdoors. Find exactly what it is and then go do it. Don't listen to anything negative people have to say because there's always going to be people who are jealous, or have failed before and didn't try again. You might fail, but at the end of the day, you're always going to come up positive, even if your business doesn't succeed. Even if the juicing doesn't do anything in the winter, which I hope it does, what I've gained just from learning goes beyond anything I could have read in a textbook.

I would really tell anyone who wants to do what they're passionate about to do it because there's not enough people out there who are doing what they love. There are so many people that come home from work every day exhausted and they don't want to do anything, and they're unhappy. They're just doing something to make money. Of course, money is super important – I'm not going to say it's not. You need to have money to get things you like in life, but it's not everything. Even if what you're passionate about isn't going to make you a millionaire, if it will make you happy, that's really great!

Go with everything! A business plan is good, but my business is pretty small so it didn't have this crazy planned-out thing, and things just worked out. Things usually work out, so always explore your options.

Very cool! And last question…do you have a motto or words that you live by?

D: Really, just doing anything and everything that makes you happy while you can, and not waiting until tomorrow. Right now, at this point in my life, I don't have a house, I don't have kids. All I have is literally myself to take care of. This point in my life is the point in my life when I need to do anything I want to do because there is going to be a point when I can't work like, 70 hours a week, which I've been doing. Because I'll have responsibilities beyond just working one day. Just do everything – anything you want to do, just go for it and do it! Because one day the time won't be there.

Danielle, it has been so much fun talking with you! You have been so inspiring too!

***

     After the interview, I looked and saw the interview with Danielle in the Vail Daily. (http://www.vaildaily.com/news/17981858-113/vail-based-main-squeeze-juicery-blends-nutrition-taste) I was really impressed with Danielle and how she had tackled the hurdles to continue going.

     What impressed me too about Danielle was how she has built a really strong network of friends and colleagues. I realized that having a strong network can be as important – maybe more important – than having a business plan. If you have people who can support you and give advice – like Danielle's friends who taste juices with her, helped develop her artwork, etc. – then you will get honest feedback plus people who will ensure you keep it "real".

     After our interview in August 2015, Danielle continued selling Main Squeeze juices at the Farmers' Market until it closed for the season in early October. She said that her talk at the Peak Women's Wellness went well! She said she was pretty nervous but it worked out great. She spoke to women about the power of juicing, why she juices, and she provided samples. She said the experience also allowed her to attend the dinners and events that weekend too. She saw several of the ladies from Peak Women's Wellness at the Farmer's Market in following weeks.

Danielle's visit with her Mom went well, too. They hiked, rafted, and went camping in Moab and Danielle's Mom came to the market with Danielle on the Sunday of her visit. Danielle said it meant so much to the both of them.

One of Danielle's plans was derailed. She was going to sell her juices in a sandwich shop in town, but then the health department called and said that was actually against code. You cannot sell your juices to a business unless they are pasteurized.

Then after Danielle did some soul-searching over the fall months, she decided to pursue her education and get a degree in Naturopathic Medicine. She applied to a program and was accepted! She will not be doing the market in 2016 as some issues arose with the health dept. She said, "I think the most important thing is that I learned A LOT from starting the company and doing the market. I learned that in fact, I do not want to own a juice shop but I am more attracted to the health aspect of things and have actually been learning juice is not as healthy as we think. What I learned is that I want to pursue a career in Naturopathic Medicine (which I think I spoke with you about) and I am currently working for an ND. I will (hopefully) open up my own practice and start that business after med school. The most important lesson I may have taken out of all of this is that just because one business plan does not go as expected, this does not equal failure, but it can build up for continual growth."

She learned she does not want a storefront as that is "more business then I prefer to do. I realized what excites me most is the medicinal side of juicing (and food). I have my BA from FSU but I still need a few more pre requisite science courses before I can apply to the university to study Naturopathic medicine. So back to school this spring."

It was exciting to talk with Danielle during the time when she was figuring out what she loves to do and how best to apply it. It is interesting that she started with juicing but then realized the part she loves about it is helping people. Danielle's new goal is to own another business – she wants to own her own medical practice by the time she is 30. I have no doubt she will achieve this because she is doing what she loves and helping people to be healthy. Cheers!

Story 7: Denise Chaykun, Travel Planner: Building the Mystery

When Jerry and I decided to get married in 1999, we were honestly more excited about planning our honeymoon than about the wedding itself! Jerry had been into traveling before we met. I had never been overseas so I was delighted when he took me on a trip to Paris for my 30th birthday. We wanted to plan something really amazing for our honeymoon.

I discussed it with one of my very best and trusted friends, Eric. Eric is well-traveled and has been to a number of exotic places. I told Eric that when Jerry and I first met, we had a memorable discussion about driving on the Pacific Coast Highway in California, something that neither of us East Coasters had done but always dreamed about. Then I told Eric we were thinking about flying to California, renting a car, and taking two weeks to drive back across the country.

"You don't want to do that!" Eric said when I asked his advice. He thought it would be if Jerry and I flew to an island for our honeymoon. I started getting really bummed, thinking our cross country trip might be a bad idea. Jerry and I talked it over, and the more we discussed it, the more excited I got about our initial plans. We talked about the places we would stop if we drove: Yosemite, Las Vegas, and the Grand Canyon, for starters. We talked about driving down the old Mother Road, Route 66. The more we talked, and the more I thought about it, I realized that while driving cross country seemed like a trip from hell to Eric, to me and Jerry it suited us perfectly. Luckily Jerry and I decided to take the cross-country drive, having realized that it was the plan that was best for us. We still talk about how much fun our honeymoon was.

My story about Eric and I discussing my honeymoon plans illustrates how personal travel is to people. Supporting someone who is traveling could be one of the most demanding customer service jobs there are. When someone is on vacation, there are so many factors involved: the weather; the food; the accommodations, including sleeping in a strange place, where you are not used to the surroundings (the softness/hardness of the bed, the amount of light that comes in the window in the morning, the damn noisy neighbor in the room next door, the lack of coffee in the room, that weird smell); the sights (why is it the major attractions are always closed for repair when I go to visit?); your fellow travelers (the crying baby on the airplane, the man with the terrible body odor on the subway, the too-loud person at the table next to you); the forms of transportation, which may include auto, air and train (and various degrees of motion sickness). Many times we go on vacation to get out of our usual life and experience something different.

However, experiencing something different can be great but it can also be awful too! With all these factors that could go wrong, it's easy to see how being a travel agent could be quite daunting.

***

In my employment experiences, people beat the customer service drum all the time. Constantly in jobs and in business books I hear, "The customer always comes first!" In my previous job history, I've worked in positions that are commonly identified as being customer service jobs – as a waitress at Pizza Hut (at which I sucked, thank you very much), as a cashier at a number of retail places including a short stint at Hechinger's Hardware store (at which I rocked, people person that I am), as a salesperson at a number of retail places, including clothing stores like Britches and Laura Ashley (where I bought way too many lacy, frilly clothes in the 1980's), and as a gift wrapper at Kirkland's. While these examples are obviously hands-on jobs with helping others – you are either in the customer's face all the time or you're doing it wrong - the thing is that almost every job is a customer service job. If you work for someone doing something, the person for whom you are doing something is your customer. For example, you may work in accounting, tucked behind the scenes, never talking to anyone but your boss and your cubicle neighbor. But you are in fact working for a customer. While your customer may be nameless and faceless to you (and you may really prefer it that way), you are likely doing the accounting for someone who does face your customer. Patients are the customers at hospitals. Astronauts are working for the citizens of their countries, who are their customers. Even while I'm writing this book, I am ever aware that you, gentle reader, are my customer.

When I think about customer service, I often think about Maslow's Hierarchy of Needs[xiii]. I learned about this concept when I was studying for my Project Management Professional (PMP) certification. While working to understand people, Maslow discovered that people have a set of motivation systems unrelated to rewards or unconscious desires. Maslow found that people are driven to achieve certain needs. Once one need is fulfilled, a person seeks to fulfill the next one, and so on.

On the first level of the hierarchy, Physiological, people have some pretty basic needs. Basic needs usually include food, water, shelter and clothing. They can also include sanitation, education, and healthcare. The needs work up to the ultimate levels at the top of the pyramid, Esteem and Self-Actualization.

When studying for the Project Management Professional certification, what first stuck with me about Maslow's Hierarchy of Needs was that when it comes to work, people may not be motivated solely by material rewards such as money, perks and raises.

Hence the reason why some people who think all they want is a high-paying job find themselves making great money but hating life. They are not achieving the esteem they seek. And they are denying the passions that make them tick.

Second, it showed me as a manager of people that even if you think you are addressing all of your employees' needs, if just one of their basic needs is not addressed, you have a problem. An example is basic sanitation needs. If you work in an office, and say you run out of toilet paper in the restrooms, you have a problem. Sure, you can pay people plenty of money and tell them they are awesome, but if they have to get in their cars every day and drive around the corner to the gas station to relieve themselves, they are going to find another job! Say what you will about this but for me, the lesson learned is make sure to address the basic needs (including sanitation) or woe unto you!

Back to travel…coordinating travel combines the skills of addressing people's personal likes and dislikes, along with ensuring you satisfy Maslow's Hierarchy Level 1 (Physiology) and Level 2 (Safety). It can be a challenge. Just like my disagreement with Eric about the perfect honeymoon illustrates, one person's perfect trip could be another person's nightmare. You want to address the person's desire for self-actualization ("I can find my true self at the beach in St. Bart's!") but you also must address their basic needs ("What do you mean I have to go to an outhouse to pee? No way!") It takes a very organized person to pull off planning successful vacations.

As someone who has been yearning to tick for years, I have been an avid reader of "O", Oprah Winfrey's monthly magazine. To me, it's the best magazine out there. I love the inspiring articles, the advice, the book reviews, the fashion, the food, everything! I was reading "O" in June 2013 when they featured things that are unexpected.

> *"Hit up Magical Mystery Tours for a surprise vacation: After inquiring about your budgets, dates, and preference, an agent will craft a custom trip, giving you the itinerary within a week of your departure. Sure, you can scope the schedule in advance, but the company recommends waiting until you're at the airport or train station. Bon voyage! (magical-mystery-tours.com) – KATIE ARNOLD-RATLIFF"[xiv]*

The concept of Magical Mystery Tours made a large impression on me since Jerry and I love to travel. A major part of traveling involves planning. Planning is the exact opposite of spontaneity – you know what's going to happen. And yes, you do need to know what's going to happen so you can anticipate what you will need – bathing suit for the beach at Nags Head, umbrella for rainy Seattle, hiking boots for the Blue Ridge mountains, etc. But that can take some of the fun and sparkle out of life.

From the Magical Mystery Tours website: "Denise Chaykun, President of Magical Mystery Tours, started the business with her friend Stephanie Whitesel. She grew up outside of Philadelphia and likes to think that she has a proper appreciation for cheesesteaks and soft pretzels, but no Philadelphia attitude. She went to Bucknell University where she majored in psychology and history, yet she's spent most of her career working with political nonprofits. In addition to loving travel, she also is enthusiastic about photography, baking cupcakes, and Hello Kitty. Currently, her dream destinations are Australia, Russia, and just about everywhere else she hasn't been yet. And yes, she also likes the Beatles and fun surprises."[xv]

***

How much do we allow spontaneity into our lives? Do we plan ourselves to death? Do we plan everything as much as we can in an attempt to gain control over a very unpredictable life? After all, we don't know when there will be a traffic accident on the way home, or a layoff at work, or bad grades from your kids, or whatever multitude of little surprises await us. Even checking the mail, something that used to be fun ("mail away and in six weeks it will come in the mail" – oh, the delicious anticipation!) is now drudgery in the form of bills and impersonal junk.

So I found the Magical Mystery Tour concept to be delightful and refreshing! I remembered this story when I started writing this book. I just knew I wanted to meet the Denise, one of the women who started this amazing business!

I contacted Denise in April 2015. After playing phone tag unsuccessfully for months, I was starting to worry that Denise and I would never speak. Then in August 2015, I received an email from Denise. "Are you available today?" I was like, "YESSS!" So it was with excited anticipation that I wrote back to Denise. That afternoon, we spoke.

Denise was really interested in what I was doing, which makes sense since she is so customer-focused. She really got me revved up about her business and my book!

***

K: I am so excited that we can finally connect! Hooray!

D: Yes! I am so sorry it has taken this long! It has been a crazy summer, and I knew I needed to set aside a time when I could slow down and focus. So it has taken a little while, but I am so flattered that you want to chat!

No worries! It sounds like you have a lot going on between Magical Mystery Tours and getting married next month. That's a lot!

D: Exactly! The whole getting married thing is like having another job. Between that, and…I'm just not very good at staying still! Recently I have been busier than usual.

No worries! Well, I am just so excited to have a chance to talk with you.

D: So fill me in a little bit more…I know you are writing the book. Please tell me who you've spoken with and where you're going with it so I can make sure I'm going in the right direction.

Absolutely! So, what I've been doing is talking with people similar to yourself who have passion or decided something was really interesting to them, and they decided to take the leap and pursue that. And so the reason I'm calling my book "Tickers" is because it's people who are doing what makes them "tick," but I also lead into the fact that "ticker" is slang for your heart. You line up what you love to do with what you actually do.

D: I love it! That's really fun! I'm excited to read it already!

Thank you! It's been a blast! I've been interviewing a number of different people. So far, I have interviewed a gentleman who teaches software training but he does it in a really unusual way. He'll dress up like one of the members of KISS (the rock band) and presents everything in a really dynamic way.

D: That is unusual!

It's so effective! I took one of his seminars, and I learned way more in his seminar than I did in any of those boring, on-line, droning on and on kind of classes! I've interviewed a lady who has a B&B that is a cross between Willy Wonka and the Hard Rock Café. I interviewed a gentleman who taught at my school and he was a track and field coach. He ended up having issues with liver disease and had to have a liver transplant. And he ended up using all the same lessons he used to teach his students to guide himself through the whole process of his illness, transplant and recovery.

D: Oh wow!

So it is a number of different passions. I tell you what, Denise, I've wanted to do this, and I had no idea how fun it would be. I'm just having a blast!

D: Oh neat! It sounds like you have some amazing stories! And you've met so many different people!

I can totally see that Denise rocks at customer service! She was so supportive during our interview. She is someone who gets excited about what you're doing and makes you feel even better about it. I can tell she is great at understanding people and helping them find what they love to do.

Definitely! My ultimate goal is to inspire people – like, don't be afraid, get off the couch! If there is something you really love to do, life is short - get out there and do it!

D: I love that! So many people say that, like, "I just can't believe you started your own company, I can't believe you're doing this!" I'm so flattered when people say that, but at the same time, there's nothing special about us. It's a fine line. You do the right amount of research, and make sure you are taking a calculated risk, and that you know what the risks are, so you don't lose the house or get someone killed, or whatever!

[Laughs] Right!

D: You figure out…win or lose, you just have to try it. Really, I don't think there is that much to lose with people trying these tasks. I guess you might look like an idiot, or something, but that's not a big deal. I think that people just don't get it. Sure, it was really scary when we started, and people thought it was crazy. But I'd do it again, start another company or something. Sure, it can be scary and at times overwhelming, but really it's not hard. You just kind of do it, and work hard, get the right people, and it…it happens!

I think a lot of people are scared to take that leap. I don't know if it is fear of failure or…I'm not quite sure what it is, but…I think – not to get off on some philosophical bent, but people don't realize how short life is. You don't get a do-over! This is our lives; you know what I mean? Take your life and do what you love!

D: Yeah! Totally! I think there's something familiar about focusing on a path, and when you are starting your own company, or doing any of those things you just mentioned, you are kind of making your own path, and there is no one driving you to do it. And if you decide you're going to stay in bed all day, or you're really unwise with money or something, nothing is going to stop you. You don't have a boss telling you not to do that, or your mom telling you not to do that, or anything. You need a little discipline to get ahead.

Yeah, exactly! I wanted to ask you if you have always loved to travel. I saw on your website that between you and your business partner, Stephanie, that y'all have been to a number of different countries and states.

D: It's really fun! All the staff at Magical Mystery Tours…I mean, it's just amazing working with them. And they will suggest something, and I will say, "I never really thought of that."

Stephanie and I went to college together. And we were neighbors. She got the travel bug a little earlier than I did. I sort of had the traditional travels growing up, like family vacations, going to Disney World, things like that. But I didn't travel a ton growing up. And then Stephanie had been to China a few times but nothing crazy. She did a semester at sea while we were at college, and that just….that opened her whole world with that one. I actually didn't study abroad. At the time, I was like, "I don't know! It's overwhelming!"

For me, once I got out of school, I was working at a political think tank in DC, and I actually ended up traveling a ton. So for work, I pretty much ended up covering most of the US. At that point, when you're traveling all the time, and especially when you're in your early 20's and you're not paying for it, you realize, "Oh, it's not that hard to travel!" You get used to living out of a suitcase, and being in airports all the time! There was this combination of work travel, and then I realized you can pretty much go anywhere you want to if you are smart about it. So that's where my travel bug came from.

Cool! One of the things I do when I research for interviews is that I go out and read as much as I can on the Internet. So of course I looked at your website for Magical Mystery Tours! It sounds like you guys got started by planning a trip for a friend. Can you tell me about that?

D: I love that you did your research! [Laughs] I usually say the same things during interviews – how funny! Now I can find something different to talk about!

Yeah, so Stephanie and I were not starting out to start a company at all. I just had a good friend who was a lawyer and we were chatting, and he was talking about how busy he was. I was talking about travel with him, and I told him, "Well, you need a vacation!" And he kind of said – and we've all heard this a lot – "I just don't have time to plan it." So I love planning people's travel, so I said "Whatever!" This is a person who earned money, he wanted to go, so really there was nothing to stop him except, "I don't want to plan it." So he's just like, "OK!"

So we were kind of joking around about it, and I said, "Well, you know what – I'm going to plan this trip for you! I'm not going to tell you where you're going! I'm just going to plan it! Just give me your credit card! And tell me kind of what you want, and your budget!" He was just the right person for this. He was like, "OK, great!" He wanted something different, something new. So we just kind of went with it!

Looking back, we had no grand plans for this at all. It wasn't like we had all this pressure or anything. It was sort of like something you do on a whim. Throughout the process, something clicked. We realized there is something magical here.   This is something you like – you know you're going to like it. It's controlled – I mean, we're not going to send you to North Korea!

[Laughs] Right!

D: And once you're…once you're past eleven, there's not that many controlled surprises. There was something just really amazing about having something come up, and you know you're going to like it, but you don't know what it is! You can't research it, you can't plan for it, no matter how much you try! You go to work, and people know you're going on vacation, and they ask, "Where are you going?", and when you say, "I don't know!", it amuses people! Everybody loves a happy surprise! So it just kind of clicked.

I had planned trips on my own, but this made me a little nervous. I mean, my friend had just given me a couple of thousand dollars to play with, so I wanted to do a good job! So Stephanie and I were bouncing ideas off of each other.

So the trip went off fantastic! We sent him to San Francisco. That doesn't seem that exotic but he was an East Coast person who had never been to California, and he had an amazing time! I mean, the first time you do this, you're not going to send someone to somewhere crazy!

[Laughs] Right!

D: I don't know…there was just all this hype over this little trip to San Francisco! We had other friends get in touch with us and say, "I want to do this! You should plan more of these!" So we
just decided to open a company, and that's it!

Oh, that's awesome! So because of word of mouth, because you helped your friend with his trip, were you getting additional people asking you about it – is that how it happened?

D: Yeah! So more people were curious. It was one of those things where we were like, "There's something here." There was something here that we don't want to let die. We wanted to see where it goes. Unlike other people starting a company, ours is unique because you don't need an inventory, you don't need a storefront, you don't need to quit your day job to get this going. So there was a lot of research involved in finding out how the hotel and travel industry works, which was overwhelming at first, but it wasn't a hugely expensive process. Initially it was a lot of friends and family.

It's interesting to note that Denise isn't making something with her business but instead is doing something. Since she doesn't need to have a physical space like a storefront or "brick and mortar" location, starting her business was easier than it would be for someone who needs a physical location. She can follow her passion and help people from anywhere!

Our customers put an enormous amount of trust in us! They were handing over a significant amount of money and saying, "I don't know what you're going to do with this!" Early on, we were so fortunate to have friends and family who knew that we had our act together, that we were good travelers, and that they could trust us. And then initially, it was definitely word of mouth. It was friends, it was family. And then it was magical! Somebody we didn't know would hear about somebody's trip, and then we ended up getting publicity and we ended up blowing up from there. It was the perfect organic growth that we needed to work out the kinks in the process and figure out how to fix the things that friends and family were willing to put up with.

Right! How cool! So what part did social media play in that? I know y'all have a website now. Did you develop that after you started getting more word of mouth?

D: It's actually kind of boring. The process of getting a website up…it took us a while because we were finding a questionnaire, and finding how to talk about it. How to provide people with the right expectations and everything. We always want a trip to be more exciting than someone expects. So we had to figure out how to talk about it in a way that if you have $1500 to spend on a trip, sure! We can plan something great and you will have a lot of fun. But with that kind of budget, you're probably not going to be going to be spending two weeks in Thailand! [Laughs] Things like that! So we were figuring out information we would need to provide people to zero in on how they like to travel and what they would want. So we explain the applications, and what we do, and what we don't do. So that took a little time.

So we were super fortunate in that there's a lot of talk about travel, and people like to post it on Facebook and everywhere else. Early on, I think our best marketing tool has been our amazing travelers just talking about their trips, and talking about how much fun they've had! Just them building up the mystery to their friends, and then having other people guessing where they are going, and really pulling other people into the experience.

That's cool! I didn't think about that! I realized the person for whom you're planning the trip would be surprised, but I didn't think about the element of them telling their friends and family, and they're like, "Where are you going?" and you're like, "I don't know!"

D: Yeah!

And then they're like, "Let's figure out where you're going!"

D: People who are planning their honeymoon, it's crazy! A lot of them have fun with the buildup with their wedding guests. They'll have a "Guess Where" map so their guests can guess where they are going! The surprise is definitely beyond just the travelers. Again, everyone likes a fun surprise!

We're really careful ahead of time to make sure we have the right information. You want to be prepared. We are very particular about not letting things slip.

That's good.

D: I think lots of people love to get in on the guessing process. And that's really fun for us to watch!

That's very cool! While y'all were developing the business, and starting to arrange trips for friends and family, I assume that you and Stephanie were still working full-time jobs?

D: Yes. Well, I think…we're organized people. So organically we wanted to do it right. You always end up taking more risks early on. You don't have to learn slowly. And luckily we haven't had too many trip mess-ups. It's not like Day One someone handed us a million dollars and asked us to plan 100 trips. If they had, we would have made some huge mistakes!

Oh yeah!

D: So we definitely both had other things going on. Steph has had two kids since we started, and we have both had other things going on and have been very busy. We figured out how to grow in a way that we could bring in other travel planners and give other options to people. We certainly have room to grow.

We have had some media mentions, like Oprah, and we were in Men's Journal last month, so we've been really busy right now. We have people who can jump on a trip that are really capable and amazing, but it's not like we have people sitting at a desk 40 hours a week waiting for people to come in.

I realized that as a Ticker, and with the path Denise chose, she could control the size of her business. She's not looking to make it a 40-hour a week vocation. She has flexibility and can work a regular job at the same time as running Magical Mystery Tours.

Right!

D: I mean, we don't aspire to get to a place like that. We want people who have other things going on, people who are traveling all the time. And really we are a little bit different from the old travel agent home.

Right! And that makes sense. One of the reasons I ask is to inspire people...I think a lot of people are like, "Well, I can't quit my full-time job!" I'm thinking, you probably don't have to.

D: No! It's funny because I get a lot of questions about that. You know, I wouldn't do it differently. When I hear somebody who just quit their job, I really wonder...I guess they must have investors or something. I don't really get it. I wonder how crazy they are to really do it! I guess to each their own - whatever works for you. It has worked fine for us, and I would certainly recommend it [working full-time while developing your own business]. Again, I guess it just depends on the kind of business you have, and the hours you need. And all that. But this was the smart way for us to grow.

So how different is it working for yourself versus working for someone else?

D: [Laughs] Oh my gosh! It is just two different worlds! There are benefits to both. I think some people would want to work for themselves. If I am ever in a job that has benefit matching or pays for my cell phone, I appreciate it that much more. Working for yourself, everything is up to you! I think one of the biggest fears is that there is no guaranteed income. You could make nothing, or you could make a million dollars – it is all on the table. In the beginning, you are probably looking at nothing, or looking at putting the money you make into the company and not making anything. So it is hugely different. You have to be a long-time thinker. It makes you really think about working smart, and what are your options at the end of the day, and what the risks are. So that one is just...there is just no comparison!

Yeah! How does that figure into what makes you "tick"? In other words, because it is something that you are excited to do, how does that affect your everyday life?

D: Good question! I think the driving force for me at the end of the day is that we are planning people's vacations. Some people take five vacations a year, and it's just a vacation. But the people we're doing vacations for may be going on an anniversary trip that they've been saving up for for ten years, or planning a trip for people who are just recovering from cancer, or a family reunion – things like that. To me, people are trusting us with something hugely important to their life. And we have to do an amazing job. That's just all there is to it.

If there are times where we have to lose money on a trip or we find we are in way over our heads, it doesn't matter – it has to be great. We have given it our all to make it great. And when we know we've done a great trip, it is just so incredibly satisfying! And it depends on who you are or what you want– some people really love planning a trip – I think we're really helping people who work have better vacations than they otherwise would have done and that's a really special thing we get to do. And we can do that because people trust us, we've proved ourselves that we want to do this, so that's something that we can really seriously, and have to, love.

Oh that's cool! Were you ever afraid or hesitant to start your company?

D: Oh absolutely! You don't know where to start. I think….you're just trying to figure it out. "If I got sued, what would that look like?" And that's so totally boring to say, but you have to look at that. You have to ask yourself, "How am I going to make money on this? How does this industry work? Is it worth trying to make money on this?" It's really scary. And again, like I said before, we weren't risking <u>everything</u>. Mostly we looked at the time, and asked, "Am I going to get anything? Am I going to get anything out of this? Or could I be working 10 hours a week at McDonald's and be bringing home a lot more?"

Right!

D: So yeah, I think you have to be smart about it. And there were times when we asked ourselves, "What are we doing? Why are we doing this?" At least in part, we finally looked back and said, "OK, this is worth it."

It's really scary, and I guess for us, we had a lot of people who asked us, "What are you doing?", and "OK, you're a company that plans mystery trips. Why would somebody want that?" Or, "You're crazy!" or "Haven't you heard of the Internet? Travel agents don't exist anymore!" I mean, we're used to it now, but there's a point where if you're having a bad day, and you hear a lot of that, it gets discouraging and frustrating. All of it is kind of scary, but you take it on a day-by-day basis.

That was going to be my next question: How do you work through that? So you just kind of took it day-by-day?

D: Yeah. At the end of the day, it was knowing where we were going, and knowing it was OK. And if we didn't have investors pushing us early on, and I'm sure that some people do have that when they have a vision for their company. I think the hardest thing is...for Stephanie and me, to be on the same page, and getting together, figuring out where we're going. It's hard! I think if it's not hard, someone is not pulling their weight, or something! Yeah, I don't have any easy answers for that one.

[Laughs] That's OK! So once you realized that you wanted to start this company, did you create an outline? Or did it just organically happen?

D: We sort of toyed with it, and outlined our plans. It was a lot of trial and error, and examination.

Gotcha.

D: I know some people do great at having a business plan and securing that, and honestly we did not do that.

Yeah! And you know what's funny...most of the people I've been talking to did not have a plan.

D: I love it! I very much am a planner, but on this one...I can see the value in writing a plan, and once a week meeting and reviewing it. But all our effort was in action and we were sort of planning things as we went. I don't know, maybe next time!

[Laughs] So what do you like best about your path? Is it the people? Or is it things that you discover? Or is it something else?

D: Being able to be part of all of these different peoples' different trips, different experiences, and seeing it through their eyes...it is so different from my trips or what I would have done. And to just see the love and the joy it brings them! It's really fun!

And no matter how much you travel there are always more things you want to do and more things you want to see. So we get a little bit of experiencing different sights or experience a different vacation. I mean, obviously we're not there! That is just amazing, and really fun!

So do a lot of people send you pictures and videos?

D: They do! You know, early on, we would freak out because we would know someone was going on a trip but we would hear nothing! And we would just be beside ourselves! And now we realize, when you go on vacation, the first thing you do isn't necessarily to report back to your travel agent!

[Laughs]

D: And there's nothing wrong with that. Lots of people have amazing trips, and just don't check back, and that's fine. But we always make sure to let people know we want to hear how a trip went. I would say about 50% of our clients send us pictures or videos. We've had people send us videos of them opening their package and their reactions. And we've had people who send us a picture every day saying, "We went to the Vatican today, and we're going to go to this place tomorrow, and we've been eating pizza!" And we just love that! On our end, we have gone through every aspect of this trip – where they're going to be, what they'll love. And it's great when they actually go through it and have this experience. So we just love, love doing that!
Of course, we always want to hear about favorites or things we can do differently. So no matter what, like anybody in our lives, if someone goes on vacation, we want to know, "What did you like? What was this like? What didn't you like? What was confusing?" Because we always want to make it better.

That's so cool! I imagine with planning surprise trips, you've probably gotten some unusual questions. What are some of the strangest questions you've gotten?

D: Oh my gosh! Well, travel planning is really personal. It is interesting the things people tell you, you get to hear a lot of things like, "I'm afraid of spiders!" or "I'm allergic to…" you name it. And all that is fine, because we want to hear it.

We've had people try to get us to hire prostitutes for them. People will try to have drugs delivered to them.

OMG! Really, people?

Oh my gosh!

D: I'm like, "No, you go figure that out! But no….no, we're not touching that one!"

[Laughs]

D: It's very odd! But you just think of all the different things that people want when they are traveling! We sort of see a mix of it. Everybody thinks of their own vacations and what they like or want, or wouldn't want. And for us it is devising, "You name it…", "We want this," or getting them to name what they want for their vacation.

Even, and this part isn't really fun, but we'll have people say, "I can't wait to go to this country" or "I can't walk more than X amount," or "I think I might be pregnant by the time we go so I can't go snowboarding!" And we're just like, "OK! We'll work with that." So yeah, you name it, we've heard it!

Oh that's funny! Who has been your biggest supporter as you've been working to develop Magical Mystery Tours?

D: Honestly, I think it's our travelers! When you see…there are certain people who just kind of click with the idea of a mystery trip. And they're coming back for more trips is amazing to us. Just knowing that they found us and they want more of us is really cool. They tell their friends; they are brand ambassadors for us! They are always Facebooking about their experiences and their travels, and why other people should do this. And just knowing that they come back and travel with us again is really, really encouraging and fun.

That's so cool! Now I know on your website, it says you and Stephanie met in 2000. But I don't see when you guys actually started Magical Mystery Tours, unless I blipped over that.

D: Oh that's funny! We should have that out there somewhere out there. I'm glad you mentioned that! We have turned 5 years old, so it would be 2010.

Woo hoo! That's awesome. You said that you have gotten some repeat travelers. People have liked their vacation, so they said, "Oh, do it again! Plan another one for us!"

D: Yes, exactly! There are people who kind of let us plan a little vacation for starters, maybe like a long weekend, and they then love it. So then they are like, "OK! Go all out! Plan something big."

While we love to plan mystery trips, we do plan regular trips for you to take. "I want to go to France!"

Oh, OK!

D: And we're happy to do that too! It's fun, and we like that. We'll have people who will do a mystery trip, and then they're like, "Oh my gosh! That was amazing! It was amazing not to have to worry about everything! It was amazing to have someone else figure out where I wanted to stay!" So they have been coming back to us for that, and that's great. The more we work with people, the more we understand what they want in a vacation, what's really fun for them. The more we work with somebody, I think, the better the trip we plan. That's really nice, too.

That makes sense. So when you're planning a trip for somebody, you're planning not just the location but the airfare, or train tickets – I guess it depends on how far they're going – and their hotel...

D: Yeah, almost everybody goes on a plane. We've had a couple of trips we planned by train for people going to a major East Coast city which seems pretty easy. So we've had a couple like that. But the majority are flights.

For every mystery trip, we're sending you there, we're planning your accommodations. People decide if they want us to plan extra activities for them. We charge a flat fee so we're never doing, like, "Well, every second of your day is planned." What usually...whether it is getting you reservations for something at the destination where you are at your location, or guided tours, or whatever. And we always ask when someone goes on a trip whether they want us to plan a lot of activities, or if they just want to wing it.

Right! So you kind of get a feel for that...probably through the questionnaires?

D: Yeah. So in the questionnaires, we specifically say, "Do you want us to plan any activities for you?" And people do want that, then we ask them to fill out another questionnaire: "What do you like?" "What kind of budget are we talking?" Really with all of this stuff, when you see there are different types of travel we have, people want such different things. It's really critical for us to understand, because travel to you might mean you're staying at the Ritz Carlton, and you have a massage, or you just want to see a new place, and you're going to wing it, and you don't know the language that you don't speak a word of – but you're totally cool with that!

We can tell by how people answer the questions...some people don't want to fill out the survey, or they'll say, "Oh, whatever, just plan it - I'm sure we'll love it!" And it's like, "Unh-uh! You need to tell us how you travel!" I mean, even with the hotel...there is nothing wrong with wanting the Ritz, and there is nothing wrong with wanting a hostel, but there are very few people who are comfortable with either! If you wanted a hostel and I book you the Ritz, you're going to be furious.

True!

D: So we interview people really well so we know how they like to travel and we accommodate that.

That makes sense! Is there anyone whose path you admire? Do you have a current hero or role model?

D: That's a good one! I just love super travelers- I just love travel bloggers. I love reading that stuff! Every time there is an article, and a person has been on vacation for two years, I love that stuff! I wish that could be me! I love it! I want to know everything they did, what they loved, what didn't work.

And entrepreneurs in general are so fun for me! I'm interested in the others like the people you have interviewed…how they do it and why they do it. I think the more you figure out this stuff the more you realize that everybody who's succeeded has made huge mistakes and probably no matter how successful they've been has been in the situation where they're like, "I have no idea what I'm doing!" "I'm pretty sure I'm failing" and "I've made a huge mistake!" I love hearing that because then I feel so much better about myself!

Being with like-minded people while you are on your journey is so helpful! I felt better about what I was doing with writing "Tickers" when I spoke with Denise. It wasn't just that she was so enthusiastic, it was that she and I could compare notes and discuss how we felt along the way. Having a common kinship is encouraging and makes you feel like you are on the right path. It could be that we are creating a network of Tickers!

I'm with you! It's so fascinating to hear…because everybody has…a lot of people have things in common but everybody seems to take a little bit of a different path so it is interesting to find out. That's what has made writing this book so much fun!

D: Yeah! I can imagine.

What sort of advice would you give to other people who want to follow their passion?

D: I think that knowing that it is going to be full with ups and downs. I mean, it is so much fun to plan vacations, but at the same time, a good chunk of my time is spent on doing accounting, and taxes, and freaking out because we don't have the right type of insurance. It's kind of knowing your strengths and what you're bad at. Right now, I'm a lousy marketer, and that is a hole we need to work on. Really, I just know I'm not going to be good at that.

I think you just have to be realistic about a lot of this stuff. You have to be willing to deal with the sticky, nasty, awful stuff and then hope that you're doing enough of the fun stuff that it all balances out!

Yeah! Oh cool. So is there anything that you've had to give up in pursuit of this passion?

D: Well, I feel like it is the perfect excuse to travel more! I can go anywhere, and it is tax-deductible!

I think it is more….you kind of put your reputation on the line when you do something like this. You feel like you need to justify that you're doing this crazy thing to people who have known you forever and ask, "What are they doing? That's just nuts! What a waste of time and money!" So I think it's that you're putting your reputation on the line and you are dedicating a lot of yourself to it. Not every job but with a lot of jobs, you know going into it you're going to get a paycheck.

And with your personal life, it's always weighing on you. A call will come in to me at 9:30 AM that there's a couple who can't catch their flight. And immediately my Sunday morning is turned upside down, worried that these people aren't catching their flight. I'm worrying, and I know that if they have a problem, and I'm not solving it, that's my fault. And that's not OK. You take a lot of responsibility and liability on yourself. And it's, it's not bad, but it can be scary, and it weighs on you.

Yeah, that makes sense. Do you have a motto, or words that you live by? Something that inspires you?

D: Ooh…I think to me, there is surprise. There is something so magical about being surprised! And we're just constantly learning more and more that there's something there, there's something magic, and we want there to be more of that!

That's awesome! Now, I first learned about y'all because I've been a subscriber to "O" Magazine, and I remember it was one of the issues that was talking about surprises in your life. And I remember your company – honest to goodness, I was

absolutely delighted! I thought that is the coolest thing I've ever heard of! What kind of publicity did you get out of being mentioned in O?

D: Oh, well thank you! We've been mentioned in Men's Health too. The thing that was amazing was that we didn't know we were going to be mentioned in Oprah magazine! We had somebody set up a trip, and they said, "We saw you in Oprah!" And I called Stephanie, and I'm like, "Oh, this person is crazy! Like, there's somebody who thought they saw us on Oprah!" And then another one calls up, and I think, "Something's up!" So I asked someone, "Can you buy me an Oprah magazine?" We couldn't find it at first, and none of us were subscribers. So we had to go searching on newsstands.

So it has been amazing! I find Oprah magazine readers to be fun, happy and adventurous people. We still have people call, about once a week, who say they saw us in "O" Magazine. It's been amazing for business. And it is a nice boost of confidence that people are tracking us.

I think it is funny that y'all were surprised by it, and that y'all didn't realize the article was going to come out that way! That's kind of interesting.

D: Yeah, that's funny! It was a good surprise for us! Actually, it was a good opportunity, and initially it was exhilarating. But then there was an immediate rush. And then we were like, "How do we capitalize on this? How do we change our marketing?" It was so wonderful…for the first few days, and then we were like, "What do we do about this?" You get this initial rush of clients, and they're not going to wait for you to get back, they're not going to wait for you to make changes on your website. It was a good but overwhelming surprise.

My last question to you is, since you shared that you are getting married: Are you going to plan your own honeymoon, or are you going to let friends of yours plan it for you?

D: [Laughs] Well, I hope this is an obvious answer, but we are absolutely leaving on a Mystery Honeymoon! Actually, Stephanie is the maid of honor, and it's really…I told her, "You are planning half this wedding already!" So we are passing my honeymoon off to Alicia, who is our next most senior travel planner. And Stephanie is planning everything else! So Alicia is off and running with this. And it's killing me! I am so excited! I keep asking my fiancé, "So, where do you think we're going?" So we keep speculating, and I keep saying, "No, it couldn't be this place because…" He said, "You need to calm down! Everything is going to be great!" So that is sort of my favorite topic right now!

Aw, that is awesome! Well, that was all the questions that I have! Thank you so much! I really appreciate it. And good luck with everything! And your upcoming wedding – I'm very excited for you!

D: Oh thank you Kim! Well, keep me updated on the book! We would be more than happy to help publicize it!

Definitely!

***

I was so excited that I finally got to catch up with Denise! Being a traveler myself, I was initially intrigued by Magical Mystery Tours because it spoke to my sense of adventure. Booking a trip and not knowing where you are going? It seemed like something that would be impossible to do but Denise and Stephanie had found a practical way – through extensive questionnaires – to make it a reality.

What hadn't occurred to me was that part of the success of her vacations for others was the ability for people's friends and families to get caught up in the fun. They could guess and speculate about where they could go.

Another connection between Magical Mystery Tours and following your path to become a Ticker is the willingness to step into the unknown and give up some control. The Tickers with whom I have spoken overwhelmingly did not know where they were planning to go or what they would do. They had to take a leap of faith and follow a path knowing what they like and don't like but not knowing exactly what that path held for them. Creative endeavors are like a trip to an unknown place. To follow your heart's path, you take with you your skills, talents, love and passion, but you may not know when you'll need to use them. Maybe like me you are a writer, and you know you are interested in talking with people who are passionate about what they do, but you don't know how to approach it. You take the leap of faith and start talking with like-minded people and see where the journey takes you.

Would you go on a Magical Mystery Tour? I asked myself that question after my interview with Denise. My husband and I have been fortunate to be able to travel to places we have always wanted to go…places we considered to be on our "bucket list" of locations to see before we die. Traveling the world, the most exotic locales we've been to were Easter Island and Bhutan (next to Nepal). Before we visited those places, we did extensive research. We planned what we wanted to see (a plane ride over Mount Everest! A tour of the Moai (Easter Island heads)!) When I think about putting the responsibility of planning one of our trips in the hands of someone else, it is a little scary. But I would totally be willing to give Magical Mystery Tours a try! Knowing that they would screen extensively to know me and Jerry's likes and dislikes, I feel they would plan a fantastic vacation for us that we would love. Denise gave me the confidence to feel that way.

I was dying to know where Denise and her husband ended up on their honeymoon! When I followed up with her later, she said, "We ended up in the French Riviera--it was fantastic! Thanks for asking. Best wishes on finishing the book--can't wait to read it." I can't wait to share my experiences with Denise, my fellow Ticker, and compare notes as we both walk our respective journeys. And I am adding to my bucket list to book a trip for Jerry and me with Magical Mystery Tours, of course!

Story 8: Shiva Pillai, Business Analyst: Happy Re-Birthday

In 2014, after I heard about the layoffs from my company, I started really examining my career. Where was I going? After seventeen years, I had worked my way from being a desktop supporter to becoming a manager. It had been an interesting journey. But I had gone about as far as I could go. I was bored, stagnant. While I loved my co-workers and even my bosses, I felt unfulfilled.

After floating my résumé, I was offered a position at a health services company, Magellan. I had two friends who worked there and was excited that I was offered a job as a Project Manager. This was the opportunity I didn't have at ManTech. I knew I wouldn't advance unless I left. So I made the hard decision to leave my friends at ManTech, and joined Magellan.

I loved being a project manager but it was not easy. First I was assigned to one project. The people in charge of the project were unwilling to relinquish their control, however. I was supposed to manage the software releases but the main players kept me out of the loop. For the first few months, I was really freaked out. I worried that I had made the wrong decision by changing jobs. I feared that I would be fired. On a short vacation to Disney with my friend, Tara, I burst into tears. Tara calmed me down and I spoke with my wonderful manager, Tammy. She assured me everything would be OK.

I was then assigned to be the project manager for the data warehouse team. The data warehouse team consisted of a dynamic team of business analysts, developers, and administrators. The change could not have been better! Instead of being shunned, I was directly involved in all of the project planning. I led the bi-weekly meetings, I stayed on top of the schedule, and I interacted with all of the members of the data warehousing team. Every member of the team was excited about ensuring the project went well.

It was there that I had the good fortune to meet and work with Shiva Pillai. He was one of the business analysts who received requests from the data users and "translated" them into the requirements for the developers to follow. When I started with the data warehousing team, I knew very little about data warehousing itself. Shiva pulled me aside and drew a diagram on the whiteboard. Immediately after he explained it, I grasped the concept on which my team was working. Shiva broke down the info into easy-to-understand pieces. He could flawlessly jump from talking with me (a non-techie) to the rest of the team (in gory technical detail).

But I was impressed by more than Shiva's communication skills. Shiva was so passionate when talking about data warehousing that he made me really excited about it, too. I so wanted to understand what Shiva and the rest of the team were doing that I bought a book on data warehousing and started teaching myself the concepts.

With over fifteen years of experience in client server and web portals across several platforms, Shiva is an outstanding Lead Business Analyst. His experience includes working with data supporting credit cards, installment loans, mortgages, banking and health care. Shiva has extensive experience in data warehousing life cycle and data marts with exceptional analytical and reporting skills. But his greatest strength lies in his ability to connect with people.

***

Later I found out that in addition to working in IT, Shiva owns several restaurants, too. How did he find the time? I became friends with Shiva and found I could rely on him to help me out on the job. I really wanted to know his story and how he became so passionate about both IT and business. I could tell he was a Ticker.

Shiva and I met for lunch at Q Barbecue where we enjoyed some ribs. Later we realized that trying to talk and eat ribs at the same time was a challenge! We persevered, and I had a really amazing interview with Shiva.

***

K: I really want to talk with you because you are passionate about what you do. And my goal is really to inspire other people to follow their passion. I always want other people to try to be the best they can be. And I think if you follow what motivates you, or what you really like to do, I think that makes a huge difference.

So I know you because we work together, but I don't know much about what brought you to where you are. You're originally from India, is that correct? Born and raised?

S: Yes, I am from India. India down south is my family. My father…my grandfather was a farmer. So my grandfather, we came to the city. My father also got into the city world. So I cannot say that my father grew up in the city, but he grew up in the country. He slowly moved over for business, for occupation into the city so that's where we were born and we were raised, and all that.

Business pretty much runs in our blood itself because we've been doing it for multiple generations. When I was with my father, the family tradition, right? You always need to respect that structure, and you just have to go with that structure whether it is right or wrong; they're not ready for a change. All that was there. So I was a big fighter of that. I said, "I cannot do this. I want to see the benefits of what I am doing."

Even from the get-go, interacting with people, I like to make…when I interact with people, I like to make them happy, no matter what it is. In whatever form it is. If it's a teenager, yeah, I comment about their dress, I comment about their beauty, no negative comments, so they feel happy. And if it is about business, if it is a customer, then I want them to feel good that I'm giving them the utmost importance as a customer.

So then my father had some beliefs, I'm just going to go over one example. My father has a sentiment of, if the first person comes in your store….we had a retail outlet where we had all the garments. And if the first person comes in and says, "I want to return something." He feels that, "Why am I getting this return customer? Why am I not getting a new customer at the very beginning of the day?" So he considers that as a bad omen. The way I consider that is, "That customer didn't leave you. That customer is giving you one more opportunity to satisfy that person. So why don't we try to make that customer very happy so she or he can tell ten other people?" So that is how I see that. We had differences there.

Differences began bubbling up. I felt compelled to do what my Dad wants me to do. But at one point I told him, "That's not what I'm going to do. I'm going to step out of the family." And I stepped out. I was the first person in my family who stepped out of the family tree, and I said, "I'm going to go out on my own, and I'm going to do what I feel like doing."

Oh wow!

S: So that was a great move. I came out to a new city. And I promised my Dad I will not continue in that business. That's when I picked up IT. That is the reason I came abroad, because if I was there in India, I need to represent my family tree. And anywhere I go, weddings or anywhere I go, parties, they would see me as my Dad's son, that's how they would see, with the family tree, right?

I didn't want to be the representative. I wanted an identity of my own. I said, "OK, I'm going to go behind what I feel and believe." So first my goal was to stay independent, then I came out to the US, after coming to IT.

Coming back to the passion thing…I was a developer. I was doing what Choudary [another member of the data warehouse team] is doing today, developing reports. And I didn't feel happy about it. Because I was always behind the scenes. I always like to interact with people. I always get clarification or give clarification. That's because I just like talking, and if I made sense, to them, and they say in a crowd, if they say, "This guy identifies with me well and I am able to clarify things with him," I like that.

Oh cool!

S: And I make every attempt to do it. Whether it is going to the countryside, and we'll talk about that, too. So I worked slowly, I changed my skill set, to saying, "I want to become a BA [business analyst]" so I could have traction with customers. So if they're happy, and they say, "Shiva is making me happy," then I feel good about it.

Mmm-hmm! [With a mouth full of ribs]

S: And I also feel that if I am solving someone's problem, even if it is a personal problem…and that's one of the reasons why I asked you what is happening with [your] job, too…because…not to be nosy, but I just want to get involved and then say, "What can I contribute that…am I making a difference?" Because that's what I'm passionate about.

The other thing that I'm passionate about is my business.

Yeah, I wanted to ask you about that, too.

S: In spite of me working in IT, I wanted to open the business [restaurant]. Today, the business is in a situation that it is above and beyond what I can make in IT. But initially when I started off, it would have been about 1/3 what I make in IT. So at that time itself, I said, "I'm going to set aside some time just for focusing on the business."

There was a lot of struggle in that too. Opening a restaurant…usually you have a lot of struggle in anything but for me, because I didn't have the immigration status, there were limitations on what I could do and what I couldn't do. I faced new challenges, different challenges that a small business person wouldn't face in America. So I faced that. I overcame one right after the other. Because I didn't give up on that passion for the very same reason.

The same reason is I like interacting with people. This retail outlet, that gives my life a renewal, a purpose, because that's what I used to do with garments and now with food. Making sure that they are happy.

Let me back up a little bit. And also let you eat! [Laughs] You said that your grandfather was a farmer, and that your father moved to the city. Now was your father following in your grandfather's footsteps in becoming a farmer, and he decided to go into business for himself? How did that happen?

S: No, my father was not a farmer at all. My grandfather made a decision that, "I'm doing farming, but why don't you do something else?" He had the money but he wanted the right folks. So my grandfather put his brother as a guardian to start off things and said, "OK, all my sons, put everybody together, work on this!" He was the one who found the money.

OK, so your grandfather was supportive.

S: Yeah.

Was your father happy with that? Do you know if that was something he wanted to do?

S: I don't know…I've never had that…when you're in the family tree, you are raised in such a way that after 10-11 years old, you are raised with the mindset that, "You are going to do this." You are not raised with the mindset that you can do what you want to do.

Interesting!

S: That is not the mindset at all in India. And within the family tree, there are strict rules which are established. So in comparison with my daughter, my daughter tells me, "Dad, I know you have a passion for business, but what if I don't like business?" So I told her, "Whether you like it or not, I am going to teach you the tools to make money and buy a business. But it's up to you what you want to do. I'm giving you this as a backup plan. So tomorrow, because I know the ins and outs of it and I've been there, so I can educate you well. I will transition that knowledge to you. Please take the time to understand that knowledge."

But she likes animals. She likes animals a lot. What I told her was, "Don't graduate going into medicine or law school just because you can make more money. Do what makes you happy in life. If you end up working in a pet store and that brings you happiness, go pursue that as a career. And whatever backup that I'm giving you, use that as an extra tool to make money."

Shiva's statement about his daughter made me think back to my interview with Samantha Martin and her love of animals!

Right!

S: Get behind your passion. If your heart says to do something…see, I can use my brain to work in the IT field. But my heart, it puts all the effort into my business. So I told her, "Do whatever your heart tells you to do. Choose a career with that, because that's pretty much your passion."
Because there is a difference between the heart and the brain. The brain will tell you, "If I become an attorney, I'm going to make more money. If I go to med school, I'm going to make money." But if your heart tells you, "[I want to work] with the animals", or [if you want to] stay with the animals, and do something, even if it is charity, go do that, if it brings you happiness!

Right!

S: Because you're going to be happy every single day. Don't just live to work, but work so you can live better.

So how did you get to that point? It sounds like, in your family, that wasn't the message you got from your father, that you were expected to go into the family business.

S: That's right.

So do you have a lot of brothers and sisters?

S: I have one older brother, and one younger brother. Both of them just follow instructions. Even if my Dad says, "Why are you talking on the phone?" they would get up and stop talking. My younger brother does this all the time.

Oh my gosh! Wow! Did you always grow up thinking, "I want to do my own thing!" What sparked it in you to say, "No, I want to listen to me!"

S: Two things. I always look for my own identity. People in the store, they would come in and ask, "Is Shiva here? Can Shiva do this?" Some customers would leave if Shiva is not there, too.

Really? Wow!

S: Because I don't talk to them as a customer. Even with the business users in IT, I don't talk to them about work only. If they have a country accent, I will talk with them about moonshine. [Laughs]

I'll talk with them about guns, common hobbies. I will make sure I establish a good relationship. For example, with the business owners, [our manager] gets nervous and wants to make sure we have a good relationship. I have discussions with them for 14 minutes, and they want to fly me there just so I can ride on their horses and shoot their guns! But we will label it a requirements meeting!

[Laughs]

S: I like to establish that relationship. That's what I kept doing. Part of when you establish that relationship, you feel more towards your passion and your own identity. When you don't, when that gets suppressed by any means, you automatically become a rebel. And I...I wouldn't say I was a rebel. I used to go out, sit by myself and literally cry. Literally cry. For many, many months. Because I'm not able to do what I want to do, I'm forced to do what my Dad wants to do. It came to a point where I said, "It's too much. I have to step out."

Because my Dad was a rich person. Whatever lifestyle I'm having today, I had that with my Dad from my childhood.

Oh wow.

S: So with the house, car, anything, any luxury I've established in the US here. I don't think me or my generation needed to work at all for our basic living because it had already been set up. Leaving that and coming out is a big move. Because when you leave the family like that, you are declaring, "I don't need anything from the family chain" and they can cut everything off. That's what happened in my case. All my wealth, everything else, got cut.

You were just literally walking away from everything. Oh my goodness! Was there a specific point in time where you remember saying, "Nope, this is it!" Or was it just kind of building up?

S: It was from 1996 to 1999. In 1999, when I celebrated my 24th birthday, I said, "That's my last birthday in this house." That night, I left the house.

So you moved to another city?

S: I moved to another city. That night, I moved to another city, and I said, "That's my last!" Until my 24th birthday, birthdays were a big deal to me. I have to wear new outfit, I have to cut a cake, I have to celebrate. I stopped celebrating my birthday after that.

Really?

S: Just because I wanted to remember that day and how it impacted my life. And I said, "I'm not celebrating my birthday anymore." Now, after all that, after 15 years, my 40th birthday I celebrated in America. And I felt that I regained some of those things, whatever comfort that I had with my Dad I regained. So my 40th birthday I celebrated because it is a milestone birthday too.

Did I have all the ducks in a row when I came out from under my Dad? No. I was literally on the street. I couldn't eat for three times a day.

Oh no!

S: I couldn't. I had very low budget on me, so what I do is morning and afternoon…morning I skipped all my breakfast, not because I wanted to but because I didn't have the money, and I didn't tell this to my parents until about 6 or 8 months. And then the sixth month, or eighth month, after I came out, my Mom came to know about it, and she started supplying funds to me. And then I became rich immediately! I was able to eat healthy, again, or at least eat! I maintained a cell phone after my Mom helped me. Obviously my Dad must have known about it, but they chose…it was hard for them too, me leaving, so they kept it to themselves. But that six months' period, I kind of determined, "I've come to the bottom of the ship. I'm going to climb up from here. It's a fresh start for me. So let me put in the seeds that I want to put in." Everything was gone, so I decided at that time I wanted to do what I like to do.

They always had preferences between kids, too. My Dad does, always. I said, "I will not have any preference between my kids. They are equal. I love them equally." Yes, there will be attitude differences between the kids, but anything that I give them is going to be equal. Despite if I am angry with a kid, I'm not going to deprive them of anything. I will give to them equally. These are some pain points and driving factors that kept me doing what I wanted to do.

We came here…it's all because of the way I interact. I used to have good communication, I went to a good school.

Where did you go to school?

S: I went to a private school. And in India, it's not uncommon, it's common that everybody goes to private school. I went to the Hill Stations. Usually when you go to private school it's local, but the Hill Stations where it was separate. It's like an 8-9 hour drive. It's like from New York you go to Boston.

I stayed in the boarding school. That way, I started living independently. The communication that I had, I always went to English-medium schools. Speaking English clearly, that helped me. I could set the expectation very clearly, and say, "This is what I'm looking for, this is what I know." So that communication helped me a lot. I started by climbing up, little by little.

So was it when you were at the boarding school when you started getting interested in IT? Did you do a lot of stuff with computers then? What was your exposure with computers at that point?

S: IT – nothing! After I stepped out of my house, it was 1999. Everybody was worried about the Year 2000 problem, Y2K problem.

Yeah!

S: So everybody was talking about IT. So I went to the open market and said, "What can I do?" Everybody said, "IT." What do I know about IT? I know nothing in IT! So I said, "OK, let me see what this IT is."

My friend was running an internet browsing center. I went and asked him, "I know you have Internet but does Hotmail and Yahoo work on your Internet?" That was the question I asked him. So I didn't know anything about Internet, I didn't know anything about IT. That was my knowledge in IT. So he said, "I have Internet, which means that you can log into anything you want." So I was thinking Hotmail was different, Internet was different. That was in 1999 when I came out.

I went and joined a course, and learned AS/400 [mid-range computer systems], which was the first thing I learned. And there was a company recruiting from the US for AS/400, so I joined the company in India. They sent me over to the US. So I came…there were branches in India and there were branches over here as well. So I got recruited at that company in India and I got sent to one of their offshore companies. They brought me over here. I worked for that company for a year, because there is a bond for that company that you have to work for them for a year, and after that, I had free will. And 365 days was enough, with my talkativeness, I had enough people who said, "Hey, come over! We can get you in. We'll get you sponsored!" So I got sponsored and continued to stay from then on.

I loved it when the other day you told the story about the…what was it, like 24 principles? Some number of things you needed to know? And you had memorized the one you really needed to know? Tell me that story again because I thought that was really cool.

S: When I joined my first [IT] job, because I know I am passionate about talking, and I know I can articulate very clearly, that is my strength. Everybody needs to identify their strength and weakness, and that is my strength. So when I studied in Pentafour, and joined the first company for [IT] work, I had another colleague who was working there. He knew a lot about AS/400. For example, if there are 20 subjects we need to know, he would probably know all of them.

But [could] he communicate? No, he could not communicate. On the flip side with me, of the 20 [subjects], I learned only one! So I didn't learn more than that. But I said, "I'm going to market myself with this one. So anything they ask me, I'm going to talk to this one and say, 'If I'm able to master this one, I think I can pick up the others.'" I can articulate in a way that you can understand. And that is my selling point.

They interviewed 33 people and they didn't want to include me because my manager knows that technically I am not that good. But he said, because people are interviewing from the US and they are not understanding the Indian accent. So maybe they were nervous? Maybe [the other candidates] had not spoken English that well before? So then it came to my turn to be interviewed; I understood them very clearly. So my manager said, "I don't have anyone to interview. I am ashamed to send you but I am going to send you because none of them got selected."

I went in and the interview started, the US guys started asking a lot of questions. So I was able to understand, and I was able to answer them back. For them, they figure, "Rather than a person who knows 20 answers but cannot communicate back to us, this guy knows one and he's able to tell one." And I said, "Given the opportunity, I will learn the other ones too." They said, "Put him on the flight! He's selected!" And that's how I came to the US. So I came only because of my communication and the passion that I had.

I'm not shy to talk to anybody. You put me with a stranger, I'm not shy. One good example: my daughter calls me Magic. So she had planned to go for her birthday party with her friend to Kings' Dominion [an amusement park], and all of a sudden her friend's Mom called and said she bailed out, she cannot come. So my daughter was worried, texting back and forth, and having a moody face. So I went to her, and I said, "What's happening? You have four or five friends lined up." And she said, "No, this girl I really wanted. I wanted [her] to come but it looks like her Dad is working, her Mom doesn't want to come," all of that.

I said, "Give me Mom's number." And I'm talking with my daughter's friend's Mom for the first time. I said, "Give me Mom's number," and my daughter gave it to me, and ran upstairs. So I was talking, and by the time my daughter came downstairs, she had her bag also with her. I told her, "I made it happen. They are going to come." "I know that already, Dad! I knew that when I gave you the phone number. That's why I packed my bags and came down!" So she was confident in me, "I know you will do your Magic!"

So you talked her into it?

S: I talked her into it, I talked her husband into it! And if I talked with her for another 10 minutes, she also might have packed up her bags and come with us!

[Laughs]

S: Because I was saying, "Hey, I'm a parent, and I'm going!" I told her, "I will go to King's Dominion with a bunch of 11 year olds!"

You're a brave man! [Laughs]

S: I went with them, and if I had continued talking with her Mom, I'm sure she would have said, "Let me come also and keep you company." I convinced her. She said, "It is a good thing you are going with the kids. The least I can do is send my daughter."

What does it take for you to have the courage to come out and make your own path, and not following the way everybody else expects?

S: In your mind, you are thinking of asking, "Did you already have a backup, or did you have something in mind for making the decision?"

Mmm-hmm!

S: "How did you make that bold decision for coming out [from under his father's rules]?"

Yeah, yeah.

S: At that point, it is only what your heart says to do. You have already given up on everybody, and I had given up on my Dad. Because I had been shedding tears for a long time. I asked my Mom, and my Mom gave me the wrong answer. My older brother didn't help me out. So it was only me and my heart.

So my heart forced me to say, "Do what you like to do. And don't do it because somebody wants you to do, somebody wants you to be something – don't be that." But did I know I would be successful at that time? Even now, I would not call myself successful. Compared to that stage and now? Yes, I am much more successful in America right now. Did I know? I didn't know anything. I didn't know if I would eat three times a day. I didn't know where the money was going to come. I didn't have any preparation. It was just, "I'm going to follow what my heart says to do. And I'm not going to follow instructions. And if I'm going to be a rebel, let me be a rebel." But now they are saying, "That is one good thing you did. You stood up, you broke the family law."

Yeah.

S: And after I came in, my younger brother came after 5 years, and my older brother came after 3 years.

Oh really? So they came to the United States, too?

S: My older brother is in Singapore, and my younger brother is in Hong Kong.

Oh my goodness!

S: So they were also criticizing me for taking this bold move, but then they saw the benefits.
Even if I need to buy anything for my wife after marriage, right, I would still have to have gotten approval from my Dad.

Oh wow!

S: Because you don't have the money. You're sitting in a family tree. They give you pocket money; they call it pocket money. They give you a monthly fixed salary. And the food and accommodations, and your outfit, everything is free because it's from our own store. So my Dad would say, "OK, I've directed all the money for this and only so much you get." So if my wife wants to get a flat screen TV, or my wife wants another sari for a function, I would have to go ask my Dad to do that. And I didn't want to do that from the get-go. That's where my independence came into the picture, too. I wanted my wife to ask me, I wanted to be the final judge of this. I wanted my wife, or my girl, to say, "I'm asking my man, and my man makes the decision."

I always fought with my Dad with that. I said, "You will not be the man for my wife! My wife is not going to respect you because you are the ultimate permission person." She needs to come to me, and we need to make a decision together whether it is right for us. And once we've both decided, we will work together to get that, and not get permission from somebody else.

That was one strong factor that I always had about my marriage life too. Once I came out, I met my wife. Mine was not a traditional marriage.

So you didn't get um…an arranged marriage?

S: My wife is from a different state. My wife is totally from a different state. We speak two different languages!

Get out of town!

S: No seriously! I speak Tamil, and she has no clue what Tamilians are. It would be like you married an Italian, and there is no relation. It's not like Canada. Italians…they have a total different language, a total different culture. I used to converse with her in the same English, the same communication I used to impress her. And I didn't even know her language, and she didn't know my language.

She came to my state. She was studying. She was doing her MSA in genetics. She happens to come to the same browsing center that my friend owned. And I used to do some part-time help at my friend's browsing center, and that's how I got to know her, and then we started dating.

And that's how y'all met! That's a trip!

S: We started dating, and I proposed to her very quickly.

Aw!

S: I think probably in the first two months. I said, "I like you a lot, and I'd like to marry you, but I cannot spend a lot of money going around." So when we would go to friendly parties or go outside to eat food, she would actually hand-deliver the money to pay the bill before we entered the restaurant. Because man needs to pay the bill – that's the culture there. That's the culture I grew up.

Right!

S: That's when the pizza trend was. I didn't always like pizza – I felt like it didn't fill you up. Now I like pizza, but back then I liked to eat Indian food. Pizza I didn't like – it didn't fill up your stomach. And it was too costly. At that time, she was my date or girlfriend but now she is my wife - "I'm going to pay for all of y'all, and you are eating this lousy pizza, and it is going to cost me thousands of rupees, and I'm not going to pay for it!" So shamelessly…first of all, I'm finding money to feed myself, I'm already begging then, but this was after six months, and my Mom started feeding me again…I still didn't want to just treat out my Mom's money for everyone. So I told my girlfriend, "You give me the money, and I will put it in front of everyone that I am paying the bill!" So I did that many times and I am not ashamed of that.

She had only given me gifts. I had not given her any gifts. Only after we came to the US did I start giving her gifts. The best gift I could do was, "I love you." I could get a greeting card for her. That's all I could afford! She believed in me. And that was a shock to my Dad, too.

So when my family asked me, I said, "Anyway, I am out of the family culture. You're cutting all the money flow, the income to me. So why should I marry the girl that you tell me?" We didn't get to choose the girl. Like my brother saw his wife on the day of the engagement. My Dad introduced them and said, "This is the girl! You're getting engaged! Now go ahead and put the ring!"

My friend Rajeshwari, I remember talking with her. She had an arranged marriage. Her parents said, "What are you looking for in a husband?" And she said, "I want someone who is taller than I am!" That must have been so different for y'all to meet and date and fall in love versus being in an arranged marriage.

S: Same thing I asked my Dad. When he asked me, "What do you want?" I'm dark-skinned, dark as in not black but dark brown – just for the record [Laughs] I said, "I need someone who is fair colored, fair complexion. That's my only requirement." That's all I asked for. I want somebody who is good-looking and fair. So that's the only request.

My older brother's wife is very fair, but their family is very poor. So my Dad said, "Maybe that's a bad decision that I did. So Shiva, I'm going to make sure that the fair complexion, I'm not going to go with that [criteria] alone. I'm going to make sure they have enough money, enough status." So the fair complexion was actually the fifth criteria, my criteria. My Dad had four other criteria before mine. Like the caste needs to be the same. When I say caste, I mean religion, religion and caste, it's the same. They need to be fairly distant, like not related; they need to have enough money and status. Then if the girl has the complexion, it's an added benefit. If it suits the first four, then they would select a girl like that. So it was not there on their list.

I was a rebel there too. I did as a kind of…I usually show off to people and say, "I did it to challenge my Dad and do it," but that's not the whole intention. I wanted a true identity for me, and I wanted my wife to say I'm the man, not my Dad. People say it is rebellion. Now it is common. I said, "As long as I can create confidence in her that she can rely on me," that's what I wanted. She did rely on me, and we are doing a lot better than what I promised. If we were living in India, it would have been different.

Now going to the previous question. Courage…you don't need to have any support or any backup plan to make a big move like that. All you need is your heart. Keep strong of your heart. As I told you, I did not have money to eat three times a day but still I made the decision. Which means, I was a beggar on the street. Literally. If someone feeds me, I would eat. I stuck to my heart and said, "I'm going to do this." And I was able to come out of it. People hearing this, they shouldn't think, "Oh, there was some support here and there. He had a backup." Nothing! Zero. That's one.

Second, you will face a lot of humiliation. For example, after I came out from my Dad, even if I go out for weddings, my older brother would come park his car. It could be a BMW or a Lancer or a Ford – Ford is a big deal in India – they could come in this car. But I will just have my motorcycle with me. And they could buy dress, garments, for every occasion. But I could not afford that because that would be fifty percent of my salary. So I stopped going to those weddings. Because they would look at me as a family member, and now that I'm disconnected, I don't get the same money and import from them. So I told my wife, "We have to sacrifice all of this." And that was also another driver that I came over to the US. I wanted to stay away from that environment.

If I knew I would be successful like this in India, if I could have made the same money in India, I would have stayed back in India. Just to show off, and say, "I was able to make this!"

[Laughs]

S: Unfortunately, my Dad has only seen when I opened the business, but he has not come in and seen all of this. But my Mom has, all my relatives have come here and they've seen what I've accomplished. Building two restaurants here.

What made you decide to build the restaurants?

S: That's the passion I have in business. And IT was not keeping me happy at all. Even today, the project that we are working in, if I'm not in the position of BA [business analyst] where I'm able to help customers, I will quit the job. Even with my previous director, I told the same thing. I like to do this. And if I see any difficulty doing this, I'm not here for the money. I will put my resignation right across. I won't have a second thought.

Today, my IT salary is only a third of what I make in my business. And I get good pay, very good - I'm one of the best paid candidates in the IT world because I converted my contracting dollars into the full-time job. If you rewind fifteen years back, I didn't have any business, and even when I built my business plan, that was only going to generate maybe one fourth of what I make in my IT. That's because I have the passion for business. I have to somehow make this work.

Working on it now…it's been eight years. Very successful - I opened another restaurant too and I will open maybe two or three more. Because I have the passion in business, I kept to it, and kept to it. With customers also, in the business, there are others of my friends also who have opened restaurants that closed. The reason is my motto is, by opening a restaurant, everybody thinks, "Oh, I need to have the best chef and then you will succeed in business!" That's not my formula.

So I do not promise the best taste at my restaurant. I do not. I tell my cooks, "Just be consistent in what you're doing." That is all. It's not rocket science to be consistent, but just give me the consistent taste. I will go talk to my customers and make sure that they are happy with this consistent food. So I don't have a chef that you can label and say, "Wow, this is a great chef!" I don't have that.

So I apply the same principle to my business too. Saying that I am passionate to talk with all of my customers. So I make my customers happy when they come in, I talk to them. I feel that they are the most important, and only because of them I'm able to run the business, which is true.

Yeah, yeah, yeah!

S: So my concept and my business is three things: Cleanliness and ambience – so when people come inside, the ambience has to be good, it has to be clean, it shouldn't be nasty. Second thing is customer service. So these are two things. Sixty-six percent goes in here. Like thirty-three percent on my cleanliness and ambience, and thirty-three percent on my customer service. Thirty-three percent on giving consistent food. Not giving the best best taste food. Consistent food. I'm not here to give you the best taste. Because you are used to your mother's food, and you will always say, "My Mom makes better than this." So I cannot meet…if I could see one person saying, "Oh, this tastes better than what my Mom makes," I've not heard that statement before! Everyone says their mother is the best cook! The tongue gets used to it.

Yeah!

S: So again there I use my strength, which is talk to customers, make them feel important, that because of them, this business happens, and answer their questions. Even now, for issues, they have an option of reaching to the manager even if they are not there in the store. Every store has an assistant manager, but if the general manager is not available, they're not going to call you. But in my store, I put up a notice saying that, "If you need immediate attention and want the manager on the phone, talk to the employee." And the employee has to put me on the phone so I can talk to the customer.

Oh, that's cool!

S: So I have not mentioned what day, time, nothing. Because that's only because of service. Again, that's again, heartfully I feel that the first customer who came to make a return, I want to make him happy. Same thing I'm doing it even today.

Oh, that's awesome!

S: Get behind your passion, and you will be successful.

So it sounds like you didn't really have an outline, like a path you knew you would follow. Like, "I'm leaving home, and I'm going to do XYZ…"

S: I only knew when I get on the Greyhound bus, I'm going to go to DC. Where am I going to stay in DC, who I'm going to meet in DC, what I'm going to do in DC, I knew nothing. And what I'm going to eat in DC, I don't know, and I don't have the money.

So when you came to the US, you came to DC?

S: This I'm saying in India. I'm using the analogy. I'm talking about when I moved to another city.

I got it. So what are the names of your restaurants?

S: India Pastry House is one, and I have another restaurant called Cholla's and Kebob Biryani.

And which one is in Charlotte?

S: Charlotte, it's Cholla's, which we have there. And Pastry House is the one I have here.

OK!

And Kebob Biryani is in Richmond, in the Short Pump area.

OK! How did you raise funds in order to start the restaurants?

S: Me and my manager at work. Same like you, he was my project manager. He was impressed with the same passion that I have. Trust me when I say this – you got me to this interview [for this book], he got me to a discussion where he said, "Shiva, let's join and open a business together!" He saw me that much passionate about business.

That's awesome!

S: I kept talking about it, the same way I talk to you, also. The same way, fifteen years back, I talked with him, too. We were always having multiple chats about that session. And one…I think in 2005 and 2006 we were always talking about it, and in 2007 he said, "I'll provide the funding." We needed only about $100-150k to open the business.

Yeah?

S: But once we started the business, we realized that we wanted at least $400,000 to go on with the business, and it was not there in the business plan. So again, that's where I started networking with people. So we introduced a concept. And everybody who gave me the money, they did not give me the money thinking I was going to be successful. They came back and told me. So how I generated money was we had the plan, we went and shared the plan with them, and they would give us the money, and the plan was we give them ten percent. Ten percent is a whole lot.

Yeah!

S: OK? That is what we give you minimum. And if you like to be a partner, you can become a partner eventually. So these are all the investors I'm talking about. But they were not just behind the ten percent alone. Because when my partner goes and talks to anybody with the same offer, he was not able to sign them up.

Hmm.

S: But when I talked to them, anybody will ask, "How are you going to run the business? What's your background? What do you feel is the most important thing in a business?" They all came back to me and said, "We didn't give you the money because you are going to make money out of it or we believe you're going to make money out of it. We know that our money is safe, you will give us the principal back. But it was purely the way you presented it. We saw it and knew, whether or not this guy is going to be successful or not, he's passionate about what he wants to do. He's not going to cheat us. He's going to do what he says he's going to do." And that is what was the driving factor for them to give the money. So it helped me – everywhere, it helped me.

Oh wow, that's awesome!

S: Sometimes I'm to the point. I might be point blank, straight up in people's face. But that has helped me a lot. In a way, when we deal with money, we deal in black and white. When we deal with friends and regular conversations, we need some ease. But I'm black and white everywhere. So when I deal with the money topic, it's very clear. They say, "Yeah, you can put money on him!" Within my friends, when we do the betting, they say, "Let's give the money to Shiva!" The reason they give the money to Shiva is that I'm going to be the judge – I'm not going to take anybody's side because money is involved.

Right! You make yourself impartial, basically.

S: Yeah. But investors I got like that. The second restaurant I opened with the profits from the first restaurant. So only the first restaurant was very hard. They asked me for three things. They asked me, "Have you done business before in the US?" I said no. "Do you have a citizenship here, or a green card?" My answer was no. The small business administration would not guarantee the loan if you don't have a green card, if all you have is a visa, they are not going to guarantee you a loan. And the third thing is, "Have you done the restaurant business before?" The answer was no. All the three questions, all the banks, told no. That was demotivating for me, but I said, "I am not giving up. I'm still going to try." So we reached out to personal investors, and we gave them some documentation in writing that we will pay them.

Yeah!

S: And that's when it all worked out well.

Oh, that's awesome!

S: And now, this restaurant cost me about $450k, and the new restaurant is a 300 seat restaurant that cost me close to $500k.

Wow!

S: And the Kebob Biryani cost me about $360 grand. So put together, it's about 1.3 million that we generate. If I rewind [the restaurant chain] Chipotle, when – I forgot his name – but when he had the first four stores, and before approaching McDonald's, he reached out to his friends and well-wishers. And he was only able to generate 1.8 million. That's all he was able to generate. But McDonald's saw the fire in him, saw the passion in him. And first invested about 30-40 million. They brought them to Wall Street. McD did all of that because McD is a big player.

They're huge, yes!

S: And after a few years, people turned. So I'm not comparing myself on that level but I think generating 1.3 million is a big deal.

Yeah!

S: To me, it's a no-man's land. I didn't have any friends, I don't have any family, even now. But friends, they pretty much become family eventually. So it's tough for us. And I was persistent about it and was able to create something.

That's awesome! That's amazing.

S: Thank you.

This is very cool! So in hindsight, would you have done anything differently? Or would you have done everything the way you have done it now?

S: I usually don't regret what I do. Whether it comes from the business, or whether it is the position I came out of from my Dad's. I made decisions before, and I don't regret for any decisions whatsoever. Because I know we cannot make the right decisions all the time. At that particular time, that was all the knowledge I had to make that decision. So I believe in me. I'm not going to complain on me, saying, "Shiva, you could have done better." The only thing I would feel bad about is if I was rude to anybody or made anybody upset. Then I would think that maybe I should have done something different so I did not offend the person. I do that sometimes. Not sometimes. I do that quite often. My threshold is minimal.

[Laughs]

S: The first time, I tell them. The second time, it goes a little stronger. The third time, I'm like, "Why the hell are you not doing it?" So it becomes rude!

Your diplomacy goes out the window!

S: I have no diplomacy! [Laughs] I have no diplomacy! I'm a straight forward person. I'm an Indian Bubba.

[Laughs]

S: Even for this lunch that you have given me, I will not think one bit that I have wasted one minute. End of the day, I seriously don't know how this is going to impact you, how this interview is going to impact you. But all throughout this conversation, I feel happy that somebody was listening to me. I'm happy with this. This is what keeps me going.

I thought Shiva's point was very interesting. How many people would be willing to spend time talking with someone else and not know what the outcome would be? How many people would be willing to talk with someone else just because they were happy to have the conversation, and not know what would come out of it?

[Laughs] That's awesome!

S: I talk with people, that makes them happy. I feel that they are happy. I don't know if it is really useful not useful, I don't know. But that is the passion that I have. That keeps me going in everything. At work, business users want to talk with Shiva, I'm happy with that. I'm giving answers to them, I make them happy. You as my project manager, my business customers, they want to talk to me. So I think this one underlying thing of…talk to people, be passionate, that's pretty much goes in every direction. It diversifies into every element. Without that, I don't think I can survive or be successful.

That's awesome.

S: I'm giving good answers?

[Laughs] You're giving awesome answers!

S: They're from my heart, not from my brain! [Laughs]

I remember you said your wife and your daughter work at your restaurant. How does that work? Does that work pretty well?

S: Again, I wanted my daughter to get into business. I'm not going to make the mistake that my Dad did and forcing her into it. It's her choice. She can do what she needs. Even with her marriage, she can do what she needs. I'm not going to cuss her; I'm always going to love her. I told her that clearly. She's going to get whatever money she needs from family support. I'm not going to deprive her of that, too. I'm good to my wife too. Even if we were to get separated, which would never happen. But even if that happened, whatever needs to go, needs to go.

I'm always thinking that the business knowledge should be transitioned. [At the restaurants] the POS [point-of-sale] system recently transitioned. All the [purchase orders] in the queue are done through iPads. So I started looking…my POS system was just a regular computer and a screen. So I started looking for iPad POS systems. Because kids always play these games in the house, "I'll cook for you, I'll serve you." So I put this program in the POS. My son and daughter, they love to come and serve me. They'll say, "What else do you need, sir? The kitchen is open." [Laughs] He's bringing everything. Mom is going to serve me.

So we play this in the family, always. The thought came, "Why can't I use this iPad as a POS system?" The kids are familiar with the touch screen and the iPad. So I introduced the POS, I installed the software, and I told my kids, "Just score it up in the POS." And they got used to it, and they became really familiar with it.

Cool!

S: And I told my daughter, "Why don't you make a training manual?" And she made a one-page training manual. She didn't know it was all going to be real. And then one fine day, I said, "OK, let's go to the store. Let's go and get started." They said, "This is all for real?" And I said, "Yeah, it's all for real!"

[Laughs]

S: So I did go, and trained two of my employees. So the motivation for [the kids] was…see they don't know the POS, but they know the iPad. They know cell phones. So I put in the software there and said, "While you're using this game" – they play all these video games, some complicated games that we cannot get into our brains on the iPad – they were good at it. So she put in the training manual when she was eleven. And she started in my store when she was thirteen.

Wow, that's awesome!

S: And the first day she said, "I am not going to do these things: I am not going to clean the tables, I'm not going to talk to the customers." I said, "You don't have to worry. You don't have to do anything. But I still pay you. All you have to do is sit and watch what's happening" – again, coming back to the customer – "any customer who's not getting attended properly, and you see the employee is not making the right answer, just make a note it for me. That's all I need you to do. And then watch whether all the tables are clean. If all the tables are dirty, just make a note saying that 'This customer left on so and so time' and then in the next fifteen minutes, twenty minutes, the table was dirty. All I need you to do is that." She said, "So it's like a spy?"

[Laughs]

S: I said, "No! Spies are hidden and you are obvious because you are my daughter! Everyone knows you are my daughter!" So she went in and sat there. And then I discovered a lot of things. The second day she told me, "I did write a lot of things. But what good is it, Dad?" I said, "You did good, you did your job. That's what I asked you to do, and you did it." She said, "That girl didn't come after fifteen minutes, that girl didn't come and wipe up, but what good is that doing us? So I stepped over and I started cleaning the table."

[Laughs]

S: So I did not tell her to clean the table, but she cleaned the table. So the second one, the customer didn't get the food on the POS on time. So she waited, and looks like these two employees went back together and went smoking. They were having a good smoke break. She said, "The customers are waiting here on the food, and there's nobody in the POS system to go check and see whether it was made in the kitchen. So I had to go into the kitchen to verify with the cook whether the food was made and then give it to the customers." I said, "That goes with your POS job then."

[Laughs]

S: She comes back home and tells me, "I think I can do this too." I said, "Don't worry, you're still getting paid." The third day, she started mastering everything, and she said, "Dad, I don't keep track of how many tables I cleaned." So the fourth day, after the monthly meeting, I told all of my employees, "She's here. Please do your stuff properly. If not, I will get her to give you instruction on what needs to be done." And all my tables are clean from that day onwards!

That's awesome!

S: So her motivation to come in was, "Dad, I want an iPad." And I said, "You already have an iPad for the family." She said, "I need a personal iPad!" Then I said, "Well, you need to contribute something to the family." So with a lot of frustration and hesitation, she came in.

And the first month she did $270. I do pay them. Anybody who works in my business. The owner is me. I get the privilege of getting the profits from it. Anybody who puts in time…if I put in time, if I do a delivery and put in time, I take a paycheck for me. If my wife does it, she gets it. So it should all come from…as you work, they all get a share from it. Like the employees. That way, if I pay you, I'm going to ask you for the best possible thing. I'm not going to ask for compromises. So if my wife says, "I'm your wife. I prepared this; it went wrong," I'll say, "No, this is unacceptable, because I paid you. So you'd better do what is right." So everybody gets paid.

My daughter got paid $270 the first month. The second month, she went up to $440 or $480. And third month, it was $898.

Wow!

S: The first month, I opened her a bank account. She has a bank account in her own name and her own debit card. And she told me she's going to spend everything, but once she started making money, she started saving it. And she told me, "Dad, I think you knew all along that this is what I'm going to be when you told me, 'Just sit in that seat and all I want you to do is make these notes.'"

What did you say?

S: I said, "Telling you is not enough. You didn't realize it at that time; you realize it now." I tell my daughter, that it was a negotiation. I will treat her like a regular employee. She says, "Dad!" I said, "There is no Dad existing. Does anyone see Dad here? It is only me. There is no Dad." This is how "mean" I am to her too.

And all the employees, when the employees give feedback about me, there is only one feedback they give. The negative feedback is, "He's to the point." The positive feedback is, "There is no BS. He is straight to the point. He's the same with every employee, whether it is his daughter or his wife. He doesn't care."

That's cool.

S: "The rules are set, and there is just one straight line. He does not have ups and downs. If his daughter is on the POS and she needs to do something that she doesn't do, he is going to question her about it." And the same rule applies. If I'm going to fine her, if I'm going to do an extra training or a free-of-charge work, I'm going to do that. I'm going to fine her; I'm not going to excuse her from that. I might be paying the fine, but I'm not going to excuse her from that. So that's what I do.

What a good preparation too for when she goes into, uh, uh, either her own business or working for someone else. She's not going to be like, "Oh well, you know, I have Dad around my little finger. He'll let me do whatever I want."

S: That is why she is able to have…she has another friend of hers. Outside of work, they go to movies, they hang out together. I can be dropping, pick up, I can do all of that. But as an employee, when it comes to the store, both of them are my employees. Their role is separated very clearly. And they know, "This guy is going to be like this. Outside the restaurant, you can scream at him and do whatever, it is totally different."

She has made a lot of money with it, and she was excited to come back. But I told her after three months of holidays, I told her, "I don't want you. I need you to enjoy your days as kids. I don't want deviations from your studies. So you've got the lesson. You have the option - whenever you want you can come back and do it. So when you have a lot of free time, let me know and we'll put you in. But I'm not going to make this a daily routine habit and have it deviate from your studies." Because studies to me, that is another tool to make money.

Oh yeah!

S: Go do that! Plus you need to enjoy as a kid, too. You need to go and watch movies. She's thirteen, hormones will be there. For now, go ahead and go to the mall, walk around…

Yeah! Enjoy kid stuff.

S: That's all. So that's how I motivated her. And my wife. The reason I brought my wife in was a different reason. My uncle, my Mom's younger brother, he passed away when he was forty-three and the wife didn't know anything. So it was a big bummer for my aunt. And then she couldn't do anything on her own. She didn't know how to open a bank account.

Oh that's awful!

S: Yeah. So that became a big eye opener for me. So I told my wife, "I cannot…whether you like it or not, I am going to find ways to train you to do it." So now my wife is the executive pastry chef, and she does all the pastries. Me and my wife, we used to work inside the bakery for a while. The two of us, we can make all the dishes there. So that was the motivation for bringing my wife.

Yeah!

S: I don't want them to do…she does only four hours every day. That's all I want her to do. The idea is not to make her work, not make her generate…. it's not all about the money alone right? She's taking care of the kids, school, everything she takes care; the entire house she runs. So that indirectly is a lot of money. If you calculate the money on the table, it's a lot of money on the table. That is a lot of other value that she adds. So I told her, "This is in preparation in a worst case scenario. If anything happens to me, I want you to be able to do things right, and be able to function. You won't get stranded in your lifestyle, right?" Once you establish a lifestyle, I do not want them to go back down. Because I've been there, and it is very hard. If you have everything, and then all of a sudden you don't even have your basic needs, that situation is very hard. So I never want them to go to that situation. I'm saying, "If this is your lifestyle, what do you need to do to maintain your lifestyle?" That's the motivation to bring my wife into the business. The entire family is in business.

Oh, that's awesome! OK, I have one more question. Do you have, like, a motto or words that you live by? Or some other kind of inspiration that keeps you going?

S: For the money part, my Mom always tells me that, "Don't cheat at all." And I'm afraid of my conscience. So even if it is a ten dollar or a twenty dollar, and somebody tries to rip someone off, I experienced, and I've been bitten before. It comes around and bites you. So that's one thing I'm very afraid of. I have fear of that, knowingly or unknowingly, I should not do it. If it's knowingly, I'll take the chance to rectify it.

But just be good to your own self, and listen to your own conscience. Be true to yourself. That's about it. I'm not a hypocrite; I don't have a different face outside. I don't do that. I'm an open book. Five minutes, somebody talks to me, they will know all the pages! "OK, I read the index, I read fifty pages, I know this guy!" And there will also be a navigation, they can navigate through the book too. So my Mom has always told me, "Do not try to cheat anybody. And do not be interested in other things, like other people's property." That's the advice she's always given me. And I live by it very strong.

Thank you!

S: Thanks Kim!

***

My interview with Shiva was eye-opening. I did not know anything about his life in India before our interview that day. He must have an incredible reserve of courage and strength. I knew he worked his butt off every day for our data management team but I didn't realize he took such an active role in running his restaurants, too. And I so admire his attitude towards his daughter. He truly believes in both his kids, but has taken care to ensure his daughter can be independent.

Changing jobs from working at ManTech, where I had been employed for seventeen years, to working at Magellan was incredibly scary. While in my gut I knew I needed to change I was also concerned I might have made a mistake. I felt like the new kid on the block. I had to reach out and make new friends, learn a completely new system and new lingo. I went from Department of Defense acronyms to health care acronyms! I wondered sometimes if I was over my head and if I made a bad choice.

Meeting Shiva reaffirmed for me that I had made the right choice by working at Magellan. I knew I was getting to know other like-minded people who loved their lives and wanted to pursue their passions. It seemed like a no-brainer to me at that point to ask Shiva about interviewing him for this book.

Ultimately, the longer commute to work at Magellan started wearing on me. It started crunching in on my time with Jerry and my time to write. Also, while I was successful as a project manager, it was emotionally wrenching at times. To me, a good project manager must make tough decisions all the time. These decisions can include firing people if they are not a good fit for the job. I had to be "tough" in order to do what was right for the project. I was doing well with it but I knew it was not a pace I could continue to keep.

Incredibly, at the time I started having these realizations, I received a call. My dear friend Robert suggested my name to a team at NCR who was working with the Defense Commissary Agency. Tom, the manager of the NCR team, wanted to interview with me. I was apprehensive once again. I had just changed jobs 6 months earlier, and now I was considering moving to another job? Would my résumé look like I was some crazy job hopper? I decided to speak with Tom and consider his offer.

I'm so glad that I did talk with Tom. My new position was as an Organizational Change Manager. This position was similar to being a project manager, my position at Magellan, but it focused on the "people" side of change. With OCM, you assess an organizational change like implementing new software prior to the change, during the change, and after the change from the point of view of the new users.

While I feel I was a good project manager, I feel like I am a kick-ass organizational change manager! Working with people to prepare for changes is something that plays to my skills – communication to make people aware, addressing resistance to new ideas, being supportive and having follow-through. It was encouraging to know that my move to Magellan was the right decision. If I hadn't moved to Magellan and instead had stayed at ManTech, it's likely I wouldn't have been at the right place at the right time to work for NCR. I really like my job, my team and my company. I am still pinching myself to ask if it is real that I started pursuing my passions and ended up not only writing a book but also finding the perfect career for myself.

I still miss my new friends at Magellan, including Shiva. But I will always be thankful to Shiva and my other co-workers for the encouragement, love and support they provided while at Magellan and afterwards.

Story 9: Dr. Constance Hendricks, PhD, RN, Nursing Professor: Breaking barriers and helping lives

On a cold December night, I stood outside with my Sorors (sorority sisters), Michelle, Emma and Dawn. We were collecting Christmas presents for a family in need. There were two little girls whose mother had tragically died right before Christmas. We gathered together to purchase presents for these girls and show them how much our Sorority, Zeta Phi Beta, Incorporated, cares about them and about the people in our community. The truth is that night we were giggling and laughing, having a ball while helping these little girls. Whoever said it is better to give than to receive was right on the money!

My journey with Zeta Phi Beta Sorority, Inc., has been one of the best things that has ever happened to me. One of my good friends, Emma, was a Zeta. My friend Caron and I were interested and were invited to attend an interest meeting held by Emma and her Sorors. I will admit, I was very nervous. Here I was, a white woman, attending a graduate chapter interest meeting for a predominantly Black sorority. I knew that Emma and my other Zeta friends, Tanya and Andrea, would be accepting of us. But what about the other Sorors?

Being from the South in the United States, I can attest that people are aware of race. You may argue with me and say people are aware of race everywhere. When I say we are aware in the South, most of us are well acquainted with the history that led us where we are today: slavery, the Civil War, segregation and the Civil Rights movement. We also feel relatively comfortable talking about race. We generally talk about it politely and sometimes with a sense of humor. Most of the people I know are comfortable interacting with people from other races. I'm no fool – racism is tragically alive and well – but I am happy to say that in the workplaces I have been, people from different races generally get along well.

Getting along well at work and interacting socially can be very different, however. I find that many people will interact socially with other people from their same race. It's more common to see people of different races out to dinner together or going to the movies these days, but honestly in the South, I usually see groups of black people with other black people and groups of white people with other white people. I'm not sure exactly why we intentionally segregate ourselves.

So I admit I was nervous when I was going to the Zeta interest meeting. This wasn't just interacting with my black friends at work. This was becoming a social proponent for all of the issues that Zetas care about. This meant being one of the only (and often the only) white faces in the crowd at events. This meant putting myself out there to be judged.

My desire to join the group won out over any nervousness I had. On December 23, 2003, I joined the Zeta Phi Beta, Sorority, Incorporated, Alpha Omega Zeta chapter. My friend Caron and I were the first Caucasian Americans to join our chapter.

My absolute favorite part of being a Zeta, besides meeting my beloved Sorors and getting to know them, is a program called Z-HOPE. That cold December night, my Sorors and I were participating in a Z-HOPE program. Z-HOPE, which stands for **Z**etas **H**elping **O**ther **P**eople **E**xcel, is an international service initiative that started in 2008, introduced by the sorority's 22nd International Grand Basileus Barbara C. Moore.

Z-HOPE has six objectives. They are:

- To provide culturally appropriate informational activities according to the Z-HOPE program format
- To foster collaborative partnerships between community organizations with shared goals
- To promote the opportunities for expansion in Stork's Nest programs [A cooperative project of Zeta Phi Beta Sorority, Inc. and the March of Dimes Foundation]
- To facilitate community service and mentorship opportunities for members of the organization
- To provide an equitable chapter recognition program for community services rendered, and
- To provide a standard reporting format to concentrate efforts and demonstrate the organization's impact

To date, more than 750,000 individuals have participated in Z-HOPE related activities and programs.

I had to know how Z-HOPE was started. How did this awesome program come into being? While I figured the person who led this great mission must be an accomplished woman with a loving heart, I was really moved by the founder's background and legacy of love born in the deep South during racially divided times. I had the honor to meet and get to know an incredible woman whom I am proud to call my Soror.

***

From the Auburn University website: "Constance Smith Hendricks received her undergraduate degree in Nursing from the University of Alabama at Birmingham (UAB) and a master's degree from UAB with a focus in Community Health Nursing. In addition, she has a graduate certificate in Gerontology from the University of Alabama, and in 1992, she was the first African American to complete the nursing doctoral degree at Boston College, earning her PhD in clinical nursing research. The focus of her research was determinants of health promotion behaviors among Alabama's Black Belt adolescents. An outcome of her research was developing a midrange health promotion empowerment theoretical framework, the Hendricks Perceptual Health Promotion Determinants Model. The framework continues to be utilized by students and research, and numerous publications by Hendricks and others cite use of the model.

In addition to multiple awards related to her professionalism and dedication to nursing, she was commissioned by Zeta Phi Beta Sorority, Inc. to develop a National Service Initiative (Z-HOPE™) and provide oversight and evaluation of the implementation. Over a 5-year implementation, the program has reached over 2 million persons with health promotion programming across the United States and in Ghana, West Africa." [xvi]

***

I just knew there had to be a great story behind the creation of Z-HOPE. After all, Soror Hendricks had done so many wonderful things with her life! I emailed Soror Hendricks in August 2015. When I reached out to her, she had just retired from Auburn University. I was thrilled by her response: "I am honored to be considered for inclusion in "Tickers". I just recently retired from AU so need a few weeks to get settled & find things out of boxes."

Allowing Dr. Hendricks several weeks to get settled as requested, I reached out to her. I was greeted warmly and settled in myself for a great conversation, and a revealing story about Soror Hendricks and her life.

***

C: Good morning!

K: Good morning Doctor Hendricks! How are you doing?

C: I'm great! How are you?

I'm doing very well. Thank you so much. Thanks again for talking with me!

C: Oh, well, I'm excited to participate!

Thank you! Let me get me questions together here. My book is about – I think I told you a little bit about it – it's about people who are really passionate about what they do. And I know that having been a Soror, I was always so excited about Z-HOPE. I always wondered where Z-HOPE started. So that's when I read up on you, and I said to myself, "Wow, Dr. Hendricks is amazing! She sounds like somebody who is very passionate about what she does."

C: I've been described that way! [Laughs]

[Laughs] Outstanding! I did a little bit of research on you on the Internet. I always like to try to do a little bit of research before I speak with people with whom I interview. It looks like you're a Charles W. Barkley Endowed Professor? Is that correct?

C: I was. I held that chair for five years. And that was the full length of the term, five years. And as I retired, I was ending my five-year tenure as an endowed chair at Auburn.

Oh, OK! That's wonderful!

C: I retired August 1, 2015.

Congratulations!

C: Thank you!

You're welcome! I was looking at your interests. It said your interests include community health promotion, minority health issues, action research, mentorship to advanced nursing scholarship, recruitment and retention in community-based health promotion intervention programs. Is that correct?

C: Yes, that's correct.

Good, good, good! I know that you worked and studied in Alabama. Were you born and raised there?

C: Yes, I was born in historic Selma, Alabama!

Oh wonderful!

C: And actually that's where I moved back to; Selma, Alabama.

That's fantastic! I wanted to ask, as you were growing up as a little girl in Selma, did you know that you wanted to be a nurse?

C: I always wanted to be a nurse. Ever since I can remember, I was…I guess I had…I've thought about this a lot. I had a lot of nurses in my family. I also had a lot of teachers. That's why I'm teaching nursing.

Right!

C: My Mom was a teacher, and her best friend was a nurse. And actually my Mom shared with me that she went to nursing school but she left. Because she couldn't handle the blood and guts!

[Laughs]

C: She quit, and actually was afraid to come home because she wasn't sure…she waited, she had graduated from high school early. You had to be eighteen to go to nursing school, and that was to go to Grady. Back in the day, to be a Grady nurse or a Tuskegee nurse was a big deal.

So she went to Selma University for two years, to the Baptist College here until she could get eighteen, and then went to Grady. And once they put her in the emergency room, she said, "This is not for me!"

She was afraid to come back home so she went to Birmingham to my grandfather's sister's house until she could build up enough courage to tell them that she left school! [Laughs] But she ended up at Alabama State, and got a degree in education, and two masters and a, whatever they call it, an EBS.

So teaching was her thing. And my Dad is from a family of ten. And five of his siblings are nurses, including one of his brothers. His brother is a retired Navy nurse now. And he has…let me see…one, two, three…my Aunt Edda, my Aunt Harriet, my Aunt Alice…so three of his sisters and a brother were nurses. And my Mom's best friend.

And so I think some way or another, I don't know, whether it was going to see them work in the white with the blue capes – back then, the nurses wore capes and hats – I'm not real sure. But I can remember I had a little dog, it probably was a…I don't know. We didn't do house dogs then. But it was a little dog. And somebody in the neighborhood cut the dog's tail.

Aw!

C: So the dog came home with the tail on it dangling. It was still there but it was dangling. So of course, I got some tape, and taped the tail up! And the tail grew back, it grew back together.

Oh my goodness!

C: But people then tried to tell me that I needed to be a veterinarian. Well, you know, animals and me, we aren't the best thing. I need human animals, not that other kind!

I kept saying, "No, I don't want to be a veterinarian!" And, you know, in the mid-fifties, a veterinarian was a foreign thing to me, and I wasn't interested. And I wasn't interested in horses and cows; that was my perspective of a veterinarian. I can remember that. I don't know, I might have been six or seven, something like that, you know, when that happened. But I have always, always, wanted to be a nurse.

The question to me, or for me, was where to go to school. I have a cousin, who was my mother's cousin, who was a Tuskegee grad who used to babysit me. And so, you know, I could see myself walking on Tuskegee's campus and being a Tuskegee nurse, with that blue cape, and you know, the way they wore their hair. And to be a Tuskegee nurse or a Grady nurse in the Sixties, well, that was the cream of the crop!

Oh wow!

C: But Grady was a diploma school; it was not a college. And somewhere, I spoke here in Selma, I think it was last year. And I stood between my Aunts, my Dad's sisters who are retired RNs [registered nurses], and Mom's best friend, who is a retired RN. And I told them that standing between them, I could feel the heat! It was magnetic. And I said to them in public, "I'm not sure which one of you is responsible for me going to a baccalaureate program rather than Grady." And my Mom's best friend said, "I think I'm the guilty one!" She said, "Because you were too smart to go to a hospital program. You needed to go to real college."

Oh awesome!

C: And I was like, "OK." And that was the difference between Grady and Tuskegee. One was a baccalaureate program and one was a three year, hospital-based program. But you didn't have a college degree when you finished.

OK, gotcha.

C: And you know, nursing is a crazy profession. There are three ways to enter the profession. You can go to a hospital program and you spend three years, and you came out as a registered nurse to write the licensed exam. You go to a community college and spend two years and come out as a nurse, same licensed exam, but you only have an associate's degree. Or you spend four years at a four-year institution, two of those which were general education, and two were nursing. And you have the same right to write the same licenses as a registered nurse, but you have a college degree.

Gotcha!

C: She said, "I'm the guilty one. I'm the one who saw that you took the four year course." I said, "OK, all these years, I wanted to know that."

[Laughs]

C: My Dad was a disabled vet. And so, my education was because I am a GI dependent. So I had the opportunity for my tuition to be paid, for my education to be paid for, because he was in the service for the U.S.

Gotcha. Was he in World War II?

C: He was in the Korean War and World War II.

Oh wow! Oh my goodness.

C: I gotta go back. I remember…you know, the older I get now, I really want to appreciate the history that I didn't pay any attention to before! I remember, and I need to talk with my Aunt, because she's the historian now, he was in two branches of service. I think it was the Air Force and the Army? So I've got to find out – that doesn't make sense to me so I've got to find out.

Yes, ma'am!

C: But I know he was a vet. When I was growing up, he was in and out of the VA hospital in Tuskegee a lot. So I learned to drive going back and forth to see him in the hospital. My Mom would put me on the highway to see him. It was a straight road, and I could drive straight, so that's how I learned, like that.

It was because of the benefits of him being a hundred percent disabled that afforded an education. The schools provided a full ride. And when my mother inquired about it, and remember, I finished high school in 1971, so it was just on the cusp of integration. Not really there, but you know....Alabama and the South were really being pushed by the threat of pulling Federal funds if you don't play this game. And so the gentleman who was the veteran's person here in Dallas County told my mother that I had latched onto Tuskegee. Because Tuskegee was my dream! Because my cousin was the Tuskegee nurse, and I had always heard about Tuskegee, Tuskegee! Well, he told my mother – and I was accepted at Tuskegee, I was accepted at Grady, I was accepted at UAB – he said, "If she goes to Tuskegee, remember that Tuskegee is private. It's a private school. She will not receive all of the benefits." And UAB was one of two baccalaureate programs in the State of Alabama. At that time, there were only two baccalaureate nursing programs in the whole State. Tuskegee was the first baccalaureate program in the State of Alabama; most people don't even know that. But Dr. Harvey, the dean at Tuskegee, helped the Alabama dean set up the program. But then Alabama was state funded, so it just grew. It was getting state money. And Tuskegee did not grow as fast because it's been a private school, and it's an HBCU [Historically Black College and University], and you know HBCUs grow like HBCUs. So even though it was the first CSN [Certified School Nurse] program, it has not grown like Alabama.

Gotcha.

C: If I went to Alabama Birmingham, I would get all of the benefits of being a GI dependent. So my mother said, "Well, that kind of ends that. That's where you're going!" And I was like, I was just devastated!

I just wanted to be a Tuskegee nurse! So the lady next door to us, Mrs. Brown, Mrs. Willie Mae Brown…Mrs. Brown, she and her husband did not have any kids – he drove a big truck that carried bricks. We have a gig company here called Henry's Brickyard. He drove it, and he always parked his big truck with all the bricks. He always delivered bricks all over the place. She was a…I guess you would call her a domestic worker. She would take in people's laundry and stuff, and she would stay home all the time. Kind of the big momma figure.

Right!

C: But on Sunday morning, Mrs. Brown would cook fried chicken, and gravy, and rice, and yeast rolls. And if you went to Sunday School, you could come and then you could go and eat. If you weren't going to Sunday School, you couldn't go over to Mrs. Brown's house to eat. Well, you know I like to eat!

[Laughs]

C: I also was the Sunday School musician. So I was always going to church and Sunday School. I was going because every week I had to learn another new song to play in Sunday School. I would get two songs together for Sunday School. Most people didn't know I used to play, and when I got old enough, my Mama stopped making me play, I learned I could sing it better than I could play it. Let me say it this way: It was much easier for me to sing it than play it. I'd rather sing and let someone else play for me. I gave up the music part.

Every Sunday, I would go to Mrs. Brown's house and eat breakfast before I went to Sunday School. My brother, on the other hand, didn't like Sunday School. So he couldn't come over there and eat breakfast! You know, there was fried chicken, rice with butter on it, yeast rolls and gravy! That was her thing, every Sunday morning. And I know, I digress a little bit!

No, no!

C: So when my mother said I had to go to UAB instead of Tuskegee, I decided I was going to run away. I was going to run away, but let me tell you where I ran. I ran to Mrs. Brown's! I didn't go far!

[Laughs]

C: So my Mom said, after I was there for a couple of hours, "Now, is Mrs. Brown going to pay for you to go to school? Then you stay over there. But if she's not going to pay, you might as well come on home."

[Laughs]

C: Mrs. Brown loved me but she didn't have any money.

But I guess, to back up a little bit further, during the Civil Rights, when we had the big march here, and Bloody Sunday, I was ten, twelve. So I remember that Sunday very well. My Dad and his sister the nurse were involved.

Oh my goodness!

C: We were at home. And I remember because…see, I think this predates you, but we used to not have ambulances like we have today. And in the segregated South, we had our own little community, you know. We had our own hospital, we had our own everything. And we kind of co-existed.

My Dad was a graduate of Atlanta College, which is now part of Morehouse. And he graduated in mortuary science. He was a mortician. And the funeral homes back in the day used to run the ambulances. They would take the same hearse to the hospital because they had a cot, same principle. And so, on Bloody Sunday, when the troopers rode horses all over the people, and beat them up, my Dad was out there with the hearse transporting people to the hospital. His sister, who is the nurse – I heard her tell her story not too long ago – was – and I'm still filling in pieces because it is so amazing – was on maternity leave. And when she heard about it, she said, "I've got to go!" She left home and went to, back down to the hospital, to Good Samaritan, which was the Black Catholic hospital. And they had that one staffed. So she went over to the other hospital, Burwell, which was another black hospital run by a black family, and she worked the emergency room there. I have lived through the experience. My church was right down the street. You always hear about Brown's Chapel where the march started. The march started at First Baptist which is down the street from Brown's Chapel. And people ran eight blocks from the bridge all the way back to the church, and then ran past Brown's Chapel to First Baptist. My church is one of those that you got fifteen steps to walk up. Well, they literally rode the horses up the steps into the church.

Oh my word!

C: And actually shot the stained glass window. We had the old stained glass windows. They shot those out. They actually threw someone through the baptismal glass. I can remember that because it took us forever to replace that glass. Every time it got shipped, by the time it got here, it was broken. It was a big thing to finally get it replaced.

OK, so you kind of have a little bit of the background stuff?

Yes, ma'am!

C: So my Mom, after President Johnson signed the voting rights act, my Mom was hired…what do you call it…appointed by Attorney General Katzenbach to be a Federal registrar. So she traveled to all of these small towns in Georgia, Alabama and Mississippi registering people to vote. And she would have to travel under the protection of Federal troopers. And she would go from Monday through Friday, and then she would come home on the weekends. We ended up having a lady live with us during the week while my mother traveled to register people to vote. She would talk about driving on the interstate, and the danger of a woman driving on the interstate. She had a '65 white Mustang with a blue interior and how the truckers would allow her to get between them on the highway. How she would ride between the trucks, and they would protect her until it was time for her to get off the interstate.

Wow!

C: Back then, my Mom stayed at the only hotel to allow Blacks to stay. The Federal Government had a contract with them. And then she had to work in the post office, or in the basement of the Federal building, if that community had a Federal building. Or most places had a post office, and that belonged to the Federal Government, not the local government. So she had to stay on Federal property. And she couldn't go get lunch. She could send the white trooper or the white whoever that was protecting her. They would go get the lunch and bring it back. Because you know, they weren't going to serve her.

So in '70, the Federal Government offered her a full-time position in Jackson, Mississippi. And that meant we were going to have to move to Jackson. Now this was coming up to my senior year of high school. And I knew I was going to be the valedictorian! It was me and one other girl, tit for tat, the whole time! And you know, and here again, I had a fit. "Oh, please don't pull me out! Please don't do that! You're taking me to this place and I don't know nobody!" You know how kids do.

Right!

C: What she did was give up that job. She stayed here in Selma and ended up going back into the classroom, actually getting a job in an adjacent county, and having to commute forty-five miles a day, one way. And she did that for like 12, 13 years until she retired. So when I look at the sacrifice she made for me, when my daughter got ready to go to the University of South Carolina, she looked at me and said, "We're going! Or I'm leaving you here." I couldn't do anything but say, "OK, we're going!" Because South Carolina was recruiting me anyway. What I said to them was, "If my daughter isn't coming, I'm not coming!"

[Laughs]

C: I was a young little sassy thing. But I said, "If she doesn't want to come here, I'm not coming." But when she said to me, "I like the feel of the campus, and we are going to South Carolina," I said, "I guess I need to accept this current job and tell my Dean that I'm leaving!" Simply because of what my mother had done for me, and I felt I could do nothing less. But you know, Denesha [Soror Hendrick's daughter] went to Carolina. She lived in a dorm and I stayed in town. It was…she could come home on the weekend and wash her clothes. I really never saw her! We had to schedule a lunch appointment on campus so we could see each other.

[Laughs]

C: I said, "I will pay for you for four years, but in four years, you need to be finished." So she finished and graduated, and said, "I'm going back home to Auburn!" I was in the middle of a post doc at Chapel Hill, and I needed to finish the post doc. I was teaching in South Carolina and had a post back in North Carolina. So I was going between the two Carolinas. Because the Carolinas are so different. I had the privilege of being inside of both of them.

And of course, she packed up and came back to Auburn, because she had graduated from Auburn High, and started the master's program at Auburn, and I stayed at Carolina and finished the last year of my post doc. And she finished her master's in one year, and went straight into the doctoral program, and three years later, she walked across the stage as the second Dr. Hendricks. At that time, she was the youngest doctoral student they had graduated at age 24. The neatest part about it was that she used my dissertation work for her dissertation work.

Really?

C: Yeah! I did my doctorate at Boston College, and I developed a theory that looks at the individuals' cognitive development, self-esteem, self-efficacy, and levels of hope as predictors of engagement in health-promoting behavior versus health-compromising behavior. And I tested the model, the model held up, so I have a copyrighted mid-range theory in the National Library of Congress. She took my theory, my mid-range theory, and used it for her theoretical framework for her dissertation.

That's awesome!

C: She used student athletes to test the theory, and it held. And so right now, I have about…I've been trying to keep up…I have about ten or twelve folks who have used my theory or pieces of it for their dissertation. I get requests to use the instruments, or what have you, and I grant permission, and they're supposed to let me know when they finish. Some do and some don't. I haven't done a good job – I need to really take time to follow up and generate an article just out of that.

Oh you should, definitely!

C: In my spare time. [Laughs]

[Laughs] In your spare time, exactly! After you received your undergrad from UAB, when did you decide to get your master's degree? Did you decide to just turn around and get it right away? Or did you take some time in between?

C: Well you know, when I went to UAB, remember, they were just integrating. I came from a parochial school where there were eighteen people in my class. And I was the valedictorian. But I went to UAB and there were two hundred people in the class! I had never been in a school with that many people in the class. And then there were only about twenty people of color in the class. And three and a half years later, only four of us graduated.

Oh my goodness!

C: But when you look at that time there…well, in the Lutheran system here, I had been exposed to white faculty because they came here. This was a Lutheran church-centered place, so we had white faculty, so that wasn't anything new to me. It was the numbers of people that overwhelmed. And when I got there, that was the first time I experienced struggling in school. Because I had never had to struggle. I had always just breezed right on. What I learned, what I tell people all the time is, the rude awakening to me was that I was average. That word had never been attached to me. "Really? Come on, now!" What happens is, when you change venues, and everybody else in the class was the valedictorian too, it changes. That whole phenomenon is what I've been studying since I finished my doctorate. Because what happens is, what I call it is…and you might find it on some of the stuff on the web…the "From Somebody to Nobody to Someone" proxy. Because we leave a place – and high school athletes do it all the time. In high school, they are the "Mr. Football" or the "Mr. Basketball". And then they go to a top-ranked school, because they got recruited, right? And then they get benched. And it's devastating! Because you are not the "Mr. Whatever" because there are five thousand more! And so, if you don't have anybody to get you over that hurdle, right there, you get stuck. Then you stay there and you fall out, you drop out of school. But if you've got somebody who can just pull you through that, and say, "Hang in there," or "Keep working hard," "Your time is coming," you can get past that. You emerge, like a diamond, as something greater than you were.

I was impressed with this proxy of "From Somebody to Nobody to Someone." It can be intimidating to bump into people who are very talented who are in your same field or interest. It's important to keep working toward your goal, even if you feel intimidated at first. Never give up!

That's awesome! So who was the person who helped you over the hurdle?

C: I'm one of those village children. It took a lot of people to raise me. I had a family; I had a family in Birmingham…my mother, that Auntie that she ran to? She was in Birmingham. And then I always had church.

So I kept people all the time. When I moved from place to place, the first thing I would do is find me a church, I find me a Zeta chapter, and I find me a good hairdresser. You know, the essential things a girl needs!

Yes ma'am!

C: I have always had that foundation. My mother's father was a Baptist preacher. So you know, I grew up in the church. And I used to follow my granddaddy because he had rural churches. And what do they do at rural churches? They feed you! I'm from the era where they used to feed the preacher in the shoebox.

What?

C: You probably don't know about that. That's just for the old people.

Oh stop!

C: Well, on Sundays, when black people get together, we always eat. You know that! We used to use a shoebox lined with aluminum foil. They would have fried chicken, they would have potato salad, and you could always count on someone having sweet potato pie. Now it's a wonder we didn't die of ptomaine! Because if you're at church all day, you know they cooked that food on Saturday! For some reason, the grace of the good Lord, we never got sick! You can't do that today! You can't just can't and not get sick! [Laughs]

[Laughs] Oh my goodness!

C: That's why I followed my granddaddy, to be honest with you. Because I knew…I followed him more than his own daughters. My mother is one of three girls. But I was the one who followed him because I figured out that they fed him. [Laughs] Between that, playing in Sunday school, and going to a Christian-based school – I was at what's Concordia College now but it was Alabama Lutheran at the time – I started in kindergarten at age three, and I continued until high school on one little plot of land. So I never knew public schools until I went to UAB. That was my public school experience.

But the church, my faith. When I was in school at UAB, it was New Pyramid Baptist Church. New Pyramid would send the shuttle, the van, and pick us up, and take us to church. And they always served dinner after church. I'm telling you, I'm a food girl!

[Laughs]

C: And they would always send the college students home with a plate. Hallelujah, praise Jesus! [Laughs]

[Laughs] Oh that's awesome!

C: You will always find the church as a central theme in my work. So when you ask me early on about the interest and minority and health stuff, you will see that my research always has a faith-based lens to it. Working in the public sector, where I was in a public institution, you don't necessarily say you're doing church stuff. But you know, in the last ten years, faith-based initiatives have become popular. Well, I was doing faith-based initiatives thirty years ago. I could see that the funding kind of lent itself to faith-based initiatives. Because awareness of our community – where in our community do we have better access to people other than the church?

Very true.

C: When you look at the Civil Rights movement, how did we get the message to the people? It was in the church. That's where they had the mass meetings…in the church. So I learned a long time ago, if I needed to get a message out, I needed to go where the people were. And I try to teach people trying to do research today, you don't ask people to come back. You must go where they already are.

That makes sense!

C: And then you will have access to people. So that was one of the foundations for Z-HOPE. I'm working my way to Z-HOPE! That was one of the foundations to Z-HOPE. Z-HOPE said, "Go where the people are. Don't have a program and think the people have to come to you. Or they may not come." So you take the message to the people.

And then what I observed in Zeta was that we would have programs ourselves. And so the challenge in Z-HOPE – hence the name, Zetas Helping Other People Excel – is that you are to present your program to other people. And if we are there, we receive what I like to call "reciprocal blessings." You know, because you benefit from the same information that you are sharing with somebody else. But if we only bring information to ourselves, we are the only people getting enriched.

I definitely understood the "reciprocal blessings." My Sorors and I experienced them during our Z-HOPE project where we brought Christmas to the family that had lost their mother.

Right! Right, so that totally makes sense why it would be "Helping Other People Excel". You want to reach out beyond just our community. It's all well and good for us Zetas to be enriched, but in order to really expand it to the community, you have to reach out to other people. And you're right, there are reciprocal blessings.

C: Right! We have to be there. We have to cultivate them. So you get the same message but you also help somebody else in the process.

Oh that's awesome! So how did Z-HOPE get started? Did somebody approach you, did one of the Sorors approach you about it? Or is it something that you thought about creating?

C: OK, and I'm going to go back to that other question because there's something else I wanted to tell you about.

Yes, ma'am!

C: OK, but let's go ahead and talk about Z-HOPE for a minute. I've actually written an article about the development of Z-HOPE. I've submitted it a couple of times to be included in the *Archon* but because of the politics of Zeta, it has not yet been published. I'm going to probably put it in a non-Zeta journal and roll with it. I wrote it while it was still fresh, because it is history. But let me just give you the snapshot.

OK, thanks!

C: Z-HOPE came under Soror Barbara Moore, the twenty-second International Grand. Now, at that time, I was a member of Soror Moore's chapter in Columbia, South Carolina. Remember, Denesha took me to South Carolina, right?

Right! Yes, ma'am.

C: I had just become a Zeta member in '96, under the Tuskegee grad chapter. I went in grad in '96, but then in '96 I left and joined the South Carolina chapter. So I was a new Zeta. So I transferred to Beta Beta Zeta in Columbia, South Carolina. And that's really…in the Southeast is where I got my Zeta grooming! I got my Zeta grooming in the Southeast region. They do a wonderful job of…we call it embellishment. So I learned

Zeta in the Southeast. And because I was a new Zeta, and I've always been an organizational girl, and we'll talk about that in a minute. During that time, when Soror Moore was planning to run, I was a member of that chapter, so the chapter was all behind her. But I'm also a nurse. I'm a member of a nursing sorority, Chi Eta Phi. I had been regional director of Chi Eta Phi before I left going to South Carolina. And at that point, when I was regional director, I think I had the largest region in Chi Eta Phi.

Wow!

C: Because I chartered probably the maximum number of chapters that any regional director has chartered. I chartered sixteen or seventeen chapters during my tenure as regional director. Most of the chapters in the State of Alabama came under me. There were only two in Alabama, I think, and that was in Birmingham and in Tuskegee. And everything else that is Chi Eta Phi came under me.

So I had some organizational skills, so to speak. I had served as Second National Vice President for Chi Eta Phi. And I was in charge of their continuing ed development and their continuing ed stuff. So I walked them through the national certification board, being a continuing ed provider. So I had some organizational exposure before I came to Zeta. And so I had planned to run for National President for Chi Eta Phi and Soror Moore was planning on running for national president for Zeta. So, as members of the chapter, we clicked. You know how people click?

Yes, ma'am!

C: We just clicked. It was actually – and it is kind of like predestination – it was Soror Moore in the position of First Anti who approved my application!

In Zeta Phi Beta Sorority, Incorporated, the title of the president is First Anti-Basileus, or First Anti for short.

Now let me tell you why it was complicated. When I was at UAB my freshman year, in the dorm – we had a nursing dorm. In the dorm, we had a rush party. They had flyers all up over the door that the rush party was down in the basement, and you're welcome to come. I just took them at their word and I went down there to the rush party. Well, it was Alpha Sigma Tau. AST, Alpha Sigma Tau. Well, guess what? Alpha Sigma Tau issued me an invitation for membership! So I actually integrated Alpha Sigma Tau. And there was another black with me who came from Tuskegee, Mary Jeter. And Mary Jeter and I didn't know each other. She was an older student coming back to school and I was a traditional, straight out of high school. We were the two blacks who they offered membership to. And we took them up on it. So I was one of the first Alpha Sigma Tau persons of color. It was in fall 1971. And I graduated in three and a half years, because I didn't have anything else to do but go to school, so I just went to school. And by the time I graduated, I was President of Alpha Sigma Tau!

Wow! That's awesome!

C: There were no black Greeks [Greek organizations including fraternities and sororities] on campus at that time. The black Greeks came to UAB maybe in '72 or '73? But by the time they came, I was already invested in Alpha Sigma Tau. I was in leadership mode. I had been their treasurer…I think I had been elected treasurer, and then ultimately my senior year, I was president. Whenever I was around Pi Kappa Alphas, the white fraternity, I'd tell them, "I'm your little sister!" They would look at me so funny. "Well, I am!" The little sisters on the UAB campus for the Pi Kappa Alphas were the Alpha Sigma Taus. So I went to all the Pi Kappa Alpha parties at their house, and the Halloween thing, and the costume thing. And they were very protective of me; nobody ever bothered me.

Oh, that's great!

C: I was their little sister. So it was cool.

What had happened was…as the children say, "What happened was…", what had happened was I got truly into the mode just like them, and you know when you graduate from college, you get married. Well, ironically, about my junior year, the guy that I had dated in high school who dumped me when I got to be a freshman, was back home in Birmingham teaching.

Ah-ha!

C: My girlfriend and I were walking from the grocery store, and this car came down the street from Sixth Avenue, and did a U-turn, flipped around and turned back. Well, he always liked fancy cars, and he was an only child, so his Momma had spoiled him. So the window came down, and lo and behold, it was my high school boyfriend who offered us a ride back to the dorm. We were about three to four blocks from the dorm. We got in his car, and he took us back. And of course we started talking. And I called my Mom, and she said, "Oh, Lord!" And in six weeks, I was engaged. And then he convinced me…like how all my life I wanted to be a nurse? All my life, my wedding was going to be on June the 10th; I was to be a June bride. Well, he convinced me…because I was in love…that I didn't need…you see, I graduated in December.

He convinced me that I didn't need to wait until June to get married, that we could get married in December. But my mother said, "You have to graduate before you can get married." So Miss Smartypants…I set the wedding date for two weeks after graduation. So we got married on December 21st. So I must have graduated in early December. So I only came home to finish up the wedding, so I never moved back home. By the time I went into my first job, I had a new name. So I never, I never lived by myself because I was in the dorm. I never was an independent adult. Because I think he knew that if I had ever realized that I could be an independent adult, it was over. [Laughs]

[Laughs]

C: I never…the first time I lived by myself was in South Carolina when Denesha was in the dorm and I moved in an apartment. We stayed married for eight years, and after that it was me and Denesha. So I never was an independent adult until I moved to South Carolina, and I said, "Oh, I'm having a moment! I'm in an apartment by myself!" [Laughs]

[Laughs]

C: Oh Lord! So from the time in the 1970s when I graduated as a sorority girl, when you get engaged they throw you in the swimming pool. All the stuff they did for everybody else, they did for me, you know! I probably had the first integrated wedding in Selma. My sorority sisters were my bridesmaids. They were white! After that, when I started being approached by the Pan Hel [Pan-Hellenic Council], I always checked on the applications, "Yes" [to the question of whether she belonged to another sorority]. Because in my brain, I sat at the table of the presidents at the Pan Hellenic. I didn't realize there was a <u>Pan-Hellenic</u> and a <u>PanHellenic</u>!

In the Divine Nine, the nine historically Black Greek letter organizations, they have a Pan-Hellenic Council. This council is separate from the National PanHellenic Conference, an organization that includes a number of women's sororities. It's important to note that a man or woman who joins one of the Divine Nine Organizations may not join another of the Divine Nine Organizations, but there are no rules that state that a woman who has joined one of the National PanHellenic Conference sororities may not join one of the Divine Nine sororities.

[Laughs] Because I didn't know that, you know? So I had been approached by the AKAs [Alpha Kappa Alpha Sorority], and when I checked it on my application, they immediately told me no because they thought I had been a member of the black Pan Hel. When I was teaching at Tuskegee, I was approached by the Deltas [Delta Sigma Theta

Sorority], and of course I filled their application out, and I checked, "Yes." Because I didn't know. And they said, "No, thank you."

I had been at church in Tuskegee all these years, all these Zetas were there. And I have to tell you, I never realized how many Zetas were in my life as a little girl. I didn't know they were Zetas but they were Zetas. Like my pastor's wife, and all those folks that had all that blue and white [Zeta Phi Beta Sorority, Incorporated's colors are royal blue and white]. You know, I never paid it no attention! And my Momma's best friend, her cousin was a Sigma...I just didn't know all that! It's coming together now.

The Zetas in the church in Tuskegee, I was a member there before I went to South Carolina. They never said anything to me. Then when I came back from South Carolina...no, let me see. When I went away to school, when I went to Boston and got my doctorate's, I was teaching at Auburn so I was still at church in Tuskegee. I went away to school in '89 and I graduated in '92. So when I came back to Auburn and went to church in Tuskegee - because I always went to church in Tuskegee, because I have family people in that church, and that's where Denesha was baptized and all that – so when I came back with my doctorate, the Zetas then decided to approach me. And so, you know, when the Soror approached me, I said, "Let me tell you up front. If you can get this fixed, then I know Zeta is for me. I've been through this two times already, and I'm not going to go through it anymore." She was like, "What is the issue?" I was like, "Look, I integrated a sorority at UAB, etc., etc. So you need to find out if I'm eligible. And then if I'm eligible, I'm all on board. That's where the Lord wants me to be." So Soror Bascome, who is a former Alabama State Director, I think she was the president at that time of the chapter. She then proceeded to contact the First Anti who happened to be Barbara C. Moore.

Oh, OK!

C: Barbara C. Moore worked on a college campus; she is the Vice President for Development at Benedict College; she understood academia. So she understood the difference between white Greek life and black Greek life. And she said, "Well, sure, she can be a member! The white sisters are not part of the Pan-Hellenic." The white sorority has its own thing, and the white fraternity has its own thing, and the black Greeks have their Pan-Hellenic. And so when she came back with that message, I said, "OK! I'm all on board! Let's roll with it!"

It was meant to be!

C: It was meant to be! And I tell the AKAs all the time, "Y'all had first dibs on me!"

[Laughs]

C: See, all of my family are AKAs. All of my Daddy's people, back in town, all of them are AKAs! My daughter and I, we are in there with the blue and white. When I lived in Auburn, there were no Zetas in Auburn. The Zetas were in Tuskegee. And so there was no Zeta chapter. I chartered the Zeta chapter in Auburn. There were no Zetas, so the organization that had the access to the youth stuff was the Deltas. And so Denesha was president of the Deltines! I was Denesha's Momma, and Denesha was going to be successful, so Momma helped!

[Laughs]

C: In fact, the day I took my pledge [to join Zeta], on Denesha's birthday, January the 12th, I can remember, 1996, was the day I was driving back from Tuskegee. I get a call from the Deltas, finally inviting me. And I said, "Oh, you are just too late! In fact, you are a few hours too late!" I said, "I just crossed! Y'all waited too late." They said, "NO!" I said, "Yeah!"

That is funny!

C: In the Auburn area, I have a lot of friends who are Deltas. And the Zetas and the Deltas work together in Auburn because we have history from way back. But that was their problem – they waited too long!

When I got to South Carolina, and finally met Soror Moore, I said, "You are the lady!" And we just kind of clicked. I tell the story in the article about two sister girls meeting up in the – what I call the pretty girl store parking lot – which was Lane Bryant. There was a Lane Bryant on one side of town that carried a better line of clothes than the other. She and I happened to meet in the parking lot. She was going out, and I was going in. We stood in the parking lot and we talked. She shared with me her intent to run, and I shared with her that I was intending to run as the national president for nurses. So we made an agreement then that if we both won that our organizations would work together. I said, "But if I don't win, Soror Moore, I will do whatever you want me to do to be successful in your administration." And we talked about it because the two groups were going to work together to do some health stuff, because that was Soror Moore's interest, the health promotion stuff. And that was my research interest so it all fit together.
Be as it may, I decided not to do some under the table stuff with some of the nurses, and they decided I wasn't going to win. So I lost by two or three votes. So I just took it and said, "OK, I'm not willing to make the deals they want so I'm not going to do that."

I didn't win, and Soror Moore won. Then it came time for her to launch her initiatives. She said, "Connie, I'm going to need you to do this!" And I said, "You know I'm your girl!" And so she knew people from all over Zeta because she had been First Anti and had traveled all over for Zeta. She knew what expertise people had. So she appointed the Z-HOPE team. She brought us to D.C.

Soror Moore knew us, but we didn't know each other. So we sat around the table at Headquarters and she introduced us to each other. She told us why she selected us, and what she knew that we had to contribute. And there were eight of us. There was Karen Gibson, who had the background in kinesiology; she brought someone who had expertise in aging and the elderly; she brought Soror Singletary, who had the United Nations connection; and she brought Darnetta Brown, an adult nurse practitioner who had some expertise in men's health. There were eight of us and we didn't know each other. I knew Darnetta. She was the only one I knew because she was a nurse and she and I were Chi Eta Phi members. But outside of that I didn't know the other people; we had never met.

We all came to that table. Soror Moore introduced us, and then she said, "Now, I would like you all to develop me a program and present it to me by tomorrow." And then she got up and left.

Oh my goodness!

C: I had brought my research stuff, and everybody else had brought their research stuff. Oh yeah, and Gloria out of South Carolina, she's an entomologist. She's the first entomologist I ever met, a black entomologist. Study of bugs! She brought all these people she knew together, and everybody brought their stuff. What I asked people to do, after Soror Moore left, was to tell everybody, "OK, everyone put your stuff in the middle of the table." So we placed it all in the center of the table and we had a prayer. And we asked the Lord for guidance, and asked him to remove the selfishness and the ego that we could function as one and begin to trust each other enough that we would share our knowledge and our fields for the greater good of Zeta. And then we just started talking.

Everybody had brought stuff. Now I tell you what I remember about Gloria's. Gloria had been working with kids in the National Science Foundation. Now of course, she was teaching them about bugs. But Gloria had developed this points system. So we took her points system and created the points system for Z-HOPE.

Oh, OK!

C: We decided we wanted a holistic approach. We wanted something for everybody. Not just women, but everybody. So everybody had a task. And we decided on the basic kinds of things, that we would do programs, and we could do similar programs. We would have a holistic approach, and we were going to do mind, body and spirit. That's how we got mind, body and spirit. Whatever we were going to do, we were going to do mind, body and spirit.

We were going to challenge the chapters not to present in their community a single focus program. That's why the original Z-HOPE said you had to do one mind, one body, one spirit in order to get your points. We were trying to challenge the chapters to present a variety of programs in their communities. We wanted you to do programs focused on women, and because we were a women's organization, it was a requirement that you do one program – if you wanted to be recognized – one women's program. But if you want to compete with the points, then you had to strategize. But then I was very aware that we needed to have an even playing field. You can't put the big chapters up against the little chapters.

Very true.

C: What we did was pull out and look at the delegate structure. We had 0-4, 5-25, 25-50, and 51+ for delegates. That's how we came up with those groupings. Someone said, "Why didn't you just do five for the Five?" We didn't think about that. No one at that table honestly thought about that. What we thought about is, this is what we use now. I was very keenly aware of the planning feature between small chapters and big chapters. So you see that structure came about so that small chapters only play with small chapters. Everybody play in your own size category.

Right! That makes sense.

C: That's how that came about. We decided on women, men, youth, and then we went around and around about whether we would use the word "elderly" or "seniors". It was clear we wanted the aged, but what was the appropriate term? The Soror who studied the aged said the current term is "seniors". We said, "Oh, OK! Seniors it is." We wanted to be politically correct. It was "seniors" not the elderly. That's how that came about. Her name was Theresa Dixon. She was a senior expert. She told us she had been working with AARP [American Association of Retired Persons] or something like that. And since I work in public health, I have this broad sense of community and population. So I was the person tasked with pulling everybody in and try to frame it.

So that was our group. We had myself; we had Darnetta for the men, she was the nurse practitioner; we had Dr. Gloria McCutcheon, she was the entomologist and she had been doing youth science camp; Theresa Dixon was my gerontology expert; and Karen Gibson was the kinesiology, the exercise expert. And so that's how the group came about. I'm looking at a picture of us with Dr. Moore at the Headquarters building before it was renovated.

We divided it up. What we did was everybody, after we decided on the basic structure, we did a template. Something I had been working with…I had gotten a grant from the American Association for Advancement of Science. They had what we call now toolkits. I pulled from that and developed this template. Whatever we did, everybody was going to leave with that template. And then we were to design our programs in that template. We had a deadline to send them back in, etc. That must have been a Friday. Then on that Saturday, we had to present what we had done to the Grand and Scarlett Black, all of the regional directors. I tell people all the time, "I do good science but I don't do pretty."

[Laughs]

C: The pretty part came from the input of the regional directors. We didn't have a name for the program at that time. We were just doing the program. Before we left that weekend, Soror Moore came back in and we made a presentation to her of what we were going to do, and she was OK with the approach we had. I think we left with a timeframe for everyone to send their stuff in. And the other thing I brought to the table was the Helping People 2020 goal. So I used those goals to make sure we addressed everything that was in Helping People 2020. [Zeta Phi Beta Sorority, Incorporated, was founded in 1920 so 2020 will mark Zeta's 100th anniversary.]

Nice!

C: That included the physical activity, obesity, tobacco, substance abuse, environmental, mental health, immunization, injury, responsible sexual behavior and access to health care. We used those to make sure…we had something to address all of those. Everybody had their own sections, and everybody had a template and also used a document called the State of Black America. I used all of those as our basic resources to give us some guidance. Soror Singletary was not at the table at the first meeting but Soror Moore brought her to the team, and then it was my responsibility to get her acclimated to what we were doing. And she brought Soror Perez to the group and asked me if I would accept her as my co-chair. At that time, she was National President of the Pediatric Association. And I mean, when the Grand brings you somebody and asks you if you will accept them as a chair, what are you going to say? [Laughs]

[Laughs]

C: I didn't know Soror Perez but I trusted Soror Moore.

By that time, I had left South Carolina and I got a job offer at Southern in Baton Rouge. I didn't come back to Auburn. I skipped Auburn and came to Baton Rouge. That is where Soror Carpenter worked, and I joined Soror Carpenter's chapter. I was in Soror Carpenter's chapter in Nu Zeta when I was doing all the Z-HOPE stuff.

I was at the beauty shop one day, and I am always a person who reads the bulletin boards. It's just one of the things I do. On the bulletin board was something about Helping Other People Excel. I was like, "I like that!" On the way home from the beauty shop, I picked up my trusty little cell phone and I called Soror Moore. And I said, "Soror Moore, how about this? Helping Other People Excel?" She said, "Honey, I like that! Z-HOPE!" And that's how Z-HOPE came about.

That's awesome!

C: Hope is one of my research concepts. So when I saw Helping Other People Excel, that was HOPE for me. What Soror Moore heard was Z-HOPE. That's how the name came about. I introduced HOPE! And she named it Z-HOPE on the phone while I was driving back from the beauty shop. She said, "That's what it's going to be!"

That is awesome. I love that.

C: Then she commissioned a graphic artist in Columbia to do a couple of designs for a logo. Then she had the whole team or some of the team when she had the regional directors' meeting in Washington. She had us to present to them. She had four designs, and I'm still trying to get pictures of those designs before they get thrown away. One of them I remember…do you remember the picture with the hands, all of the little kids' hands?

Yes, ma'am!

C: That's one of them. And the other is what we have for Z-HOPE. I don't remember the third one. I remember the little hands; she liked the hands. I didn't like the hands. It was the regional directors who pushed it towards the logo we have now. Stacy said we needed to move the Z over and have the Z over the O. That was her touch to it. That's how we got the Z-HOPE logo instead of the little hands. The regional directors chose the logo.

Soror Moore strategically took us to every region. She had to have this ready to launch by the first regional conference which was going to be in the Southeast in November. From that November, the rest of the year, we went to every regional conference and held Z-HOPE training workshops. But somewhere along the way, before that, and I know that person will emerge again, told me the design that you see, with the framework of overlapping circles that we use?

Yes, ma'am!

C: Some Soror sent it to me and said, "Soror Hendricks, this is what you are saying." I said, "Oh yes, that is cool!" And so, she tweaked it. She took it and made it pretty.

I think it's cool the whole Z-HOPE from start to finish was just a big collaboration. I figured when I read that you had helped with initiating – not that I thought you did it completely by yourself- but really you put it together along with Soror Moore, and Soror Moore brought together everybody. And heck, y'all didn't even know each other before she brought you all together. That's amazing.

C: We didn't. It was truly a collaborative birth from the collaborating minds of the Sorors.

This is a great story about networking and the power of collaborating with others!

Soror Hendricks, I'm going to have to wrap up, but I wanted to ask you one quick question before I let you go. What advice would you give to other people who have a passion or desire to make something happen?

C: Don't give up.

Awesome! Love it! Thank you so, so, so much! I really appreciate you taking the time to talk with me!

C: I think you got a lot more than what you asked for, but, you know…

Oh, I really got some amazing information! I'm so excited! My goal is to get people excited and have them feel like, "I have something I want to accomplish; I can make it happen!" I think you're an inspiration for that.

C: Well, I wish you much success in your endeavors, and I thank you for thinking of me to be included!

***

Soror Hendricks – Dr. Hendricks – could not have been nicer and more encouraging. And what a legacy she has! When I reached out to her, I had no idea that her family had been involved in Bloody Sunday with the Civil Rights movement. Also, I didn't know that she too had been a member of a "white" sorority before she joined Zeta – just like me!

After our interview, Dr. Hendricks updated me on her upcoming activities. She is being inducted into the Tuskegee University Hall of Fame in April. She was also inducted into the American Academy of Nursing and will be inducted in the Zeta South Central and Alabama State Zeta Hall of Fame. In addition to completing the Leadership Selma Dallas County, she is now building a new School of Nursing Program at Concordia college Alabama in historic Selma, AL as the Dean of Health Sciences & Director of the Department of Nursing. She may have retired from Auburn University, but as you can see, this amazing lady is still vibrant and active!

I had a wonderful time talking with Dr. Hendricks. While I had wanted to talk with her about Z-HOPE, I learned so much more. This kind of amazing discovery is one of the main reasons why I love being a Zeta. I am so blessed to have the chance to get to know women – and men – I may never have met before. I am so enriched from the experience, and I am thankful I too can add to the Zeta experience.

Story 10: Sarada Jammi, Dance Instructor: The rhythm of life

Manakin Sabot is a quiet, rural suburb west of the Short Pump area in the West End of Richmond, Virginia. While there has been a lot of expansion since I first visited this area over three decades ago, it still looks like a small country town to me. Past Satterwhite's restaurant, down a winding path, there is an incredible temple, filled with exotic beauty. It was here in this that Jerry and I were introduced to kuchipudi, an Indian classical dance.

***

When I had started working at Magellan, I met Ameya. Her kind smile and friendliness won me over quickly, and we became friends. I learned that she and I both graduated from the College of William and Mary – although, I believe she was probably born around the year I graduated! Our age difference was irrelevant and we became friends. Ameya and I bonded over our love of all types of cuisine. Often we would go to lunch and talk.

It was over over some delicious pho at an amazing Vietnamese restaurant in the West End that I talked with Ameya about Tickers. I had just finished interviewing Shiva, one of our co-workers, and was telling Ameya about how well it went. She shyly said, "You know, this might be selfish. But you should talk to my mom."

I knew that Ameya's mother was a dance instructor. Earlier in the summer, Jerry and I were invited to attend a dance recital by my then manager, Umakanth. His daughter Lilikith was performing for the last time before leaving for Virginia Tech.

Jerry and I entered the temple. We were greeted warmly, and were invited to stash our shoes in the coat and shoe area. We grabbed our seats and awaited the performance. Neither of us had seen Indian classical dance before. This dance was so much more involved than other dances I had seen or experienced. Lilikith's facial expressions, her hand movements, her footsteps, everything was so involved and yet so graceful. I was mesmerized. My favorite dance of the evening was when Lilikith danced while standing on a brass plate. She clung to the edge of the plate with her feet and never missed a beat.

So when Ameya suggested over lunch that I speak with her mother, I had an inkling of her talents. It turns out that what I knew was really only a small part of her dedication to dance.

***

Sarada, Ameya's mother, was introduced to dance by Smt. Shantha Balagopalan in Dhanbad, India in 1976. In 1985, she moved to Madras, where she received training under Padmabhushan Dr. Vempati Chinna Satyam at the Kuchipudi Art Academy in the true gurukulam style, living in his home. In 1987 she moved to Kuchipudi Kalakshetra, Visakhapatnam, a branch of the Academy. After moving to Singapore, she returned to Kalakshetra yearly throughout the nineties for advanced training. In 2000, she spent a whole year honing proficiency in expressions, choreography, and theory at Kuchipudi Kalakshetra under Hari Rama Murthy and N. N. V. Satyabhanu, and worked towards translating the theory from Telugu, the vernacular, to English.[xvii]

Note: Smt. is the equivalent of "Mrs", an honorific given to married women in India.

***

This single-mindedness can be defining to one's life. Ameya's mother, Sarada, lives and breathes dance. But even though I knew she had this passion, our interview was filled with surprises.

It took us a while to coordinate our interview. I have a "phone phobia" which means I can often procrastinate when it comes to calling people. Ameya said her mother has a similar phobia. When we finally reached out to each other, I asked Sarada (whose name is pronounced like 'Sara-the') where we should meet. "Would you like to meet for lunch?" I asked. She agreed, and said she would serve lunch at the temple. I was so excited because I love Indian food! And home-cooked – or temple-cooked – food? Yes! I came to the Sri Sai Temple bringing an offering of Clementine tangerines for the Gods. We ate lunch first, and then we sat down for the interview.

***

K: Let's go ahead and get started. I'm going to pull up another chair so the recorder can sit. Because sometimes I have a tendency to talk with my hands, and I don't want to knock the recorder over!

First of all, thank you again for sitting with me. I really appreciate it. Ameya had told me so much about you before I even came to see the performance that I saw.

And then, when I came to see Umakanth's daughter perform, I was just blown away. I had never seen Indian dance before, and it really wowed me. I was like, "Holy moley!" It is so beautiful, and so intricate, and so unlike anything else I had seen before. I didn't have much comparison. I told Ameya, "It is sort of like belly dancing but it's so much more intricate than belly dance!" So I wanted to talk to you.

Before I interview anyone, I always do some research online. So I looked you up on Google, and you came up under the site specifically – and please forgive me if I mispronounce anything...

It was under the Kuchipudi Kalakar web site. And so you were one of the featured people who was on there, so they had your bio. And I thought, "This is super! I can find out all about you." So it said that you had always known that you wanted to be a dancer.

When did you first see people perform dances? Did you have a specific memory?

S: My father is a musician. So we lived in India, in the northern part of India. He was a scientist. So we lived away from the actual hometown. He used to teach music at home. And then we used to have these artists who would come from the South to perform. And whenever we had a performance, he would drive us wherever we had to go.

Ok!

S: It was not a four wheeler but he had a scooter so he used to take us. And then we used to watch. But I don't know if that really interested me. Because from when I remember, I remember that I used to love dance. I used to go to the movie theater or something, and when a nice song starts, I would forget it was an auditorium or anything. I would start doing my own dance. And my Mom always tells me that I used to gather all the little kids in my neighborhood. I was hardly four or five, but all the littler ones I would gather and teach them something for some song.

Oh cool!

S: And then we used to invite everybody to come and sit down. Parents would sit and then we used to do some dance.

So the first time they really felt I was deeply interested, I was about seven and a half or eight years old when one of the greatest dancers of all time, Dr. Pragyasa Ponmada, she came to Dhanbad, the place where I was born. My father went and told her, "I have a daughter who is interested in dance. She says she's ready to come with you."

Dhanbad is further away from Calcutta on the East side. This lady is from Chennai, which is in the south. So it was two days of travel to go there. So he said, "She said she wants to come and stay with you and learn." She said, "OK, you bring her tomorrow." She was doing a demonstration. So she said, "You can bring your child so I can talk to her and see." She was expecting somebody who would be seventeen or eighteen, and she sees a little kid. She says, "What, she's a child! I cannot take her. It's too far and I keep traveling. I cannot take such a small kid. If you have somebody who can come and stay with her, I will certainly teach her." So my parents didn't have anybody at home who could leave with me. And I have siblings, and my father was here, so my Mom couldn't go. So the search continued. And then finally, when I was fifteen years old, I completed my high school. In India, in tenth grade, you graduate from high school.

My master, Dr. Padmabhushan Satyam, had come to Calcutta. And my father took me to Calcutta to see the program. It was about six hours of train ride. And then there he asked my master if he could take me and teach me dance. He said, "Let her finish her schooling first. At least basic education she should have." And then he said, "In dance, you may earn; you may not earn. You may be successful; you may not be successful. But you come from a family where your Dad is so highly qualified." My sister is a doctor. "So everybody is so highly qualified. Why do you want to go into a line where there is no certainty?" My father told him, "She just wants to dance. So I don't want to discourage her. Let her." So he said, "Let her finish her high school. Then at least she will be able to do her work by herself, take care of herself. Then you can drop, and she can live with us."

So then, as soon as I finished my tenth year class, in 1985, I was fifteen years old. My Dad took me to Chennai, and then we went to the master's house. The school was called Kuchipudi Art Academy. And then my parents were thinking I could continue my regular education as well as dance class. But he said, "If she has to stay, then she has to stay in the house. I cannot allow her to go out. Because it is a responsibility. We don't know how things will be outside. So she can live here."

So I was living with them. We call it gurukulam. "Guru" means master; "kulam" means their house and family. So in gurukulam you just stay and you just are a member of the family; that's it. You may not be related by blood, you may not be anything, but you know you are all one family. We don't give money or anything.

But you were like a member of the family. You would cook together and eat together, and do chores?

S: No, they would cook. You would just do your dance. That's all.

Oh, OK!

S: About twenty to twenty-five kids would be there all the time. There are no more masters who are like that. He passed away about three years ago. Nobody does that anymore because it is too expensive. It's a big responsibility. It's not easy to manage your own kids, to think about them.

Yeah!

S: So that is how it was. So morning, you just wake up. He would never wake you up, he would never tell you you have to do this or do that, or anything. You wake up and go. We had like small attached huts where he used to teach the class. And then we had a big hall. He used to sleep in one of those attached huts. So if you wake up in the mornings at four and you go there, he will teach you dance. If you don't go there, he will not come and wake you up.

First round used to start at four or four thirty; it used to go until six thirty or seven. We take a shower, our basic stuff. And again at eight thirty the regular class would start, and the day students come. From eight thirty until one thirty used to be that class. Then at one thirty, about two o'clock we would have our lunch. Then at four o'clock we would have class again, and it used to go until six. From six thirty, we would have a class until nine.

Oh my goodness!

S: At nine, he used to start his school and he had a special class. I used to sit and watch that. So by the time he leaves the hall, it would be about eleven thirty or twelve, sometimes one, sometimes one thirty. Because we didn't have any separate rooms. Nothing private in the dance hall. No special attention or anything. We were just living there. So that is how we learned.

I believe in gurukulam. Especially in these arts, when you live with them, the more you observe. Maybe you don't realize, but in the long run, that is what will help you grow. You watch them teach, you watch them. But it's not easy to live. Most people will drop out because nobody will give you any good treatment.

It almost sounds like – this isn't exactly the same – but like the military, where you're in barracks, in a way. You just get up and train and train.

S: You have to be passionate. Otherwise it's impossible. No one ever gives you anything, like, "Oh, she is precious." You want it, you have to show that you really yearn for it.

Let me ask you something. You were interested in dance when you were about seven and a half, but then you completed your schooling. And it wasn't until you were about fifteen and you had graduated…were you still dancing between age seven and a half to fifteen?

S: I did learn from one of the, you'll have it on my website, Shantha Balagopalan. I went there for a year or year and a half. But being a musician, my father, he felt that she was…see, some people don't have the beat.

Gotcha!

S: She was having some issues with the beat because he used to play drums for her. And he felt, you know, because I was so interested that it was not right to put me with somebody who has some problem with the beat. Because dance is all beat.

Definitely.

S: So then he said, "You know, we will look for somebody." And every summer, we would travel to the south, keep asking people. Everybody would say, "Yes, we are ready to take her!" But everybody would say, "We need to have somebody to take care of her." So that happened from when I was seven to when I was fifteen; eight years. So we could never find one until finally I found one.

**That's awesome! Sounds like your Dad really believed in you. He sounds like he was a big
supporter.**

S: My Dad, my parents, both of them. The thing that really awes me about them is that my father always said, "Just do what you love to do. It may not be an easy path, but certainly you will be successful."

Oh, that's awesome!

S: "But when you are trying to do something, just do your best. Put in 100%. Not, 'I tried but it didn't happen'." So when my sister wanted to do her medicine…she's also just like me. When she was ten or twelve, she used to tell, "I want to be a surgeon."

Oh wow!

And she is a cancer surgeon. So he used to always say, "If you believe in yourself, it will happen." It might not be right now, but you have to work on it, and you will have it. And my uncle knew my brother was not so focused on what he wants to be. He was like, "I want to be an engineer, just study and then work." But my sister and myself, we were both very passionate. And she did what she wants to do.

So everybody used to, even his colleagues, used to tell [my father], "She is so good in studies. Why do you want to go and put her into dance? There is no future in India arts!" In India, there is a lot of art and a lot of culture. But if you want to be financially successful....I don't know about here, but in India it is very difficult to be financially sound person being an artist.

Honestly, it is very similar here. Often, people will be like, "I want to be an artist." And people are like, "Well, good luck. You're not going to be able to make any money from that." So it sounds very similar to Indian culture.

S: That is the reason everybody had discouraged, "No, you can study. You can be independent and have a regular job!" But somehow it never, never made me...[Laughs]

I don't care about money also. Maybe that is the reason it is easy for me. And then, the way I was...my parents never bothered about money or saving, or you know, that you have to be rich or anything. Maybe that was the influence. I don't know.

Sounds like it.

S: I enjoyed with my master because it was nothing but dance.

So you really enjoyed that?

S: I really enjoyed that. And he also never demanded – you believe me or not, I don't know – more than ten, twelve thousand students have passed through his school; he never took a single penny from anyone. Never.

Wow!

S: He never charged for teaching dance; he never charged for people living in his house. But he demanded passion. You have to have the passion to work with him. Otherwise you cannot live there. I think you know that my parents finally put me in the right place to help me!

Yes! How long were you there?

S: I lived in his house for like three and a half years. But my health didn't cooperate that much. Because so many hours of dance and the food habits. So my health, it started giving me trouble. He had a branch in a place which where my sister was studying; it's called Kalakshetra, and it's close to Hydrabad. When he had a branch, what I did was I moved there so I could be a day scholar. I could go in the morning, come back and live. The same routine, the routine didn't change much. I used to go in the morning at eight and back in the evening at five thirty or six, sometimes come back at eight o'clock. It was all seven days of the week, the whole year. I wouldn't go back home. Then I was there for almost three, three and a half years I was there.

So the difference between being in the gurukulam where you you were living there and then moving to Hydrabad, what was the difference? Less hours of the day?

S: What was the difference? It was more like your habits were regularized. But I was living in a hostel where they would give us breakfast and lunch, everything. There, because of the number of hours I would put in for dance, it was my master and his wife who had to cook for so many people. So she used to take her time to do it. So they had a school year, and he knew some people who were board members of a hostel, so he went and talked with them. And then he moved me there. So I went there.

That is where I got married. Then we went to Singapore. And from there I used to go every year, and then stay in the Kalakshetra for a couple of months at least, practice, and then go back. So there was never a gap. But it wouldn't be as intense because it was only two months or three months.

So when you got married, because you were staying near your sister but away from your parents, right? Did they arrange the marriage for you?

S: No, no. I was not staying with my sister; we were in the same town. She was in the medical hostel and I was living close to my dance class. I met my husband in my friend's house. They used to rent a small portion of his house so I met him there. What attracted us, I don't know. He is an engineer so he used to work in the shipyard in the automation department. So he used to work there. Somehow we got together.

Initially I was not interested in getting married because back in India, in those days, I'm talking late eighties, nineties, that time, once you get married, the families would not encourage you to go out and perform.

I was wondering about that!

S: So they wouldn't encourage that. So that's why I was more to be by myself. But then I met him and his Mom also, she is eighty-five. She also had trained in dance back in the forties, fifties. So she was also interested in dance. And his father also has a very similar nature like mine. Like, he was an attorney, but he never demanded money. They were very similar ideologists. So I think that is what made him feel comfortable with me.

So I told him when he proposed to me, "I am not going to go to office. I am not going to earn money. I want my dance class. I want to live mine. If you are ready for it, fine. Otherwise…" And he has lived up to it. He has never demanded me to work, he never demanded anything from me.

That is wonderful.

S: He has always cooperated whatever I do. [Laughs] So he has been…I think that is the reason I have been able to do what I want. Because I have this ability to…

Yeah, and the support. That means a lot.

S: My mother and father supported me and my sister, and all. Same as I was supported in my parents' side…initially with my mother-in-law, there were some issues because she felt, you know, you need to have two jobs; two salaries will make your living a little easier. Otherwise he's having to struggle. Eventually she is realizing that it doesn't work with me.

[Laughs] So she came around?

S: She came around!

Good!

S: She's fine with it. So that's how it continued.

So when you…it sounds like not long after you got married, y'all moved to Singapore?

S: Mmm-hmm.

Now, were you able to continue dancing there?

S: In Singapore, I used to teach in one place. One of my master's students, she was teaching there. From my master I came to know that she was there. I went and met her, and I used to help her teach the juniors, help her with the classes like that. I used to perform with her and everything. So that was good.

Oh, that's great!

S: It was not difficult for me. Then after that, in 1996, 1997 I think, Ameya was in school at that time. She had to write about parents and their careers. So she said, "My Dad is an engineer; my Mom is a dancer, an Indian classical dancer." She was in kindergarten then. So the teacher called me. "She wrote that you are a dancer. Are you?" [Laughs] "Yes, I am." Then she said, "We are looking for classical dancers because the Ministry of Education has said we need to introduce Indian kids to Indian culture." Because in Singapore, there is a huge Indian population. Not people from India India, but in Singapore there is one group who speak Tamil. Their roots are from India. So for them, they need to be exposed to Indian culture. I said, "Yes, I am interested." So then I applied, and I was working for ten different schools working through the Ministry of Culture teaching Indian dance.

So when you say different schools, were they different locations? Was it all elementary schools or high schools?

S: Elementary school kids. So I used to go to about four and five schools. At each school, it was like an extra-curricular school activity. Children would sign up and then I would go out and teach them. And at the end of the year, they would have a program at the school. And then they would go on to the national level where all the schools would compete.

It was a totally different experience. They didn't want the whole set of training which would take years together. They just wanted something simple which will be done in a year's time.

So it...I mean, this may sound basic...but it was not anything like the gurukullam where...it was more like a day program?

S: Yeah, just two hours. I had to come up with a short program of what I would do. And then I would give them the music which I would...so I used to find a piece of music. They usually preferred instrumental. So I used to find some music, and then choreograph for that. Based on the choreography, what are the steps, what all movements are required. I used to plan that, and then plan the class, and then teach the children, and then we used to present. So that in one way was good for me and good for the children because it gave them an exposure to Indian dance. Some of them would get interested, and then they would come to Retaliax to get in-depth knowledge. There I would teach as I do here. Like regular class, where the children go through the whole nine yards.

Was it ever hard? Did you ever have children who weren't interested? You came obviously from a background where everyone was very passionate.

S: It was different for me. It was a little bit difficult because I couldn't understand how to make such a huge subject so small. So for me, that was the first problem. Then the second thing was, you know, how to group the steps and all so they understand how to do the basic items. I think I struggled for maybe a few months and then I could kind of figure it out. And in between, I always had support from my master.

Oh, that's great!

S: We had the principal there, and I used to talk to them, so that way it helped me know how to mold them. And it became easier.

So there wasn't a guidebook on how to do a shortened –

S: No!

So you were pioneering this sort of program?

S: Yes, and it was good. Because then I understood that everyone doesn't need to have the whole…because it's one thing if you want to, like my students have been learning for eight years. So in one year, what can I teach? Not much. So I finally figured out in one year, you can do a little of this, this and this, and I could be happy with that. Initially, it was a little disappointing. I felt I wasn't doing justice to it.

It does sound, on the flip side, that you were giving these children exposure they wouldn't have had before. And some of them did become serious students?

S: Oh yes! They did come and learn. And they…actually, what I see is most of these school kids, they would learn many other things. Self-discipline, they would learn confidence. They would learn to observe more. Dance is all visual. You have to see, and you have to copy it.

Right!

S: So they would develop that kind of stuff, and they would be more successful, the teachers would say they were more successful. So that is how I learned that we are learning many more things, not just dancing.

So here also, that is what I tell the parents. "You think you are sending them off to class and I take too long. But what happens is they learn, and they are more well-rounded. And it's very good for them in the future." I don't expect everybody to sit and teach dance like me. It's a good thing to have confidence. It's a good thing to learn to observe and learn things, because everything cannot be taught. To get discipline is good. That is all the side effects.

And most of them, they really go to all these specialty school programs. I think it helps them develop their IQ. Maybe it helps them to develop more that, you know, they are more focused. I don't know. Most of the children go to Godwin [a well-respected school in Richmond] or AP [advanced placement, the placement of a student in a high school course that offers college credit] programs or things like that. I think it really helps them. Ameya and another student went to William and Mary. One went to Cornell, then one went to Berkeley. Everybody has gone to good schools. So it certainly makes them more disciplined and more self-motivated, things like that. You learn much more.

That's awesome! After moving to Singapore, you would return to Kalakshetra yearly. And then, it sounds like in 2000 you went back to India?

S: Yes, I was there for one whole year.

Please tell me about that. How did that come about?

S: That was when we decided to move from Singapore. We were thinking of it for quite some time. Then in 2000, my husband came here as a student. He did his MBA. So then, I said, "Let me go back to India. I can stay and practice." That way, financially also, it would be good. For me, also, I could focus on what I want to do.

That is when I was like a full-time dance student. Same like before, I used to go in the morning at eight. My children used to go to school so I would pick them up from school. Again, take them to class after that. In our dance class, it's more like a family. Even now, when I go to India, I go stay with my master. They cook the food also and they will take care of; we practice. I will teach also, everything. It is more informal. When we are in the class proper, it is more formal. But otherwise, outside it is a more informal relationship. I personally feel that when you learn in that manner, when you have a more informal relationship with your master, you learn more.

That makes sense.

S: Even when…if I teach my students as a student, we would just say, "OK, good. You are doing good." But when I feel it's my child, we are never satisfied with them.

[Laughs] Right!

S: We want the best.

I guess you have more invested, so it's not like, "Oh, that was fine." It's more like, "Oh no, I know you. You can do better."

S: All my students, I don't know, somehow I have that will and wanting like they are my own kids. That is how I am bonded to my master and his family. So that's why I go back. I used to stay there and perform. At that time, I performed a lot, in 2000, because my mother in law was there to help take care of the kids. I used to travel a lot and perform, practice, everything. It was good. It really made me live my dream one more time.

Oh, what a great opportunity! That's fantastic.

S: When we moved here, I took it more seriously. I did not want to do what I did in Singapore and go to the schools and all. That was maybe a different opportunity but I didn't want to go in that direction. I wanted to stick to my original, you know, what I want. And Gods' grace, it has been good.

Oh, that's wonderful! So when y'all moved to the States…it sounds like your husband was already here because he was getting his master's. Then what year did y'all move - was it 2001?

S: 2001.

And then when you moved, were you in Virginia then?

S: No, we first moved to Illinois. That's where he was studying. In the university, I did perform. I think I did two or three performances. And then the next year, 2002, April, we moved to Richmond.

Oh, OK. When you moved, I imagine since you've been involved in dance, were people already aware that you were studying with your master and already be involved in dance? Or did you talk to people when you got here?

S: No, I actually I have been lucky all the time. So my friend was already here. She was teaching just three or four kids. She was just starting her bachelor's degree. She did accounting, I think. She had a little ten month or one-year-old baby, so she was finding it difficult to cope with the family and studying, and this. So she was looking for someone on whom she could leave and do the stuff she needs to do. So it was good. Also, the parents were also very happy, because they wanted someone who was more reliable. So I started teaching.

We had about four or five kids. And then we did a summer camp, where we did six or seven hours of dance class every day. Same like the gurukullam but you come in the morning, stay the whole day, and in the evening the parents come to pick them up. So they enjoyed that. That I started. And then, it has been good since then.

Now my friend has her own school. She…we figured out that our ways of teaching are a little different. One…even if we come from the same school, we have difference. I decided to be on my own, and she decided to start on her own.

You each have your own dance schools, but it's not like you are competitors?

S: No.

Because you have different styles?

S: No, the style is the same. But I don't like to change my basic stuff. I want my kids to come at least three or four times a week. But most of the Indian parents are not ready for that. They want it once a week, maybe a half hour or an hour. So I don't take them when they don't take it seriously.

When they cannot put in the time, I don't take them. So she took care of that kind of kids.

OK, so that's a good balance!

S: And then, my master came every year. Sometimes he came and teaches for my kids also.

How did that make you feel when he came?

S: Oh, it is good. So that is how…we are all together, but little differences. It's not that we are under one school name, but what we do is the same thing.

When you were studying, and it was the gurukulam style, it sounded like it was more normal for students to start when they were fifteen, or old enough to take care of themselves. Is that the case here? Or do your students start younger?

S: See, for dance, it is good to start when you are about seven because your body is more flexible. You can learn better. And then, you know, you need about ten years to train. So by the time you are seventeen or eighteen, you will be there to perform. I didn't have that opportunity then so I started late. So I think students…I was particular that they have to be age seven until two or three years ago when one parent was really on me that they want to have a five-year-old join. And then, surprisingly, that kid did really well.

Oh good!

S: So that changed my opinion that I should not just push kids away because they are not old enough. Maybe I should start at five and let them go at a slower place, let them learn as they grow. So I have five-year-olds now, at least five. I cannot take any more.

[Laughs] Yes, that would be challenging!

S: Yes! Once they join kindergarten, they can observe and do it. It's very difficult. And Indian dance is very…it's very similar to sports. It's very rigorous. It looks graceful but it is really rigorous and requires a lot of energy. And because of the stamping and all we do, your legs have to be really strong.

I've taken dance class before, but never Indian dance. Do y'all do a routine where you warm up? Are there stretches?

S: No, we really didn't know all this. I didn't know all this. But now, after many of us have had issues with the knees, we kind of made it a routine with them to stretch before class and after class. But usually, our system, we have to do a few steps, so that is a kind of warm-up. Then, we do the items. It's really a two-and-a-half-hour long class. They get time to do all that. But I didn't know for a long time that you had to do stretches.

So when I saw the performances, one thing that I noticed was that they seemed like very intricate routines. And it also seemed like it wasn't, um, how do I say it? Sometimes you see a dance performance and it will be the same steps repeated. In some of the dances, and tell me if I'm wrong, it looks like it is very intricate where it is almost like a script. Is it choreographed?

S: Yes. It is choreographed.

Do you use, do you have to write the choreograph, or is there something that's like a traditional choreography?

S: There is nothing written. I don't have anything written.

Oh really? Oh wow!

S: Most of it is…most of our Indian Hindu tradition comes orally. So most of it is oral tradition.

Interesting!

S: I don't have anything written.

Nothing's written down? It's all up here! [Taps head]

S: Now Ameya is working with me to document most of the steps. So at least we will be able to give something to children who leave so that they will have something to refer to. But I don't have anything written.

So, do you call them routines? Or would you just call it a particular dance? For instance, I was particularly impressed with the dance on the plate.

S: Brass plate.

Yes! Do you call it a dance or a routine?

S: That is called the Tarangam. So these are basically songs about Lord Krishna [a Hindu god]. They describe his childhood. He is supposed to be very naughty and they have a lot of stories about him. So these are the stories they describe. And at the end, basically, he says…all these songs are written by one poet. So he connects to the Lord through these syllables where we have all these dance. That is how they are connected, and they are all performed on the plate. So that is called the Tarangam.

So there are particular steps that are always done?

S: These are all done by my master. Most of them go back to him. He has actually…see, in kuchipudi dance, it was not, they wouldn't allow women to dance until recently.

Oh really?

S: Because all are male. Because for us, dance is more of devotion. It's more of a prayer. When we do the service, we say…it's like, you know how we treat our God, how our prayers go. Just like you treat your guest. You invite them, you ask them to wash their feet, you give them food. Then you know, after that, you will have some entertainment for them. You will sing, you will dance. After the prayer service is over, then we bathe the Lord. Then we do the prayers, then we give the food, then we offer dance, we offer music, we offer everything. So this is a part of the service.

And for us, when you have your menstrual cycle, you are not eligible to go into the temple. For four days, we do not go into the temple. So that is the reason women are not eligible to dance. In this tradition – not in the other Indian dance traditions. But in kuchipudi. It comes from a small village where only males dance. But my master, his guru, he told him, "Until we teach it to ladies, we cannot see the grace in this art. They will keep it as a folklore, they will not teach it as classical dance. So for that, you need to teach it to, introduce girls, to this." So then he was exiled from the village.

And he moved to Chennai. He had to walk…you can read about it in the kuchipudi web site. It's amazing. He is one and only one. So he moved there, and then he read this whole text on dance. It's like the model text of dance. He correlated how kuchipudi dance is based on this, and then he worked with the Government of India to make sure that, it is one of the Indian art forms. Previously it was folklore. So until the Sixties, no women, no women performed. It is only since the Sixties. Maybe late Fifties, early Sixties they started introducing women into this.

You had said that your mother-in-law did dance. Did she do kuchipudi?

S: No.

I guess it wasn't since you said she did it in the Forties and Fifties.

S: That was called Bharatanatyam. That does not come from the drama tradition. That's a different art form, a different style altogether. This particular art form is only for men to perform.

Do you ever get any resistance from people?

S: No, no more. Earlier, in the village, they wouldn't…but now in the village, they are teaching ladies. It has been accepted. Things have changed. So that is how it was. That is why you will see that all my former masters were men.

OK, that makes sense then! I wanted to ask you about something that I read. It was talking about…that you had spent time translating theory from Telegu to English. I'm confused…is it like a translation, like you are translating a language? Or is it like you are translating…

S: Most of these…as I told you, most of this is oral tradition. So when they learn, what they do is they will make notes. And most of them write in our mother tongue. Many of us don't know the language now, the youngsters. So I used to sit down and listen to all that and then translate it into, those meanings into English. So those children who do not read the words can also benefit. So I did a lot of that work in India when I was there in 2000. I worked on it then.

How did you create your current dance studio? Is it part of the temple here?

S: No, no. I do teach at home. We have the garage, right? I made the flooring and everything. I have my own place so I can do it at my own time.

That's wonderful!

S: Only on weekends I do it at the temple.

What kind of modifications did you have to do to the garage?

S: We had to finish the walls. I put some insulation down. I came up with my own design because children dance barefoot and on the concrete it would be difficult. So I put some insulation, raised the floor and then put a wooden floor.

So what do you prefer: dancing or teaching?

S: I love teaching. I love it. My passion is teaching dance. It's not performing. I don't like to perform.

So it really is the teaching! OK! That's interesting because I would have thought that the love of the performing kept you going.

S: No. I don't like…I have performed a lot, but that is not my…I am not passionate about getting onto the stage.

Interesting! So you're passionate about dance, but more passionate about the dance itself rather than doing the dancing?

S: Yes. I enjoy dancing by myself or I enjoy teaching. That's it.

But not performing in front of people?

S: No.

So, it sounds like you didn't really have an outline when you were that seven-and-a-half-year-old to where you are now. Did you really have an idea of where dance would take you?

S: See, for a long time, from when I remember, I wanted to teach. So I think I have been doing that for…even when I was learning dance, I used to teach the younger students. That's it. But I didn't have any passion to reach here, I didn't have a plan like that. As long as I am able to dance, that is good enough. [Laughs]

Very cool!

S: I had one…I always had a dream. In Pittsburgh, we had a big temple, an old temple. I think it is one of the oldest temples in the U.S. There my master did a lot of dance programs, like his students. He was also basically an educator, not a performer. So they did a lot of dance dramas, we called them dance ballets. He did a lot of those then, and he conducted a lot of workshops there. So I always had a great desire that at some point I would like to do a workshop there. But somehow it didn't work out. And there are already great teachers in Pittsburgh. So now I'm not bothered about that.

[Laughs] OK!

S: When I was in India, that was a passion I had. But by the time I came here, they already had great teachers.

So what have been some of the challenges you have with keeping the dance studio going?

S: See for us, in the Indian community, the biggest problem is parents want the children to learn dance as an extra-curricular activity. So when we demand the time…see, it is like going to school. You don't go to school once a week and get where you are today. You have to go every day. Especially with dance, the biggest challenge is that it is so physical. The body has to get used to it. And Indian dance, it has a lot of expressions, a lot of expressions. A lot of lyrics which you have to express.

I always tell my kids, that's what my master told me, that it should become like walking. Like you know, when you walk, you just walk. You don't have to think: You have to lift your leg; you have to stretch it out, you have to put it – you don't have to do that. Same way, you need to do your footwork. Whatever has to be done by the feet has to become a mechanical thing where your mind doesn't have to think. That is when you will be enjoying that song, the lyrics – that is when you can get involved and express.

Gotcha!

S: You need a lot of practice. And Indian parents – they want their children to excel in dance, in music, in karate, in X, in Y, in school. There is a lot of pressure in school. A child will be in second grade and they will expect the child to do fourth grade math. Indians are really crazy about that. That is the biggest challenge.

The second thing is – take Likitha, for instance. She learned for ten years. She went to college. I don't know if she is really going to continue this. So that…I feel, you know, I wouldn't say it was wasted effort. But certainly I want somebody to be like me who will continue. Most of the parents, they also don't encourage the child to continue. "Yeah, you have learned, you have done your program, that is enough. Now you need to move on." But move on – what happened to all this time you put in? What happened to all this effort, the effort the child has put in? So that is the biggest challenge for us. But I don't know –at some point, maybe someone will be there who will come back.

There are some people. Ameya came back [to dance] after college. In college, for the first two years, she was not too into it. Now she has come back, she has more passion than before. I have another student who learned for two and a half, three years, then went to school. She went to college; now she is doing her PhD, and now she has come back. So I hope more and more children will do that. But I personally feel the parents are the problem. For us, it's all academics. And how much is the paycheck. So that is the biggest hurdle until we teach our children to just live what they want. But we don't teach our children to do that. We want them to have the status, what car you have. It's a challenge; that is the biggest challenge. It bothers me all the time.

I think that's one of the things that makes it so hard, like we were talking about before for people to pursue their passion. Because they feel so much, um, outside force saying, "No! You can't be a dancer. A dancer doesn't make money. You should be a…" you know, whatever makes money.

S: Everybody wants their…I don't know, at some point, somebody will be there.

Yeah, definitely! So who has been your best supporter? It sounds like you've had a number of people who have been your supporters: your father, your husband...

S: I don't know. Somehow everybody has been with me. Everybody to date.

What advice would you give to other people who want to follow their passion?

S: Follow your heart. See, when the mind starts speaking, you have so many calculations. But when you are just following your heart, there is no destination. There is no need to perform. There is no need to prove yourself. There is nothing, but you will achieve everything because you will be enjoying it to that level.

Very cool! I have one last question. Do you have like a motto, or words that you live by?

S: [Laughs] You have to be passionate about what you're doing. That's it. You need to just...see, when you are doing something, thinking it is work, you cannot enjoy it. When you do it because you just enjoy it? I'm not bragging or anything, but somehow with Gods' grace, I am able to do what I love to do. So I come to the temple around three-thirty in the morning. The latest is four. Here, it is a lot of work. We do a lot of meditation. We call it japa. It means chanting and all that. And then we shower the Gods and we dress the Gods. [There are statues of the Gods in the Temple.] I don't know if you observed it or not.

No, I haven't.

S: So all that, that takes a lot of time. So by the time I am done with my routine in the temple, usually it is at least one thirty or two in the afternoon. Then sometimes I get time to rest. Other times I don't. But usually these days I try to rest. Again, at five, my dance class starts. And then, when my dance class is done, it is about nine.

Wow!

S: But I don't know. I think because I love whatever I'm doing, I don't feel drained out or "Oh my God! When will I get a break?" I feel I am living a break every day because I'm enjoying what I'm doing. But if you don't enjoy it, what happens is you need to stop and go for a vacation. You need time for yourself. But what I am doing is really for myself. I think that's – that's what's important for more and more of us to do. My master always said, "Don't dance because you want to be famous. Don't dance because you want to get money out of it. Dance because you want to dance. Everything else will come behind it." Everything else – see, once you are a dancer, see, I'm...some money you need; you will get it. People will know you. You will be…everything else will happen. Everybody cannot be as great as Michael Jackson, as popular as him, or as somebody else. Certainly at your level, you will be, and if you are destined to be somebody like that, you will. You don't need to do anything.

So I always tell my kids' parents, I don't tell my children, no, but I tell their parents, "Don't push them. Just let them enjoy." See, when they come every day to class, what happens is they connect, they make their friends. This is all what makes them enjoy for a longer time. But when you are saying, "OK, five to six is dance class, six to seven is karate, seven to eight is…," you are giving them exposure to something where they need to relax, and you are making it more mechanical. But things have changed. Too many expectations! I always complain about parents.

[Laughs]

S: Especially…I don't know that much about American parents. Indian parents especially want the child to…I don't know what they want from the child. In school, they have to be first. In dance, if any other child is dancing better than her, the mom is already worried. How can everyone do the best? And karate – "Did she get the black belt? Did he get the black belt?" Come on! They are human beings, right? Give them a break. I hope someday parents understand that they cannot do that to the kids.

I hope so, too!

S: They come and tell me, "You tell them, they should do this." That's enough!

Thank you so much, Kim.

Thank you! This is fantastic – amazing!

***

    After our interview, Sarada gave me a tour of the temple. She explained each of the Gods to me and told about each of their stories. The statues of the Gods are washed and dressed, and have food offerings presented to them. The temple itself is absolutely beautiful. I was so impressed and honored to have this tour and this time to talk with Sarada. I felt joyous and at peace when I left the temple, in addition to having a happy, full belly.

    Sarada's story is one of a pure love for teaching dance. She was fortunate to have people in her life – her father, her husband and his family – who supported her dream. But she still had to have the courage to pursue life and her passion on her own terms.

After our interview, Sarada took me through the Temple and showed me the statues of the Gods. She explained what each God represented and their stories. Her love and devotion shone through her words. I was very honored to talk with Sarada and to hear about her amazing journey. And I sent a big "thank you" email to Ameya for encouraging me to meet her Mom!

Conclusion

So where did Tickers take me?

Tickers took me to a new full-time job. As much as I loved working as a project manager for the data warehousing team at Magellan, I had too much on my plate at the health care company. I was trying to manage data warehousing, which was a full-time job, plus juggle managing two other projects. Combined with the fact that the health care company was located 48 miles away, which meant an hour commute for me each way every day, I felt drained. Having too much to do and not enough time made me feel defeated every day.

One day, I received a call. One of my good friends, Robert, had recommended me to another defense contractor. NCR had just won a contract with the Defense Commissary Agency to support a major software implementation. They wanted to talk with me about the position and ultimately I took it.

Leaving Magellan was a tough decision. While I loved working with Shiva and Ameya and the rest of the team, and I had a super amazing manager, Tammy, the commute was too long for my liking, and I was really interested in the new challenge with NCR. So with a heavy heart, I left Magellan. But I was really glad that I had met and gotten to know this amazing group.

In an interesting twist, the job I was offered was not the job I was expecting! I was offered a job as a Change Manager. In software, a change manager is usually synonymous with configuration management, or ensuring that software changes are made in a controlled and documented fashion. This new position, however, was as an Organizational Change Manager. As it turns out, I couldn't have asked for a more perfect job! Instead of managing configuration changes, Organizational Change Management is about ensuring that people are aware of and ready for software changes. It involves the people side of making a change rather than the software side. This position fell in line with my goals to coach and motivate people. I couldn't believe my good fortune! My job as an Organizational Change Manager is perfect for me. I am working with people to help them transition as a new software program is introduced. I use my writing skills to draft articles. And I coach the executives as they go through the new changes.

Through Tickers I have discovered how much I love talking with people and hearing about their stories. I absolutely loved speaking with all of the interviewees for this book. I used my digital recorder and transcribed all of the interviews word by word. Their answers to my questions were so amazing that I didn't want to use the wrong word so the transcription part was painstaking. But as you can see from the results, it was oh-so worth it.

So I am a Ticker. I am now a writer. I am on my path to being an Organizational Change Manager, an author, a life coach, and a motivational speaker. I know more about who I am and where I want to be. It is pretty amazing how far I have come, and I feel really excited about waking up every morning!

The tough parts of our lives usually feel super sucky while we're going through them. Many of the Tickers with whom I spoke were impacted when the economy tanked in 2008 (including Bill Smith, Aimee Hartle, and Samantha Martin). When they had to reconsider where they were going, they reassessed where they wanted to be. These trying times can actually become turning points. That's what happened to me when the layoffs happened to my team. I can't say I enjoyed that time of my life – it was confusing, upsetting and downright hard to go through. But without that experience, I would never have written this book – or be working at my current job, which I love!

The best advice I received from the Tickers includes:

"Why not make the most of every single moment that you're here? Because if you don't know what happens to you after you die, then of course you need to make the most of every moment that you're here." ~Bill Smith

Why not be everything you can be? Many of us have so many resources available to us but we don't make use of them. We can tell ourselves, "I'm too tired" or "I don't feel like it" or "Ooh, look at Pinterest!" I'm all for having down time – in fact, I think we need some rest and relaxation to function well – but are you using all of your talents, or are you squandering them to watch a rerun of "The Big Bang Theory"? Only you know the right balance of work and relaxation you need. But if you know you are slacking and could be doing more with the precious moments you have, why not get your butt off the sofa and start making the most of every moment? Life is so short, and we sometimes live like it will last forever, one commute to work to workday to night in front of the TV, lather, rinse, repeat, after another. But guess what? It ends. Live like you mean it.

"Don't worry about being right or wrong. If you like a beer, tell me why you like that beer. Is it sweet? Once you can say that, then we are getting somewhere." ~Aimee Hartle

Know yourself and what you like and don't like. If you can be comfortable in your own skin, and make decisions for yourself, you will get closer and closer to your true self and what makes you tick.

I'll admit a few things, gentle reader, that I feel awkward disclosing, but here it goes: I love filling out forms. Having a paper or electronic form in front of me and filling out all the fields is something I enjoy to do. Most people hate filling out forms but somehow in my heart of hearts it makes me happy. I think it is for me a joy of starting and completing a project successfully. Yup, I admit that my tendency is kind of strange but I know myself and I don't shy away from filling out forms if it will help other people.

So what you like may not be as weird as filling out forms, or it may be weirder. Whatever! As long as you don't hurt others, find out your own likes and dislikes. The more you know yourself, the closer you are to finding your passion. And then you can find your own inner joy of (fill in the blank).

"Pioneers are people that pay for it, who come up with ideas – they don't do things like everybody else. They make their own notebook, they make their own toilet suitcase, they design their own houses, and they don't build like everybody else. They come up with something unique. They make their own mailbox; they have their own portfolio. Instead of making a bio like everyone else, they find one that fits them and they make it. There are very few pioneers." ~Don Aslett

If your passion calls you to an unusual place, that's great! Many of us want so much to fit in and not "rock the boat" that we will hide the unusual things we like to do. No one wants to be judged as being a "weirdo" for fear of rejection. But if the passion that tugs at your heart is unusual, don't let that stop you! Most people who hear there is a Museum of Clean or a cat circus or a vacation tour company that doesn't tell you where you will travel will raise their eyebrows in surprise! Cleaning can't be fun, right? Cats don't listen to anyone, and everyone wants to know where they are going when they are ready to travel! However, if you know in your heart you can do the unexpected, then do it! The world will scoff at you until they see you doing what you set out to do. And then when they see your "crazy" idea working, they will be amazed! Don't be afraid to be amazing…it's what you were meant to do.

"If you fail, it's good. If you make mistakes, it's good. If you don't try, it's not good. So it doesn't matter if you are great at everything. It matters that you are open to try anything." ~H. H. Leonards

No one likes to fail. We generally want to be winners, to be the very best. But the thing many of us don't realize is that failing is important. Failure shows us what we still have to learn. When you stop trying, you stop opening doors. And as I learned at the Mansion on O Street, you want to try all the doors because you might open up to something quite magical and special.

"I always preach the gospel, especially in running or track, where you can't control your opponent, do the best you can and let rest take care of themselves." ~Weldon Bradshaw

What is your opponent? An opponent is defined in Webster's Dictionary as, "Someone who competes against or fights another in a contest, game, or argument; a rival or adversary." When you pursue your passion, you are not just going after what it is that makes you tick. You are also always fighting off "opponents". Time can be an opponent. After all, we only have a certain amount of time on this Earth as humans. And unless you are psychic, you don't know how long your time will be.

Expectation can be an opponent. Society or family may be dictating to you, "You must work in an office in order to be respected" or "You must do 20 extra-curricular activities to be considered for this school" or "Stop wearing that bear costume...you look ridiculous." Your opponent can be as trivial as junior middle school peer pressure ("All the cool kids are wearing this!") or as serious as finding out you have cancer ("We can't say how long you have left.") What makes the pursuit of being a Ticker is not just having the courage to do what you want but also to have the courage to face your opponents and deal with them and life's expectations in your own way.

"I'm a big believer in...this is what you're going to do every day for the rest of your life, for like, how many hours a day? How can you not?" ~Samantha Martin

While I am a big believer in education, I also think there is something bad that kids are taught in school. It is delayed gratification. We're told if we focus on our homework, then we will get a treat. We're told if we go to college then we can get a good paying job. On the face of it, there's nothing wrong with learning delayed gratification. In fact, in some ways, we need more of this in today's "I want it now" society. But we can also take it too far.

Sometimes in pursuit of a good life we can forget to live right here and now. Yes, we should save up for retirement. Hopefully many of us will live that long and we will need the money to take care of ourselves and loved ones. But what if we take that too far? What if we sign ourselves up for a career we hate, one that sucks the life being out of us? That is not a healthy way to live, either. If you work in a job you despise, you can become stressed out and miserable. It can impact your well-being, both physically and emotionally. There should be a happy medium, a life balance where you are both being responsible (saving money, paying taxes, getting regular medical checkups) but also where you are living your life right now (flying to Tahiti, trying to learn a square dance, eating at that really cool restaurant), and not delaying your gratification until a later date. The thing is, only you know what that life balance is for you. You can tell by how your body feels. Is your jaw clenched all the time? Are your guts churning? Do you feel like you want to hit someone? These could be signs!

It's true that you usually do what you do for a living every day for many years of your life. How do you want to spend your time? If you feel in your guts that you hate your job but you have an end goal to get to a better life or a better occupation, then maybe the right choice for you is to plow forward to your goal. Maybe you need to work at the sucky job for right now because your kids are in college and you want to pay for their education. You have a goal in mind, to work to help your kids, so maybe your choice is to carry on because at this moment your kids and their well-being is more important to you than loving your job. But if you are in a horrible job and just hate your life right now, what are you getting out of it? Maybe it is time to start thinking about what your end goal is. If you are working just to make money, and your soul is suffering as a result, it's time to invest in yourself. Life is too short to do things you hate to do! To quote the company L'Oreal, "You're worth it!" Use the hours of your life like capital and invest in YOU.

"You need to have money to get things you like in life, but it's not everything. Even if what you're passionate about isn't going to make you a millionaire, if it will make you happy, that's really great!" ~Danielle Fernandez

Yes, of course money is important. But it doesn't mean the pursuit of money should overshadow everything else. Growing up in America, many of us get bombarded with advertising that says, "Having the right stuff is happiness." And we buy into it without examining what we really feel. Sure, buying that expensive designer purse might be thrilling in the moment. But is that a sustained happiness, or just a sugar rush type of high – here one minute and gone the next?

I'm not saying not to buy expensive purses (if that's one things you love to do)! What I am saying is to listen to yourself, not the ads, and "hear" what makes you happy. Do you smile a lot when giving people instructions, for example? Does an interaction like that leave you feeling a little lighter? Or do you look forward to cutting vegetables and cooking a big meal? I don't know you so I may not hit on the right example, so you should consult with the biggest expert on you – YOU! What makes you smile or feel excited or just a little better about yourself or your day? Focus on that. There may be many things. Listen to them. Maybe one of those feelings is trying to clue you in on what makes you happy. Then, when temptation calls and says, "I want that Kate Spade purse!" or expensive car or whatever, think again about what makes you really feel happy. If that expensive purchase doesn't get you closer to your happiness, your true happiness and not just the giddy excitement of "I want that!", then walk on by.

Going after a job just because you think you will make lots of money is just as foolish as buying the expensive thing. Likely, if you don't like what you're doing, the perks of the big bank account will feel hollow. You can try to justify it to yourself by saying, "I'm a big so and so, I'm well-paid! I'm a success!" And to the eyes of the world, you may look like a success. But if that career isn't bringing you true joy or happiness, you are not really successful. You may be a deluded fraud. The Bible says, "If I speak with the tongues of men and of angels, but do not have love, I have become a noisy gong or a clanging cymbal." Your love and passion are your guides to ensuring you do not fall into that trap. Be filled with the passion and love you have, and not with material things or empty titles.

"I think the more you figure out this stuff the more you realize that everybody who's succeeded has made huge mistakes and probably no matter how successful they've been has been in the situation where they're like, "I have no idea what I'm doing!" "I'm pretty sure I'm failing," and "I've made a huge mistake!" I love hearing that because then I feel so much better about myself!" ~Denise Chaykun

It might be tempting to look at someone who has made it in business as an entrepreneur and say, "Wow! It looks like they did everything right. I bet they are just smarter than I am, or just had everything fall into place for them!" The fun part of success stories is in the before and after comparisons. For example, Steve Jobs worked on computers in his garage and then built the multi-billion-dollar Apple Corporation! Another example is Joy Mangano, the subject of the movie, "Joy", who created a home shopping empire by peddling mops at local stores! These stories can get you revved up and excited to take a great idea and be the next "big thing". The part most of us tend to gloss over is the hard work, hours of time, and the trial and error it generally takes to move from the garage or the local store to becoming successful.

Truncating a success story by glossing over the part where the entrepreneur does a lot of hard work reminds me of a famous skit from the television show, "Seinfeld," where the characters tell a story and say "yada, yada, yada" in between. In one scene, George's girlfriend says, "So I'm on 3rd Avenue, mindin' my own business, and, yada yada yada, I get a free massage and a facial." At first, George admires this succinct way his girlfriend has of speaking. She literally makes a long story short. George is fine when her short story sounds innocent, but later when she says, "Speaking of ex's, my old boyfriend came over late last night, and, yada yada yada, anyway. I'm really tired today." Suddenly the story sounds like his girlfriend has been cheating on him, and then George wants to know the details. In the second story, "Yada yada yada" omits some details that George considers important to know!

With stories of success, whether it is career-wise, relationship-wise or even something like dieting, most people want to know the "yada yada yada" version of the tale. "You look so good! How did you lose the 60 pounds?" is something you might hear. Generally people want to hear a quick, succinct answer: "I did a weight loss program!" Most people don't want to hear the whole story. "Well, I joined a weight loss program! I was excited when I lost ten pounds quickly, but then I plateaued. I freaked out and starting eating badly but then I saw a program for an exercise and I started following that. It was really hard and I struggled every day, especially when my co-workers brought in doughnuts, and when we had the birthday party for my son. But then I continued to work out and diet every day." Sure, the second version is what really happened – frequently weight loss stories (or relationship or career successes) do not happen overnight. But we don't usually want to hear all the struggles and the effort. We'd prefer to think it is something easy.

Denise's comment speaks to the hard part of pursuing your passion. While doing what you love to do can be rewarding, it is still hard work, and there are times when you will screw up. And that's not a bad thing! Actually, as I found with the Tickers I interviewed, failure or roadblocks pop up frequently in their stories.

Bill Smith started his business but got frustrated and found it to be a "depressing puzzle" at one point. Don Aslett wrote some books that hardly sold at all. Samantha created a children's zoo only to discover she doesn't like children and started hating her job. But these issues that at first were obstacles eventually became jumpable hurdles to these Tickers. Bill did figure out the puzzle and created the perfect work-life balance for himself. Don changed his focus to write other books with topics which were successful and resonated better with his audience. Samantha focused on working with the Acro-Cats which brought her happiness while bringing joy to other people (and not forcing herself to work with children exclusively!). It is the roadblocks and the failures that help Tickers better define, "What do I really want to do, and how can I make this work?"

Know that if you try, you will fail. And that's OK! In fact, it is better than OK because failing means you are closer to knowing the true path that will work for you. Later, when someone asks, "How did you succeed at doing what you love to do?", you can start by giving them the "yada yada yada" version of your story. The wise ones, the ones who want to know what it really took to succeed, will dig deeper and find the real work behind the dream.

"Even for this lunch that you have given me, I will not think one bit that I have wasted one minute. End of the day, I seriously don't know how this is going to impact you, how this interview is going to impact you. But all throughout this conversation, I feel happy that somebody was listening to me. I'm happy with this. This is what keeps me going." ~Shiva Pillai

You may know what your passion is, and what makes you tick, but you may not know what's next for you or where your passion will lead you. In following what makes you tick, you may have to try out a few things before you find what works for you.

This was true for Shiva. He knew he loves talking with people and he enjoys making them feel happy. When he left his father's family business to live on his own, he didn't know what he wanted to do. But he trusted his gut. He knew he liked helping others so he started helping his friend and his internet business. This lead Shiva to an IT company, even though Shiva wasn't passionate about IT and knew very little about it. Shiva's love of talking with people and putting them at ease lead to him being selected to come to the United States, not based on his knowledge at that time but based on his people skills. No matter what challenges have come Shiva's way, he has had confidence in his love of people and his ability to please them and it has lead him to a lucrative career in both IT and in the restaurant business. And he has a wonderful, loving family whom he is encouraging to find what they love, also.

Anyone who wants to be a Ticker can follow this. When I took the leap and moved from working for ManTech to working for Magellan, it was scary. But I knew I had the confidence in my ability to be a leader and also to be a "people person". I knew working with people and helping them to achieve on the job motivated me. It has ultimately led to me becoming an Organizational Change Manager. And I know this passion and trust I have in myself will lead me to become an outstanding life coach, speaker and author. I would want to do these things even if no one paid me. That's what keeps me going!

"Don't give up." ~Constance Hendricks

This is such a simple statement, but it carries a great deal of power. It's easy to follow your passion when you have a day when everything is going your way, and everything seems to be "clicking". But you have to muster the passion to continue to work hard and focus on the days that suck, too. There might be days when you just aren't feeling it. For example, Danielle mentioned she turned down a fantastic trip to Europe so she could start Main Squeeze at the Vail Farmer's Market. Shiva could have said to himself, "Well, if I go out on my own I will be cut off, so I might as well stay here and work for my father." The easy way is not always the best way. Ultimately if Danielle had gone on her trip, and left her friend to run Main Squeeze, it could have turned into a disaster and ended her business before it began. If Shiva had just stayed in the family business, he could have ruined his life by stifling his need to help others in his own way.

There were times when the Tickers ran into issues with the economic downturn that happened in the 2000's. Bill Smith was impacted by the downturn when his part-time job was suddenly reduced to a no-time job! Samantha's traveling business with the Festival of Cultures wound down because of the economic downturn. While it is easy now to look back and say, "Wow, the economic downturn actually helped Bill and Samantha in the long run because they had to reassess their plan and figure out another strategy!", I'm sure at the time they may have felt like, "Well, this blows! Now what?"

The answer is to never give up. If you feel in your guts that you are following your passion, and you really want to give it a go, never give up. Yes, you may run into roadblocks and have to change your plans. But that's OK...as we discussed before, roadblocks and failures are part of what gives us the directions to move forward. But if you give up, you will never see your dream grow, and that can be devastating to your well-being. There's a saying that if you never buy a ticket, you will never win the lottery. And that's true. If you never give yourself a chance to dream, to follow your passion, you'll never achieve it. You need to be your own motivator and believe in yourself. As Dory says in the movie "Finding Nemo," "Just keep swimming!"

I had a hard time with this concept for a while because I kept thinking in what I call "all or nothing scenarios." I was thinking that in order to follow your dream, you had to have a dramatic turn in your life, quit your day job, and start from scratch working on your passion. For me, it would have meant quitting a job with a good salary, benefits and stability to pursue writing. But I already have a lifestyle that I like, and I am one half of the marriage of Kim and Jerry, and that marriage requires money to sustain the lifestyle. For me, coming home and saying to Jerry, "Well, I quit my job. Now I'll be a writer!" was not the best option. (Hello, D-I-V-O-R-C-E!) I found what works for me is what I call spoon digging.

This concept comes from Martha Beck, a noted life coach whom I consider to be super awesome, relatable and wise. In a video she made in 2011, she talks about how to move towards your best life while still working in a job you hate. She fields a question from a woman who asks, "How do I take steps from a secure salaried job that is hated...toward a career path that would be joy-filled but initially without monetary income? How's this done when there are people relying on the current income?" Martha wisely points out that you don't have to choose one or the other, and explains what she calls the Monte Cristo effect. She talks about the character from Victor Hugo's book,

"The Count of Monte Cristo" who is imprisoned but spends 20 years digging his way out with a spoon and then escaping. Martha says we can do the same thing by continuing to support our loved ones while working at the non-fulfilling job while spending a few minutes a day working towards our passion.[xviii]

Right after the layoffs at ManTech, I found the video from Martha on the Monte Cristo effect. It made a huge impression on me! I felt like I had found the keys to my freedom. I kept working at ManTech but started sending out my résumé and asking around about job openings. This lead me to my position at Magellan. At the same time, I started a journal. I named it my "Dig Spoon" journal. Just to make it official and symbolize the Monte Christo effect, I used a hot glue gun to glue a plastic spoon to the front of the journal.

I started writing down what I wanted to do….how great it would be to interview like-minded people who were Tickers, people who were doing what I wanted to do. I didn't spend a lot of time at first. I would spend 15-20 minutes a day thinking about what I loved to do and what got me excited about Tickers. I didn't give up. Instead, I picked up my metaphorical spoon and started digging. And a year and a half later, I'm writing about it and sharing it with you!

Know that you should never give up. If you are in the position to make a radical change and you want to (and know you can) pursue that path, terrific! If, like me, you have people counting on your income, however, you don't have to take a leap. Sometimes it just takes a few scoops with your spoon.

"My master always said, 'Don't dance because you want to be famous. Don't dance because you want to get money out of it. Dance because you want to dance. Everything else will come behind it.'" ~Sarada Jammi

You can't fake passion. I think people try to fake happiness by surrounding themselves with material objects and by keeping themselves so busy they have no time to reflect. But you can't fake to yourself a real passion. You either love it or you don't.

For me, I have a number of passions. I love to cook. For a while, when my friend Jen and I had our catering business, Food for Thought, I thought I wanted to cook for a living. It turns out catering was too demanding for my liking. You spend so much time and effort with the tasks outside of cooking – working with clients, coordinating menus, shopping, setting up the catering area, billing, etc. – that in my opinion it overshadows the joy of cooking. I continued catering for a while though because the excitement of cooking for others and seeing them light up when they ate our food was terrific. In the end, I couldn't fake the fact that while I love cooking, I hate catering.

If I had ignored the fact that I didn't like catering, I could have pushed myself. I did have some delusions of grandeur at one point: "Jen and I could be the next Martha Stewarts!" I could have forced us to do more and more catering gigs, asking for more money each time. And we could have advertised like crazy in order to become well-known in Central Virginia. None of this would have changed the fact that I hate catering. In fact, I could have forced the business so hard that I would have burned out on cooking altogether. And that would have been a shame because I still love cooking for my friends and family.

I think what Sarada is saying is that following your passion should come from a pure place. Yes, if say you pursue acting, it is fun to daydream and say, "I could become famous! I want to be an A-lister!" But that's not coming from a pure place ultimately. In other words, if you love to act, and dream of being rich and famous, that's OK, but don't make it your goal to be rich and famous. Ultimately at the end of the day, your best bet is to work for the love of the acting and not for how you benefit from it.

I still love to cook. But I know now that I love it because I like to cook my way. I don't want to literally cater to someone else's needs. Friends have told me that they can taste the love in my cooking, and that feels better to me than a huge paycheck or being on Food Network.

Throughout my conversations with the Tickers, there were some common threads.

I asked all of the Tickers I interviewed whether they had an outline or business plan for their path.

I was really surprised to find that most of the Tickers did not have an outline or a business plan when they started. I have read a number of business books that practically insist that you have a plan but in reality, I think it starts with a feeling rather than starting with an outline.

Bill Smith didn't know what he wanted to do and in fact, he had resisted teaching CMMI. And ultimately for him, he knew he could be a great instructor for someone else, so he decided to be the great instructor for his own company. James and Aimee started with working at craft beer festivals and just decided one day, "Hey, let's try opening a bar!" H felt a calling and took a leap of faith and a handful of credit cards to start the Mansion on O Street. Constance saw the Tuskegee nurses and felt such an admiration that she wanted to become one of them. Don just wanted to earn money while he went to college and figured everyone needed a cleaner. Shiva just knew he was miserable and couldn't carry on under his father's thumb. Sarada fell in love with dance and knew she had to learn. Danielle and her partner knew they wanted to make juice but they jumped in without a specific plan.

If you know what you want to do, certainly it doesn't hurt to have a plan. But if you don't have a complete, detailed plan right away, that's OK too. The Project Management Body of Knowledge includes a great concept called Rolling Wave Planning, which enables you to plan for a project as it unfolds. You may start with a high-level plan and then make detailed plans as you get closer to your goal and as you learn more. As you try different ways to make your vision happen, you will have successes and failures. Document these! As you move forward, you'll find what works and what doesn't. But if you say to yourself, "I can't start until I have a plan!" then you may be allowing yourself to procrastinate. I say it is better to jump in and get started with a bit of analysis and then use rolling wave planning to adjust your vision as you move, rather than set up your own roadblock by insisting you start with a completed, detailed business plan.

Social media, social networks

All of the Tickers with whom I spoke use social media in one way or another. Almost all of them have a website presence on the Internet. Danielle used Facebook for Main Squeeze. H uses her website and an email newsletter to communicate to her dedicated community. Samantha helps her cats send Tweets to their followers and even started some Twitter "wars" between the kitties! She and her crew also use Facebook to recruit volunteers for their shows, let their audience know about upcoming appearances, and when they were raising money on Kickstarter for their new bus, they used Facebook to keep everyone up-to-date on their progress. Bill made videos on YouTube initially to get noticed for Leading Edge, his CMMI training business. James and Aimee use Trinkin, the website for locating local craft beer bars, to list their daily menu of local and imported beers and wines.

Social media has many advantages. Many social media outlets, like Twitter, Facebook and Instagram, are free and it is easy to set up an account. Plus there are so many people using social media that it is a great way to reach a wide audience. Tickers can share pictures, videos, information about upcoming events, and read the feedback from their audience. Aimee said social media can also create desire in your audience. Websites usually have a cost involved but they also offer the ability to share information, pictures, videos, schedules and events too.

The downside to social media is that any fool with an account can post whatever they want on your site. But I think the ability to reach a lot of people effectively can overshadow this downside.

Writing books can be helpful too, as Don Aslett and H have realized. While the printing business is currently having some issues keeping afloat, a book can be a great way to enhance and promote your passion. Self-publishing is easy to do nowadays.

A sense of humor will take you far

Many of the Tickers have incorporated humor, delight and surprise in their passions. Bill uses humor to teach CMMI, a topic that can be as stale as dry toast. Dressing like a member of the band KISS definitely catches people off guard – in a good way! Don uses humor in his books, his company and his museum to make the subject of cleaning engaging. When you see his toilet-shaped briefcase, it immediately makes you giggle. Delighting in the amazing objects in the Mansion on O Street is such a wonderful feeling. It can make people connect with one another as they ooh and ahh over the incredible and the kitschy objects. Sharing a surprise by planning and speculating over a mystery vacation can also bring people together as they try to guess where their friends will travel. And presenting a trained cat who decides instead of performing to run in the audience and find a human friend can bring laughter to an audience of Acro-Cat fans.

When we laugh together, we can share our passion and bring other people into our world. That is how people who are interested in a subject that may not initially connect or resonate with you can suddenly make you fascinated in a subject or look at it in a fresh way. To feel joy, delight or just plain tickled engages us emotionally.

People at different points in their careers

It seems funny to say that people at different points in their careers is a common thread! With the Tickers with whom I spoke, however, it was interesting to note similarities in their story arcs, and that I could identify where they were.

James and Aimee with Bucket Trade and Danielle with Main Squeeze are at the beginning, "Gelling" stage. They are still experimenting with what works for them and what doesn't. While James and Aimee started with one location in Chester, Virginia, they decided to branch out and have a second location in Petersburg. But they found that they had to separate during the day as James would work in the Petersburg location, and Aimee would work in the Chester location. At the time of publishing, they are thinking of consolidating both places into one larger location in Petersburg. Danielle, in the meantime, has realized that while she loves juicing and the benefits it brings, she really is more interested in the health aspect than the business aspect of juicing. She's forming a career path where she can focus on the nutritional benefits of juicing and living a healthier life by pursuing naturopathic medicine. For James, Aimee and Danielle, their businesses are fluid and changing frequently.

Some of the Tickers' stories illustrate a time they had established who they were and how they operate, but had to change or reevaluate their approach. I call this the "Readjusting the Sails" stage. Weldon Bradshaw's world upended when he had to face a terrible disease. He had the skills from being a great coach but he had to change his world by applying what he knows to himself. Shiva had to change his path when he made up his mind to leave the family business and follow his heart. Constance had her heart set on becoming a prestigious Tuskegee nurse when she learned she had to attend a different college. Bill realized he couldn't keep working part-time for his company or else he would lose the work-life balance he had achieved. Each of these Tickers had to figure out a new way of doing what they were doing, or metaphorically readjust their sails to catch the changing winds.

Many of the Tickers' stories describe a gutsy, determined focus on achieving their goals. I call this the "Go Hard or Go Home" mentality. Denise continued working on scheduling mystery vacations even when others told her they thought she was nuts. Samantha kept pursuing her love of animals even when her family was not supportive of her dream. Sarada had a determined focus to make dance a part of her life, one which she was able to pursue despite health issues and time constraints along the way. It took courage and determination to keep moving towards their dreams despite the obstacles along the way.

All of the Tickers have shown they have the ability to be flexible in the face of change. Every one of them had to make tough choices (quit the pet shop job when offered a movie role for rats, move away from family to live with a dance teacher in another city, max out the credit cards to buy the perfect place in D.C., for example), struggle with money issues and economic downturns, make sacrifices, and face days when they may have wanted to give up. But all of the Tickers persevered. And none of them have stopped moving and growing. Each one of them has future aspirations, new challenges to face, and hopes of something new and different in the future.

I started my journey to become a Ticker by asking lots of questions. I didn't know what to expect as I began scheduling interviews and talking with the Tickers. The fact that I would have a really great time working on the book has just blown me away. Talking with each of the Tickers was really fun! I got excited hearing their stories and they in turn got me excited about sharing their stories. As I reread each interview, I gained new insights. I kept thinking, "OMG! I can't wait to share this with other people!"

One of the experiences that touched my heart happened right before publication. My friend Randy and my niece Erin edited the book for me. Randy asked if he could share the chapter written by Mr. Bradshaw with a friend who was dying from cancer. I said, "Of course!" Right before publication, Randy said his friend had passed away. He said he believed his friend drew comfort from Mr. Bradshaw's story. This touched me deeply and made me realize that the reason I wanted to write Tickers was not just to learn for myself what it means to tick, but also to share what I learned with others and help them on their path.

And here I am, a year and a half after the layoffs that kicked off my journey! In that time, I changed jobs twice and found a career as an Organizational Change Manager that I love. I also have written a book and realized that I love to write if it involves talking with other people and figuring out what makes them tick. And in doing so, I myself have become a Ticker.

Follow-up Questions about Tickers

In reflecting on the stories, ask yourself these questions:

- Did these Tickers choose their path, or did it choose them?
- How did they move from the "idea" phase to the "action" phase?
- Are they any different than anyone else, including me?
- If I figure out how the Tickers found their path, could I use that information to find my own?
- How do the Tickers get other people excited about their passion?
- Would following a passion lead someone to take a different or new approach? Would that lead to something new? Is that an innovation?
- How can innovations improve the world? Can it make the world better for others? Can Tickers influence people to see the world differently?
- What's more important – the Tickers or the thing that makes the Ticker tick? Or are they the same?
- How do Tickers identify what they want?
- What's the catalyst?
- What did the Tickers know that all of us should know?

Find Out More about the Tickers

If you'd like to know more about the wonderful, amazing Tickers interviewed in this book, please check out these sites!

Bill Smith, Leading Edge Process Consultants
http://www.cmmitraining.com/index.html

James and Aimee Hartle, The Bucket Trade
http://thebuckettrade.com/

Don Aslett, Don Aslett's Cleaning Center, Museum of Clean
http://donaslett.com/
http://www.museumofclean.com/

H.H. Leonards, The Mansion on O Street
https://omansion.com/

Weldon Bradshaw, "My Dance with Grace," Hume-Lee Transplant Center at VCU Medical Center
http://brandylanepublishers.com/wp/book/list-all/memoirautobiography/my-dance-with-grace/
http://www.vcuhealth.org/transplant/about/spotlight/WeldonBradshaw.html

Samantha Martin, The Acro-Cats with the Rock Cats, Amazing Animals
http://circuscats.com/about.html#.Vudg7JMrKi4
http://www.amazinganimals.biz/

Danielle Fernandez, Main Squeeze Juicery
https://www.facebook.com/MainSqueezeJuiceryCO/?fref=ts

Denise Chaykun, Magical Mystery Tours
http://magical-mystery-tours.com/

Shiva Pillai, Hot Breads
http://vaindian.com/hot-breads-richmond-va.aspx

Dr. Constance Hendricks, Auburn University
https://cws.auburn.edu/nursing/pm/hendricks-c

Sarada Jammi, Kuchipudi Kalakar
http://kuchipudikalakar.blogspot.com/2011/05/sarada-jammi.html

Kimberley Eley, KWE Publishing LLC
www.kwepub.com

[i] Rybar, *Yahoo Answers, 2009,* "What does what makes you tick mean?"

[ii] Susan Adams, *Forbes,* June 12, 2013. "Disconnected From Your Job? So Are Two Thirds Of Your Fellow Workers." http://www.forbes.com/sites/susanadams/2013/06/12/disconnected-from-your-job-so-are-two-thirds-of-your-fellow-workers/#4021f0432512

[iii] Wikipedia, "Protestant Work Ethic," https://en.wikipedia.org/wiki/Protestant_work_ethic.

[iv] Samuel Gregg, *Mercatornet,* January 21, 2014. http://www.mercatornet.com/articles/view/did_the_protestant_work_ethic_create_capitalism.

[v] https://www.youtube.com/watch?v=isLlOlqpykM&feature=youtu.be "You Know You're CMMI Maturity Level One When…(Project Management PAs)", posted by Bill Smith, Leading Edge Consulting.

[vi] https://www.youtube.com/watch?v=jFfFQ9XU7Jw "Death by PowerPoint", posted by Melodee Mabbitt, with thanks to Alexei Kapterev, of Real Time Strategy.

[vii] Paul Anka, "My Way".

[viii] http://www.mormonwiki.com/Don_Aslett

[ix] http://www.washingtontimes.com/news/2011/dec/27/museum-of-clean-ready-to-shine/#ixzz3RZNPJHTA

[x] http://www.omuseum.org/index.shtml The Mansion on O Street website.

[xi] http://www.collegiate-va.org/Page/Our-School/News/Reflections The Collegiate Schools website, Weldon Bradshaw, "Reflections."

[xii] http://smallbusiness.chron.com/being-entrepreneur-challenging-32802.html, *Houston Chronical,* "What Makes Being an Entrepreneur So Challenging?" Tanya Robertson, **Demand Media.**

[xiii] http://www.simplypsychology.org/maslow.html, Simple Psychology website, "Maslow's Hierarchy of Needs."

[xiv] http://magical-mystery-tours.com/3-book-a-trip-to-who-knows-where/, Reference to the O, the Oprah Magazine June 2013 article, "Be Surprised!" from the Magical Mystery Tours website.

[xv] http://magical-mystery-tours.com/about/, Magical Mystery Tours website, "About" page.

[xvi] https://cws.auburn.edu/nursing/pm/hendricks-c, Auburn University, School of Nursing website, Constance Smith Hendricks, PhD, RN, FAAN biography.

[xvii] http://kuchipudikalakar.blogspot.com/2011/05/sarada-jammi.html, Kuchipudi Kalakar, profiles of Kuchipdi instructors.

[xviii] http://marthabeck.com/2011/01/coach42day-hated-job/

Made in the USA
San Bernardino, CA
27 July 2017